Chupacabras

and Other Mysteries

by

Scott Corrales

Introduction by Marc Davenport

Greenleaf Publications
P.O. Box 8152
Murfreesboro, Tennessee 37133
USA

Manufactured in the United States of America

Library of Congress catalog card number
97-68468

ISBN
1-883729-06-8

Contents

Preface

One of the most significant books I read during my formative years was John A. Keel's *The Mothman Prophecies*.[1] I remember the cloudy Saturday afternoon I headed to Farmacia Miramar, in San Juan's Miramar sector, across from the glittering Condado Lagoon, to scan its considerable book section. I emerged with a glossy new paperback portraying a fearsome-looking, bat-winged creature on its cover. I was thrilled at the concept of a lone investigator facing the unknown in its myriad guises, and at the undeniable visual power of Keel's unmatched prose. I have read *The Mothman Prophecies* many times since 1976. I consider it the most significant book in ufology to date.

Now another creature of the same epic proportions as Mothman has risen from the depths of mystery to haunt the island where I first read Keel's book. This time the scope is island-wide. The media glare beats down on the elusive beast, politicians demand an investigation into the riddle, and a lone investigator—Jorge Martín—faces down a cryptozoological conundrum and the very real danger posed by rogue UFO research groups.

I wrote this book to enable you, the reader, to understand the strangeness of the situation Puerto Rico and the world are experiencing.

Scott Corrales
Bradford, Pennsylvania

Acknowledgments

Any page devoted to acknowledgments must begin with sincere gratitude for the research conducted so selflessly by Jorge and Marleen Martín. They have devoted thousands of hours, without benefit of outside funding, to tracking the Chupacabras (Goatsucker) and every manifestation of the UFO phenomenon that has been recorded in Puerto Rico. These investigations have never been easy, and, on one occasion, placed their lives in jeopardy. The recognition shown to them at UFO conferences in the United States, Europe, and South America is testimony to the sterling quality of their research.

Greater love hath no man than to clip newspaper items and record television and radio broadcasts for his nephew. That statement best describes José Valdez, who has, since 1991, kept me abreast of the situation in Puerto Rico through a flurry of correspondence and packages so profuse that the United States Postal Service should accord him preferred customer status.

Thanks are also in order to Dr. Rafael A. Lara Palmeros, Director of Research for Mexico's Centro de Estudio de Fenómenos Paranormales (CEFP), for providing access to his limitless files and insight on the UFO situation in Latin America; Dr. Oscar Rafael Padilla, for information concerning manifestations of the Chupacabras and related creatures in his native Guatemala; and Mr. Willie Durand Urbina, of the Puerto Rican Research Group, for providing us with an interview with original witnesses to the Chupacabras.

Introduction

Although my study of UFOs had spilled over into subjects like crypto-zoology for decades, I had never heard of the Chupacabras (literally translated "Goatsucker") until I met Joyce Murphy at a UFO conference in September, 1995.

Joyce owns Beyond Boundaries, a travel agency that organizes tours to the Great Pyramid, Machu Picchu, Stonehenge, and other locations where adventurous truth seekers might expect to learn or experience something extraordinary. She had read my book, *Visitors From Time: The Secret of the UFOs*, and my wife's book, *Lost Was the Key*.[1,2] Because both of our books dealt with the possibility of what can only be called "time travel," Joyce thought Leah and I would be the perfect husband-and-wife author team to lead a research expedition to Puerto Rico, where numerous citizens recently had been reporting encounters with "dimensional doorways," and "time warps." Both Leah and I saw an opportunity to search for real answers, and agreed. Arrangements for the expedition were made. The Chupacabras was discussed as a possible area of investigation, but, at the time, I had no idea how much of our research time would be devoted to it.

At the last minute, Leah fell dangerously ill. Her doctor forbade her to travel. Feeling extremely guilty about leaving her, but nevertheless feeling heavily obliged to give the ten paying expedition members the adventure they had bargained for, I reluctantly opted to make the trip without her.

I arrived in San Juan on February 10, 1996. I quickly fell in love with the beauty of the islands and the breathtaking warmth and visceral lust for life of the beautiful, almost childlike souls of Puerto Rico. My first scheduled engagement was dinner with the other members of the expedition, and with the island's foremost investigators of the unexplained, Jorge Martín and his enchanting wife, Marleen. I found all of them to be charming, and quickly gained the utmost respect for the Martíns and their work.

Jorge wasted no time in conveying to our group the fact that the most urgent area of investigation on the island right then was neither UFOs nor time travel, but the mysterious Chupacabras, which had been killing animals all over the island, and had created a sensation. Some of the killings had occurred that very day, in areas not too far away from our hotel.

Swallowing my disappointment at not being able to fully pursue my original line of research, I apologized for Leah's inability to accompany the expedition, then seized the moment and made a plea to the group. I said it appeared we had an unforeseen and fortuitous opportunity to work on the cutting edge of research into the unknown. I acknowledged that some of them had traveled thousands of miles and spent hundreds of dollars to spend a week investigating UFOs and time warps. Then I asked how many of them—after hearing the incredible testimony being offered about the so-called Chupacabras—thought that, in the interest of science, we should shift gears a bit and attempt to capture one of these creatures—or at the very least aggressively try to obtain photographs and pursue other physical evidence to prove or disprove its existence. Every one of the ten members of our expedition agreed enthusiastically.

We did hunt UFOs, interview contactees, and measure magnetism in remote locations said to contain doorways into other dimensions. One member of our team even swam across a lake reputed to be the portal to an underground alien base to try to take underwater photographs. But nearly half of our week-long investigation hinged on pursuit of the elusive Chupacabras. With Martín's aid, and with the full cooperation of Mayor José Soto of Canóvanas and his directors of education, civil defense, and public relations (complete with an official-vehicle escort), we were able to obtain priceless interviews with several firsthand witnesses. They appeared completely genuine, and their stories all fit together very well, even though they did not know each other. They all described the creature as about three or four feet tall, with powerful hind legs, large, almond-shaped eyes that looked wet and black in daylight and glowing red at night, and a strange row of spines or feathers from the top of the head to where a tail would be (no tail was reported). We were also able to collect actual physical evidence in the form of hair samples that may well have been left behind by one of the elusive creatures.

Tragically, as of this writing, no definitive result has yet been forthcoming concerning the hair samples.

I tried to have them submitted to the National Forensics Laboratory in Ashland, Oregon—the world's foremost authority on identification of unknown animal hairs—but was unable to overcome the requirement that all specimens be submitted by an American law-enforcement officer in charge of the investigation of a crime. Plenty of crimes had been committed in Puerto Rico (many livestock were killed or removed), but I encountered difficulties in communicating with the local authorities at all by long-distance telephone with my limited grasp of the Spanish language, let alone convincing them to sign an official report stating that a "monster" had killed their citizens' animals and drained their blood.

One Japanese laboratory issued a vague statement that the samples did not conform to any species they knew of, but displayed certain similarities to wolf hairs. (There are no wolves in Puerto Rico.)

Employees of two different American laboratories offered to perform identification tests, then disappeared. Neither of them left forwarding address-es. I have been forced to conclude that both must have intended to use labora-tory facilities without the permission of the owners, and their deceptions were subsequently discovered, which caused the immediate termination of the tests in question and the employees as well.

At the present time, we are all waiting to hear the results of tests spon-sored by the popular American TV program *Strange Universe*, whose produc-er, Scott Catamas, promised to have my samples analyzed if I would tape a segment of the show for him—which I did.

I think I can safely speak for everyone in our expedition when I suggest that we needed much more time to conduct our research properly. Much more evidence must be collected before any solid conclusions can be drawn about what the mysterious creature is and where it came from. We need to deliver a live specimen—or at least a corpse—to qualified scientists for serious labora-tory study. Until we are able to do so, all we can do is continue our efforts to capture the creature on film; collect, catalogue, and analyze the various bits of goo and hair found at its many "crime scenes"; document its victims; and, of course, record and compare the testimony of eyewitnesses.

It would be easy for me to sit in my armchair and declare that the Chupa-cabras is nothing more than a relic of the dinosaur era, which, like the coel-acanth, simply has not yet been encountered and categorized by zoologists. Some of the facts do support that hypothesis. The creature's powerful hind limbs, scrawny forelimbs, and three-clawed hands are consistent with what we know of dinosaurs. If it does, indeed, have chameleon abilities attributed to it by witnesses, and if it can jump as high and run as fast as some witnesses have claimed, it might well have escaped detection for centuries in the nearly impenetrable jungle of the El Yunque rain forest.

And now something appears to be wrong in that rain forest. Our expedition spent two nights there, searching the jungle with night-vision equipment. We walked for miles, stopping to scour the landscape with our equipment every few hundred feet. During the entire time, the only creatures any of the members of the expedition spotted were one dog (on the road leading into the park), one snail, and one tiny, sleeping bat (in a picnic shelter). We saw no birds, no monkeys—no other creatures of any kind. The forest that should be teeming with life appeared to be almost empty, and this could spell trouble for an animal with the voracious appetite for blood that reports of the Chupacabras' many victims imply. It is perfectly logical to conclude that such a creature, thus deprived of its blood supply, would venture into the farms and settlements surrounding the rain forest to feast on the easy pickings of the huge numbers of chickens, rabbits, and other small animals kept by the residents there.

But other factors do not add up.

Several witnesses swore to us that the Goatsucker's eyes emitted *beams* of light that illuminated the nocturnal landscape like flashlight beams. That is not consistent with what I know of biology. Although fireflies, glowworms, fungi, deep-sea fishes, and other life forms do have bioluminescent capabilities, none of their lights are as powerful as flashlight beams. Of course we know very little about the structure of dinosaurs' eyes. Perhaps they all contained some mechanism for emitting powerful light. But at the moment, we have no evidence on which to base such an assumption.

Many who saw the Chupacabras said it has a web of skin connecting its wrist to its knee or ankle, that this web forms a "wing," like that of a flying squirrel when it raises its arms, and that this structure allows it to glide like a hang glider. But some witnesses insisted that the Chupacabras has a levitation capability that allows it to float through the air like Superman, in level flight without flapping wings, and without any other visible means of propulsion. One witness claimed that the extremely rapid movement of small, feather-like appendages along its backbone propelled it like a bumblebee, but his claims were not corroborated by any other witnesses, and such flight seems to be physically impossible, given what we know of aerodynamics. While Hindu yogis, mystics like Arthur Ford, and even a few modern-day hypnotherapists are said to have achieved true levitation, this ability has not been demonstrated to the satisfaction of mainstream science. Perhaps all dinosaurs could levitate—but, again, we have no solid evidence on which to base such an assumption.

Despite numerous face-to-face sightings of the animal standing on the ground and the documented killings of hundreds of animals, I know of *no* footprints known to have been left by the creature. I personally crawled through the backyards of witnesses on my hands and knees and questioned numerous others without finding anything but dog, goat, and chicken prints, and shoe marks. Unless the animal has some kind of wide, pillow-like structures on the bottoms of its feet—which none of the witnesses has reported—it should leave footprints. Hawks and eagles spend almost their entire lives above the ground, but even they sometimes leave footprints at the sites of their kills.

Perhaps there are other enigmatic details that would further contradict the "relic-from-the-dinosaur-age" hypothesis, but I think you get the picture. At present, it is no more provable that the "alien pet" hypothesis, the "escaped genetic experiment" hypothesis, the "interdimensional traveler" hypothesis, the "devil's agent" hypothesis, or any one of a hundred others. We simply do not know the answer—yet.

But, as Agent Mulder, of *The X-Files* would say, "The truth is out there." That includes not only the truth about the mysterious Chupacabras, but also the truth about UFOs, Bigfoot, and numerous other mysteries that have baffled researchers for centuries. How do we find it? One way is by examining the evidence we have already.

A lot of that evidence has been hidden from most investigators behind a simple, but highly effective wall called "the language barrier"—the confusion of tongues that thwarted human endeavors in the days of the Tower of Babel, and that is still thwarting us today, in spite of jet airplanes, TV, and the internet.

That is why I was so pleased when I discovered that Spanish-English translator Scott Corrales, the author of this book, had been devoting hundreds of man-hours to documenting and distributing data gathered from the encounters so many local people have had with the mysterious beast in question, and with other fascinating inexplicable phenomena in Puerto Rico, in the rest of Latin America, and throughout the world.

Chupacabras and Other Mysteries is a landmark work because it boldly crosses the language barrier that has kept so much important data hidden from the entire English-speaking world. It builds a bridge to our wonderful, passionate, loving neighbors to the South, thus allowing English-speaking readers around the world to access some of the incredibly rich and varied reports of meetings with the unknown that have been experienced throughout the Spanish-speaking world. Much of the information contained in it first appeared in a photocopied volume called *The Chupacabras Diaries*, self-published by the author, and in numerous articles that he penned for Spanish and Latin American (and a few North American) magazines.[3] It does not pretend to solve conclusively the riddles of the Chupacabras or any of the other enigmas that populate its pages. It simply presents the available data in an interesting, easy-to-read style.

This book is likely to leave any reader forever and unalterably changed. Change can be good.

Marc Davenport
Murfreesboro, Tennessee

...all these men are being drawn closer and closer to ontology, to an examination of the question that lies beyond the simplistic, "Can these things be?" The real question is, "Why are there these things?"

—— John A. Keel *The Mothman Prophecies*

Chapter One

The Opening Rounds

For more than a century now, Puerto Rican peasants have sung fervently: Líbranos, señor, de este terrible animal! (Deliver us, Lord, from this terrible beast.) It is a song accompanied by the syncopation of numerous drums (called *tumbadoras*) and the percussion instruments available in the rural reaches of the island at the time. Folklorists all but dismiss the possibility that these lyrics might be anything other than the result of an ardent Christian urge to be delivered from the devil, who is described in bestial terms. But Puerto Rico's long history of paranormal phenomena can lead even the sternest doubter to read between the lines of this peasant song.

For decades, Puerto Rico has experienced a level of paranormal phenomena beyond that usually felt elsewhere in the world. Major documentaries like *OVNIs Sobre Puerto Rico: Documento Confidencial* alerted the world to a situation in which bizarre creatures, UFOs and their occupants, and religious phenomena played out on the same stage—or in different rings under the same tent. Animal mutilations presided over the weirdness of the early 1970s, mirroring the stateside UFO wave of 1972-73, while, at the same time, people disappeared in the rain forest known as El Yunque. "Men-In-Black" walked into business offices, and presumably alien craft crossed the skies with impunity. One UFO even paused to be picked up on a TV commercial for a rum distillery while the camera was left running all night in order to capture a perfect sunrise from the top of a building in the heart of San Juan.

The modern age of weirdness kicked off with the alleged crash of a UFO in the El Yunque Rain Forest in 1987. Soon afterward, a massive underground detonation rocked the southwestern tip of the island, attracting the attention of the military. Amaury Rivera had his abduction experience in the same area a year later. (Controversy over Rivera's story threatened to destroy the ufological community in both Puerto Rico and Spain, and has indeed left it badly divided.)

Two years after that, 1989 began with sightings of the enigmatic, repulsive "vampire birds." They appeared in many different parts of the island simultaneously. Naysayers came forward and alleged that they were common island birds with rooster spurs grafted into their beaks. This improbable statement seemed to quell the incipient furor, but the fact of the matter is that government officials confiscated not only the birds in private hands, but even film that was being developed at a Fotomat store.[1]

Both 1990 and 1991 witnessed the return of the UFO phenomenon and its attendant manifestations to the Adjuntas area, a mountainous region famous for its coffee-growing plantations, and its high-grade copper (still unexploited). It was at this time that Laguna Cartagena, an unremarkable, kidney-shaped body of water near the towns of Boquerón and Cabo Rojo, became the alleged entry/exit point for a subterranean/submarine base that reputedly exists deep below its surface.

The outrage over the UFO sightings reached such extremes that the mayor of Adjuntas, perplexed by the viewings and doubtlessly irritated by the sheer volume of sightseers pouring into his normally quiet town, demanded President Bush order an investigation into the phenomenon accosting his constituency. It is unknown if his request ever made it to the White House.[2]

The 1992-94 period witnessed an intensification in the number of UFO sightings, encounters, and abductions. A mysterious "aerostat"—a kind of barrage blimp loaded with surveillance equipment and tethered to a ground station—was launched high in the air by federal authorities not far from Laguna Cartagena. This action was ostensibly to help win "the war against drugs," but it raised countless suspicions that the aerostat was being utilized to detect UFO activity and other paranormal events in the area.

The appearance of triangular UFOs similar to those reported over the Hudson Valley in the 1980s intensified during this period. In 1994 a diminutive alien was reported to have been shot and bludgeoned to death by farmers. They placed its corpse in a freezer to become the strongest physical evidence collected on the island to date. Unfortunately, the party in possession of the cadaver is unwilling to relinquish it for study—chiefly out of fear that it would be confiscated by federal authorities.[3]

This high level of strange activity would continue into 1995, when excited reports of a monster would begin to spread across the island.

Chapter Two

The Merry Month of May

Jorge Martín's message on the answering machine on the afternoon of May 17, 1995, carried a certain ring of urgency. When I returned his call, the first thing he said was, "Do you have any idea what's going on down here?!"

For the next 45 minutes, Jorge and his wife Marleen, Puerto Rico's foremost investigators of UFOs and other strange phenomena, briefed me on what had been going on during their investigations in the central region of Puerto Rico's mountainous interior. Since March, animals of all shapes and sizes had been mutilated in the municipalities of Orocovis and Morovis. The authorities were stumped, and no clue as to the perpetrator's exact nature had been found.

This new wave of mutilations that disturbed the normally peaceful Puerto Rican spring was different in many respects from the classic 1975 wave investigated by Salvador Freixedo, who lived on the island at the time. Only a few cases presented the extrusion of organs that characterized the "mutes" of the American Southwest (admirably documented by Tom Adams). These new, gruesome developments left animals entirely bloodless through a single, neat perforation found on some part of the body.

The result of the Martíns' dedicated research, compiled by commuting between San Juan and the scene of the crimes, can be appreciated by reading a mind-boggling special edition of their magazine, *Evidencia OVNI*, that was entirely dedicated to the mutilation phenomenon. Martín made it perfectly clear, in his editorial column, that the special edition did not intend to sensationalize the issue—rather, it hoped to provide a series of factual events to help the reader reach his or her own conclusions.

The Orocovis mutilations were first brought to light by Arnaldo García, a radio-show host and journalist with Radio Cumbre, and an affiliate of San Juan's WKAQ. While the popular perception remains that these events began in March, they had, in fact, been taking place in scattered locations over a period of time. One year earlier, for instance, a number of deer at the Mayagüez Zoo had been found mutilated and bloodless. At the time, concealing this fact from the public was considered prudent.[1]

The mutilation wave also had a strong component of high strangeness in the form of bizarre humanoids resembling the so-called Grey aliens popularized by stateside ufology. One of these creatures, in fact, was the first to be reported during the Orocovis flap. A police officer investigating a dead sheep on the property of Mr. Enrique Barreto suddenly became aware that something was staring at him from the shadows. The "thing" was generally humanoid in appearance, three to four feet tall, and had orange-yellow eyes. The police officer ordered his partner to stop the squad car they were in, jumped out, and pursued the creature. Immediately he was engulfed by a sense of nausea accompanied by a pounding headache. He was rendered so helpless that his partner had to come to his rescue.[2]

At six o'clock on the morning of March 26, Jaime Torres encountered a similar creature in the field where Mr. Barreto's sheep were kept. Torres, an avid UFO enthusiast, had come to the area the previous evening in the hopes of learning more about what was going on. He and his brothers had repeatedly seen UFOs since December 1994 from their home in Orocovis' Barrio Gato. A nocturnal sky watch, he felt, represented a good chance at seeing more UFOs.

In the early hours of the morning, Torres realized that a round-headed creature with elongated black eyes, a fine jaw, and a small mouth was resting on a tree limb not far from his position. This unusual being had chameleon-like pigmentation, alternating from purple to brown to yellow, while its face was a dark, greyish color.

According to the lone witness, the creature made a curious gesture. It moved its head from side to side and produced a sibilant hissing sound that caused him to feel faint. Overcoming the sensation, he managed to see the creature drop from the tree limb and rush off into the dense foliage. Torres decided to abandon the site as well—quickly.[3]

"José Vega" (pseudonym), a neighbor to the Barreto property, claimed to have seen a similar creature at a distance, while keeping watch from a tree limb, as journalists and investigators covered the terrain where the slaughtered sheep had been discovered. Vega confessed that, although he had been looking at the creature through binoculars, it left him deeply shaken and made him feel ill.

The news division of TV Channel 11, in San Juan, reported that, on the night of May 11, a gargoylesque creature had been reported by a policeman and other individuals waiting at a bus stop in Santurce—the hub of metropolitan San Juan. Armed with his truncheon, the policeman struggled bravely against the five-foot-tall creature outside the building that houses the water and sewage utility, Aqueductos y Alcantarillados. The nightmarish creature had allegedly been devouring a rat before squaring off with the policeman. The creature flew straight into the air, snatching the billy club out of the policeman's hand with its claw. A similar creature was allegedly seen flying over the De Diego Expressway by drivers caught in an afternoon traffic jam. No doubt many of them envied its freedom of movement!

Reports issuing from the Fajardo area, where the El Conquistador Hotel complex is located, indicated that local residents were concerned by chilling screams and howls heard in the night skies, seemingly produced by something flying over the area.

On May 15, 1995, Martín interviewed Mr. Dolores Torres in the mountain community of Barranquitas. According to the gentleman's testimony, he had stepped out to his backyard momentarily to cut some fresh plantain bananas for dinner, when everything around him became brightly lit in shades of yellow, orange, red, and white. When he looked up to locate the source of the polychromatic display, he was stunned to see a transparent, cylindrical object less than two feet long suspended from a cable that vanished into the sky.

The next thing Torres became aware of was that a large, black shape was flying or floating toward the cylinder. He was able to distinguish a grey-faced, humanoid figure sheathed in a black outfit. The figure, whose eyes had the curious detail of being shut, approached the farmer, who took a few swings at it with his machete. The cylinder and the black-clad figure disappeared, leaving Torres badly shaken and in need of medical treatment. During his interview with Martín, he declared:

> Look, people have come here to tell me that the thing I saw was the Chupacabras that's been killing all these animals. Others tell me it's the devil. They're both wrong. These creatures are extraterrestrials...what use could the devil have for a cylinder with a cable attached to it? Something's definitely wrong here.[4]

Mr. Torres was not alone in his speculation regarding an extraterrestrial origin to the entire situation. The strangeness of the animal deaths in Orocovis' Barrio Saltos had many wondering if the federal government would step into the confusing and frightening situation to investigate, particularly after it was learned that a representative of the US Department of Agriculture had inquired into the situation, and that his superiors in Washington had developed interest in the matter as a result of media items issuing from the island.

By now, both the farmers and townspeople of Orocovis were convinced that they were faced with an extraterrestrial menace. Fifty goats had been slain in the town of Comerío, south of Bayamón, and the creature responsible had been identified as three feet tall and hairy. The means by which the animals had been slain was common to all others on the island—incisions around the neck, through which blood had been extracted, and, in some cases, the absence of certain organs, such as the heart and the liver. Stories flew all over the island about the monstrous "*Chupacabras.*" Literally translated, the word means "Goatsucker."

On May 19, 1995, the inhabitants of the beautiful lake town of Patillas were dazzled by a UFO that flew over the Valle Real urbanization. According to Moisés Picart, the vehicle lit up the hillsides and disappeared shortly afterward. It did not correspond to any known commercial or military craft. Amazingly bright objects were reported over the neighboring communities of Comerío and Barranquitas, where another high-strangeness event had transpired.[5]

Earlier that same week, an elderly sugarcane cutter, hard at work in the fields, suffered a heart attack after fending off an attack by a monstrous, winged creature (which may or may not have been the Chupacabras) in broad daylight. A police report indicated that the man had been carrying out his work at Barrio Palo Hincado when the "bird" (for want of a better description) assaulted him from behind.[6]

Don Francisco Ruiz, a cattleman in the town of Humacao on Puerto Rico's eastern shore (south of the Roosevelt Roads Naval Facility), was stunned to discover, on the morning of May 22, that three of his goats and their young lay dead without a drop of blood in their bodies. Officer Stephen Alvarez, a spokesman for the police department, said the dead animals were found in the Punta Santiago section of Humacao. Puncture marks were discovered in the goats' necks, foreheads, and legs.

The results of Mr. Ruiz' crude autopsies on his animals, performed on the spot, demonstrated beyond any doubt that the carcasses had been completely emptied of blood. This was the first case to take place outside the mountainous central municipalities of the island, but it would by no means be the last.

Chapter Three

Into the Realm of Beasts

Perhaps no single portion of paranormal studies evokes more reactions —positive and negative—than the appearance of strange beasts, ranging from winged entities and oversized felines to grotesque, hairy, simian creatures. They elude police and hunters, yet become plainly visible to suburbanites emptying trash. They have been seen hurling 55-gallon drums at their pursuers, yet also appear to have a ghostly, insubstantial aspect that allows them to vanish almost instantly. They have been reported in every location possible, from the tropical rain forests and high mountains to the heavily congested streets of metropolitan areas.

Many investigators have shunned research into these apparitions. It is a surefire way to achieve disrespectability, even among fellow sleuths of the unknown. The scientific/academic establishment scoffs benignly at these reports, confident that what is not known to it is not knowledge. Meanwhile, to this very day, thousands—perhaps hundreds of thousands—of witnesses around the globe continue to report encounters with physical entities that defy explanation.

In the restless years between the two world wars, journalist H. T. Wilkins visited the Belgian city of Bruges, and looked into a most curious story regarding an ancient monastery once occupied by members of the Dominican order. At the turn of the century, Wilkins' host told him, the monastery had been turned into a boarding house for the use of students and tourists. In many cases, paying guests refused to stay the night because of a foul-smelling apparition described as "damned inhuman."[1]

Not relishing the prospect of losing more customers, the owner contracted a crew of builders to break up the stone floor of a cellar believed to be the root of the problem. Nothing was found underneath the cold medieval stones, but when the cellar walls were broken, the builders discovered an alcove containing bones that were not the least bit human. A pathologist was summoned to examine the disquieting find. After careful observation of the bones, the pathologist declared that they belonged to an adult, rather than an infant. Aside from that, he was unable to say much more about the monstrosity.

Wilkins was told that, once the bones were removed to the Belgian Medical Museum, no further disturbances were reported. He ended his treatment of the subject by speculating whether or not the remains were those of a creature resulting from "some nasty amour of the unnatural type denounced in the books of the Pentateuch, or the remains of some horrible thing teleported to Bruges from some world in space."[2]

This quasi-Lovecraftian account might be dismissed as a fanciful Gothic anecdote related to a visitor to a foreign country. But could those bones, lying in the dusty ossuary of some European medical establishment, be physical proof that non-human creatures slip in and out of our world?

Perhaps the man-apes known as Sasquatch, Yeti, Ucumari, etc. constitute the greatest and best-known variety of mystery creature, and the only kind whose study has received a tacit nod from officialdom. Anthropologists have even gone as far as establishing its identity as the *Gigantopithecus*, an anthropoidal creature that may have survived into modern times by keeping clear of *Homo sapiens*. The historic record contains mentions of these beings. They were used by the ancient Medes and Persians as ferocious battle animals, and Nearchos, Alexander the Great's admiral, encountered communities of them on the barren shores of the Persian Gulf, living in crude huts made of whalebones. Medieval bestiaries faithfully included them under such headings as woodwose, wild man, vampire, and other demi-human categories. Bigfoot may have given rise to the Nordic myth of giant trolls. All this appears to point to an elusive, physical being that has been encountered repeatedly throughout the centuries.

Argentina's Salta region has played host to a number of hairy-hominid sightings for many years. This rugged, mountainous region could not differ more from the Sasquatch's forested Pacific Northwest. Its arid, desolate landscapes meet vast salt deserts, such as the Puna de Atacama, where rainfall is almost nonexistent.

According to Dr. Rafael Lara Palmeros, Director of Research for Mexico's CEFP, Dr. José Cerato and geologist Claudio Spitch discovered the footprints of a Bigfoot-like creature at an elevation of almost 16,000 feet in 1957. The prints, according to Spitch, were so large that they precluded the possibility of having been made by a human being. A month later, José Santolay ran into the alleged maker of the footprints—a large, fur-covered creature that terrified him by emitting sharp cries. Authorities looking into Santolay's claims surmised that it could have been the *Ukumar Zupai* described in the legends of the Coya inhabitants of the region.[3]

Seventeen years later, Benigno Hoyos, a worker in the vicinity of the Arízaro salt desert, had a face-to-face encounter with one of these creatures, and fired at it with his gun.

According to anthropologist Silvia Alicia Barrios, hunters have successfully apprehended live specimens of Bigfoot's southern cousin. One such case involves the capture of a family of Ukumaris—a mother and two offspring—by Andrés Olguín. The two young Ukumaris were allegedly turned over to a Paraguayan zoologist.

In late December 1993, repeated Bigfoot incidents surfaced in New Mexico. Among them were sightings of a large, hairy creature near a major highway; a white Bigfoot; another similar creature stalking a herd of elk; and, more amazingly, a report of a large man-ape that hurled a dog over a six-foot fence. Bigfoot was also active in Pennsylvania during January 1994. It caused a flurry of excitement there for a number of days.[4]

The files of Pennsylvanian researcher Stan Gordon include a 1995 case in which a young man, home alone in a part of the state notorious for its manifold Bigfoot sightings, ran barefoot across a freshly-tarred driveway to get away from a screaming creature prowling in the vicinity. Unlike its counterpart on the Pacific coast, the Pennsylvania Bigfoot has shown an inclination toward appearing in suburban areas close to human habitation.[5]

Also among the Pennsylvanian sightings are some that border on the paranormal. In one case, three-toed creatures were seen in the proximity of a UFO. Other entities could be pierced by flashlight beams, as if not really there (holographic projections?). In one classic case, a woman heard what she thought was the sound of a raccoon or dog rattling through cans on her porch; when she went outside to inspect, she was confronted with a seven-foot-tall, hairy ape. The woman fired almost point-blank at the creature, which "just disappeared in a flash of light...just like someone taking a picture." Gordon notes that many involved in UFO/Bigfoot cases have experienced strange presences in their homes and other occult manifestations.[6]

Noted authors Jerome Clark and Loren Coleman discussed the appearance of one of these man-beasts at a séance in Poland during the 1920s. According to the testimony of Colonel Norbert Ochorowicz, witness to one of these apparitions, the ape-like creature often caused fear among the sitters, but did not have an evil disposition and expressed "goodwill, gentleness, and readiness to obey."[7]

During the earlier wave of cattle mutilations in the mid-1970s, Puerto Rico was also visited by the ubiquitous big, hairy monsters. Many witnesses to these Bigfoot-type creatures agreed that they ranged in height from four to seven feet, had black or brown fur, presented a generally humanoid appearance, and had a penchant for destroying plantain and banana trees by tearing them open to extract their nutritious sap. One witness managed to fire his pistol at one of these rampaging creatures. It had no apparent effect. An issue of *Enigma!* magazine featured a photograph taken of this apparently vegetarian "smallfoot." It was christened *El comecogollos* (roughly translated as the "banana tree eater," a most unwieldy moniker) by the irreverent island media. The creature's existence and exploits, however small, became a regular feature in local comedy shows.

The *Comecogollos'* apparently placid nature and vegan ways did not mean that the other hairy hominids under investigation were equally peaceful. A document obtained by Jorge Martín deals with a preliminary investigation into one of these cases, in which a Bigfoot-type entity embarked upon a spree of raids against animals kept in hen houses, pens, and hutches in the community of Trujillo Alto. The Alamo family, who witnessed one such raid on their property, described the hairy intruder as having glowing, blue eyes and greater proportions than the *Comecogollos*.

Another "manimal" nearly caused a resident of Rexville, a suburb of San Juan, to have a heart attack in the summer of 1991. Eduardo Velasco stepped out to his backyard one day, only to discover that the 18 rabbits he kept in neat hutches had been ripped to pieces by the fury of some powerful, unknown entity. "It" had torn its way right through the resistant wire of the hutches to reach its prey.[8]

Winged Wonders

To many, winged humans and humanoids belong strictly in the realm of myth (Daedalus and the Garuda) or in the literary domain of magic realism, as exemplified by Gabriel García Márquez' *A Very Old Man with Very Big Wings* or Pedro Prado's *Alsino*. Cryptozoologists and Fortean researchers, however, know these flights of fancy are firmly grounded in sightings of weird, often hostile anthropomorphic figures that move through the air with wings entirely too small for their size and apparent weight.

The island of Puerto Rico is the heavyweight champion of apparitions of these strange, winged wonders. Some cases go as far back as the turn of the century, while others have occurred—too close for comfort—in this very day and age.

On April 23, 1995, Reynaldo Ortega, a resident of Naranjito, Puerto Rico, where a Mrs. Quiñones had encountered winged oddities previously, saw a gigantic bird standing on the roof of his house. Ortega had gone out to look for a small goat on his property, since the epidemic of animal mutilations on the island was at its greatest virulence. Ortega described the winged oddity as a creature between three and four feet tall, with the body and dense, black plumage of an eagle, a thick neck, and piercing eyes. The nightmarish raptor had an even more peculiar characteristic Ortega would never forget: it had a wolf-like muzzle instead of a beak.[9] This "griffin" (for want of a better description) did not harm the terrified onlooker.

During the early 1990s, residents of the communities surrounding the mysterious Laguna Cartagena reported seeing a ghastly, bird-like creature perched on a metal fence. The grotesque avian had leathery wings, scales, and a horned head. The witnesses produced sketches of what they had seen. To a great extent, it resembled a pterodactyl—a flying reptile thought to be extinct for millions of years.

Pterodactyl-like birds have been reported elsewhere on Puerto Rico from time to time. One witness recalled that, during her high-school years, while she was walking down a street with friends in broad daylight, she experienced a sensation of time slowing down around her. This bewildering effect made it seem as if her companions were speaking and walking in slow motion, and made the air appear rarefied. In the clear sky above, she saw a large, winged creature flap its wings and issue a cry that was apparently not subjected to the time-lag effect. Once the bird had flown out of sight, time resumed its normal speed.[10]

At the time of her encounter, she had no knowledge of, or interest in, pre-history. Only after later learning about pterodactyls in school did she realize she had seen one. The experience has remained in her mind to this day.

Chapter Four

June Bugs

As the month of June began, the media seemed to lose interest in the Chupacabras and in the constant animal slayings. The threat of another water shortage was on the horizon. (Puerto Rico was very nearly left waterless in 1994, when excellent weather produced no rainstorms to replenish cisterns and reservoirs.) Political intrigue between one party and another and the very real threat posed by the discovery that the US Navy intended to build a huge radar array in the southwestern corner of the island fueled controversy. Such concerns understandably drove interest in the Goatsucker to the back burner. But the brown mailer deposited into my mailbox on a sunny Saturday contained a cassette that proved the critter was still at large. Only now it was the skeptics' turn to have their say.

Perhaps emboldened by the success of a UFO conference held at the University of Cupey on June 3 by former-ufologists-turned-apostates Andrew Alvarez and Orlando Rimax and disbelieving zoologists and psychologists, the skeptics felt they could make their case on the national airwaves.[1]

The cassette began with obvious disappointment in the voice of José Valdez—my uncle and correspondent for my *Samizdat* newsletter in Puerto Rico. He warned that it had been a mistake to tape the live call-in show because the guest speaker obviously did not have the first idea of what he was saying. An hour later, I was forced to agree.

The host, parapsychologist José Enrique Acosta, announced in a somewhat affected tone that the subject of the evening's broadcast was to be that of the "vampires" afflicting not only the island, but also the rest of the world. His guest, zoologist Edwin Velázquez, had apparently studied these cases in Mexico, Brazil, and Thailand. However, in these other countries, certain people had not tried to make an issue out of the mutilations by alleging extraterrestrial intervention and other supernormal conditions, as had been the case recently in Puerto Rico.

The zoologist stated that his study of Puerto Rico's "vampire" problem dated back twenty years, when he had been employed with the now-defunct Safari Park Zoo. He had been invited by the media to determine exactly what had caused the mutilations in the Moca region during the 1975 wave. Apparently, after a search of mountains, valleys, hills, and dales, no cause that could not be attributed to dogs was ever found. Then he promptly added that even cats and mongooses were responsible for the mysterious killings!

At this point, I could feel my interest in the recording rising.

The slain animals were neither desiccated nor bloodless, as had been alleged, the zoologist contended. Blood was still in evidence within the organs. The signs of attacks to the muzzles of beef cattle were indubitably caused by canine assaults.

In an incident investigated in Toa Alta, the death of a number of heifers had been attributed to an itinerant mandrill. The zoologist pondered this, and decided that, if dogs had not caused the carnage, a mandrill would constitute a fitting replacement indeed, since mandrills are carnivorous, and the configuration of their teeth is that of a carnivore.

The host asked his guest why these things appeared to come about every two or three years, providing UFO believers with the theory that, when lights are seen in the nighttime sky, dead cattle usually litter the ground the following day, particularly in Mexico.

Pausing for a moment, the zoologist replied that, if one looks closely, one will notice a refractory period between the so-called waves, the last one being the Adjuntas sightings of 1993. This time span could be understood as a period of catharsis or release that the popular mind demanded in order to cope with worldly tribulations. Belief in UFOs could best be seen as a safety valve of sorts, and people who would ordinarily never consider visiting the mountains of Orocovis were now doing so as a means of escape.

The program continued:

> Host: Many people have said that the creature drags itself along the ground, lives in caves...is there anything to this belief?

> Zoologist: Not everyone can describe a creature they see at night, and their imagination fills in the blanks by association with other things. It happens very often in the Laguna Cartagena region, where feral monkeys escaped from a research institution. A person seeing one of these apes in twilight would believe they had seen a little man, thus confusing the real for the fantastic.

> Host: ...people must learn to banish their fears, as can be witnessed by the situation created around vampires, bloodsuckers, and an entire array of creatures.

> Zoologist: This is dangerous, because when the humble, ignorant people of our rural areas hear that there is a bloodsucking creature on the loose, they believe it. Hysteria sets in. We should not be so sensationalistic. The media, for whatever reason, only gives one part of the story rather than the whole story.[2]

After a commercial break, the host returned with an additional guest, journalist Arnaldo Ginés, of Channel 11, on the telephone. He had been invited because he had investigated the Orocovis "vampires." He stated that, even though he had seen dead animals, and a bull had died before his eyes, neither he nor his cameraman had noticed anything unusual.

Throughout the remainder of the program, the host and the zoologist continued to debunk, flagrantly, the idea that anything unusual had happened.

They insisted that the victim animals simply had died of bites from dogs or other animals. They suggested that disease might have been responsible for one animal's death. They denied that the victims had been exsanguinated, as many witnesses had claimed, and even suggested that the puncture wounds reported might be from barbed wire! Callers reminded them that some wounds were deep enough to reach into the victims' lungs, that the flesh was not torn as in dog bites, that signs of struggles were inexplicably missing, and that corpses did not decay normally, but their arguments were brushed aside. Also brushed aside were callers' attempts to bring extraterrestrials into the conversation.

When the recording ended, I rewound it and played it again and again. I still could not believe what I was hearing. The callers had the skeptics pinned against the ropes from the very first call.

Throughout the broadcast, the host and the zoologist tried to support the "feral dog" theory, which was no more supportable than the ridiculous "swamp -gas explanation" Dr. J. Allen Hynek had suggested many years ago (and later regretted bitterly) when pressured to explain away a dramatic UFO encounter. They forcibly invoked contradictions to support the dog-bite theory, and sought last-minute solutions (the animals being sick) to rescue themselves from the deepening water they were getting into. As Muad'Dib says in the memorable banquet scene in Frank Herbert's *Dune*, "I never saw a man drown around a dinner table before."

The callers represented a cross section of the island's demographics. Caller #1 was a middle-aged woman, obviously knowledgeable about the subject of unidentified flying objects, but quite willing to concede that animals such as the legendary Tasmanian Devil could cause such havoc among bovines. The host and guest mounted an ineffective defense when they sought to deny that any UFOs had been reported in the Orocovis area, because the networks had been broadcasting such testimony for more than a month!

Caller #2, a middle-aged, soft-spoken woman, triggered the skeptics' defenses in a spectacular way, prompting the host to become discourteous. The insistence that it had never been anything but dogs with sharp canines behind the Orocovis slayings became a mantra rather than a theory.

Caller #3, a middle-aged man, asked why dogs, feral or otherwise, had not caused similar damage before. Rather than limiting himself to answering the question, the zoologist took the offensive by challenging that belief in UFOs, previously described as a safety valve or mental alibi for a distressed population, caused these periodic manias. The pitfall lay in the fact that no mutilations were ever reported during the refractory periods when people were not "hallucinating Martians," so to speak. The host responded to the demand that he furnish proof of the validity of his own field, parapsychology, by making an arrogant remark aimed at putting the caller down.

But the coup de grâce clearly belongs to Caller #4, a medical technician who challenged the zoologist's expertise by saying that a televised autopsy had prompted experts to say that something was definitely unusual about the bull that remained both uncorrupted and free from rigor mortis. Reeling from the verbal punches, the zoologist had no course left but to issue a vague threat of verifying the story with the veterinarian who performed the autopsy.

Caller #5, a grandmotherly woman, appeared to be the only caller to go along with the pooch-oriented scenario the skeptics had set up, only to add the whimsey that a lion could have made the single puncture mark. Chagrined, the skeptics were forced to agree with her, but took advantage of the conversation to direct a few blows against believers in any extraterrestrial intervention in the Orocovis scenario.

Only Arnaldo Ginés' statement that the killings appeared to have abated in the Orocovis region rang true.

I do not know if Dr. Acosta ever revisited the subject on a subsequent program, but after a brief lull, the killings would begin anew.

Chapter Five

The Witnesses

By August 1995, there was no shortage of serious, genuine, and often frightened witnesses who had seen the strange creature dubbed the Chuacabras with their own eyes. Although some of the things they described seem impossible, investigators who have interviewed them find it extremely difficult to disbelieve them because they are so obviously concerned and serious, and they stick to their stories, even in the face of ridicule.

The numerous interviews recorded by researchers would fill many volumes and become redundant, but the following interview serves as a good representative example for readers. The two original witnesses questioned are Ms. Madelyne Tolentino and her husband, Mr. José Miguel Agosto. The interview was conducted by Lucy Plá and José Manuel Rodríguez, of the Puerto Rican Research Group, on March 20, 1996 in Canóvanas, Puerto Rico. I am grateful to Willie Durand Urbina, of the Puerto Rican Research Group, for providing this material:

Lucy: Good morning. My name is Lucy Plá, and my companion is José Manuel Rodríguez.

MT: Good morning. My name is Madelyne Tolentino Maldonado.

Lucy: What is the name of this neighborhood?

MT: Barrio Campo Rico in Canóvanas, Puerto Rico.

Lucy: On what day did you see the Chupacabras?

MT: Sometime around the second week of August 1995.

Lucy: At what time?

MT: Approximately 4:00 PM.

Lucy: Where was the creature?

MT: Facing my mother's house. [Note: Madelyne's mothers' house is the first
floor of Madelyne's home.]

Lucy: What was it doing?

MT: I was helping my mother, since she was getting ready to move into that
location. I noticed that a vehicle was about to park right outside the
house. I looked to make sure it wouldn't block access to the house. Then
I noticed that the fellow driving the car was frightened. His eyes opened
wide, and he started backing out. His attitude led me to believe that
someone was going to hit him or mug him. It made me go up against
the glass window, which, you can see, is quite wide, and faces the front
of the house. I then became aware of that creature, walking on two legs,
apparently having come quite a distance, from the corner. It would seem
that, when the creature became aware of the car, it did not want to get
too close to it. It stood in front of the window, through which I was

looking outward.

Lucy: Was the creature aware that you were looking at it?

MT: At first, no. Later, I deduced, by its eye movements, that it was, indeed, looking back at me .

Lucy: What change did you observe in its eyes?

MT: It moved them constantly, side to side. It dawned on me that it had no whites to its eyes.

Lucy: What color were they?

MT: Dark grey. [In an earlier interview, Madelyne said the eyes appeared black.]

Lucy: Did you notice anything else about them?

MT: They were damp and protruding, running up to its temples, and spreading to the sides.

Lucy: How tall was the creature?

MT: About four feet, more or less. At the time, it was walking like a human, on both legs. Its arms were drawn back into an "attack position," as though it were a [TV] monster.

Lucy: How many fingers did it have?

MT: It had three long, skinny fingers. The arms were also very long. They were drawn back, but I had the impression that they were very long.

Lucy: And its hair?

MT: Rather short, and close to its body. Rather well-combed, in fact. I noticed that it appeared to have been burned by something. It had some round things on its body, and the region seemed ashen, as if something had burned it right there. The burn mark revealed pinkish-purple skin, as if the top layer had fallen off.

José: As if it had been shot?

MT: No, no, no, not a shot. It looked like it had burned itself with something, and among the ashes you could see this pinkish-purple skin.

José: People are saying someone fired a shot at it.

MT: Yes, I know, but the gunshot incident was much later—around September.

Lucy: What about the creature's legs?

MT: Its legs were very long and skinny, and I could see three separate toes...like a goose's foot, that has a little thing between the toes.

Lucy: And its nose and mouth?

MT: For a nose, it had two little holes, and its mouth was a slash. It was closed. At no moment did it open its mouth, so I saw neither fangs nor teeth.

Lucy: What else did you notice about the creature?

MT: I noticed something odd in its lower back. It looked like it had feathers—something that didn't match the rest of its bodily characteristics. I thought, "What the heck is that?" because it did not match the rest of the body.

Lucy: How were those "feathers"?

MT: They were like feathers, but flat on its back. At no point did they rise. Do you know what I'm saying? [In an interview conducted by Marc Davenport in February 1996, Madelyne said the "feathers" became erect and moved rapidly from side to side.]

Lucy: Yes, I do. Were they joined by some sort of membrane?

MT: Yes, and it looked reddish, like a mixture of copper with brown and other colors.

Lucy: What else did you notice?

MT: It was such a weird creature that I even got down on the floor to see if it had genitals. It had nothing at all—it was "plain" and sealed. I laughed, and said to my mother, "What the heck is this? Does it defecate through its mouth after it eats?" It made robot-like movements, as if being controlled by someone.

Lucy: And its arms were in an attack position all the time?

MT: At no moment did it lower them.

Lucy: What were its movements like?

MT: Slow, as if guided by remote control. Like a robot.

Lucy: In other words, neither human nor animal movements.

MT: No. And when I noticed the look in its eyes, I shouted, "My God!"

Lucy: You screamed?

MT: Yes, because it shocked me. To tell you the truth, had that thing appeared in front of me, I would have run, but since I was behind the glass, and there was a gate outside the glass, I thought, "That thing can't harm me in here." Meanwhile, when my mother heard me scream, she decided to go out and grab the creature....The thing took off running. I'm not sure if it was because I screamed or not.

Lucy: Then what happened?

MT: I noticed that it kind of hopped, like a kangaroo. But it wasn't a kangaroo! It plunged into the woods over there, where you see that palm tree. [Note: A street faces Madelyne's mother's house. Across the street, an empty lot contains a palm tree, a wire fence, and a machine shop belonging to Madelyne's husband, Miguel.] My mother ran after it. I went outdoors, but I stayed far away, where the car was parked. I thought, "I'd better stay here, since I have no idea how that thing is going to react." My mother was where you see that concrete pad. A boy who works for my husband is always willing to deal with animals and keeps a pair of gloves in his car. He put them on and went into the woods to catch the creature.

Lucy: Then what happened?

MT: He says that, when he tried to grab the creature, it whipped out what I thought were feathers. He says that they stood straight up and that they were very long spines.

José: Like a rooster's comb?

MT: Yeah. He says that it stood straight up and didn't move. The spines changed colors.

Lucy: What else happened?

MT: He says he pried its mouth open and saw that it had really large fangs.

Lucy: Fangs and teeth or what?

MT: He told me that they were fangs and teeth. He kept on trying to grab it and the thing ran out of the woods. My mother was also in there trying to catch it. There was a kid on a bicycle who went crazy when he saw the creature. He threw broken bottles at it. My mother shouted to a neighbor, "Catch it! There it goes!" But when I looked—and I believe this today—that creature has supernatural intelligence.

Lucy: What makes you say that?

MT: Well, because when the creature heard what my mother shouted at the neighbor, it started running much faster than it had. Its feet weren't touching the ground. It was as if it had been suspended in the air, floating. Then it disappeared down that other street facing the church.

Lucy: Were there other witnesses?

MT: That same evening, two drivers who run the church buses saw the creature. They say its eyes were lit in the darkness. Apparently it can "turn them on" at night. I told my mother, "Look, let's keep quiet about this and not say a word to anyone, or they'll think we're either crazy or liars."

Lucy: Where was your husband?

MT: He'd gone out to look for parts. When he returned, I couldn't hold back, and I told him. He said, "My God, that's what I saw this morning!"

Lucy: Have you had any further experiences with the creature?

MT: I ran into it again on January 4 this year [1996]. I was returning from K-Mart on Route 185. I began smelling a powerful odor, like battery acid, inside my van.

Lucy: When you first saw the creature, did it give off that smell?

MT: Yes, but not so strong. It's a really strong smell, like Malathion, poison. It suffocates you. I was trying to swallow and I couldn't feel my throat. I was driving along with my two-year-old, and he started gagging in the van. He would not stop coughing.

Lucy: Did you feel that your throat was burned, numb, or what?

MT: It felt numb. It's like taking a Chloraseptic® tablet.

Lucy: Did you feel any strange sensations in your eyes or skin?

MT: No, just my throat.

José: Did you feel faint?

MT: No, but I felt that, if I stayed there, smelling that reek, there was no telling what would happen. Then I told myself, "The creature must be still roaming around here."

Lucy: What time was it?

MT: Around 7:00 PM. Beyond the race track, in front of Canóvanas' Barrio Cambalache, right there, on the right, I saw the creature. It was standing in front of my van, as if wanting to cross and enter Barrio Cambalache. I saw that its eyes were lit. They looked like Christmas lights.

Lucy: What color were they?

MT: Like fire—orange. They were a shocking sight.

José: How many times have you seen it?

MT: Twice—and I would rather not see it again.

Lucy: Please look at this Chupacabras drawing. Were its eyes like this?

MT: Yes. Yes, something like that. [Note: Lucy showed Madelyne the drawing in Compuserve® under the title CHUPA_GIF. in the Latin American Forum Library.]

Lucy: What happened?

MT: I hurried back home. I felt deathly ill because the odor had suffocated me. I arrived feeling very nervous. Miguel, my husband, asked me, "What is wrong with you?" I told him, "Look, I just saw that creature again." He asked, "Where? Where did you see it?"

Lucy: What did Miguel do?

MT: He told me, "Well, I'm heading over there. I want to see it in the dark." He went to find my uncle, and they both went off to the place.

Lucy: Did they see it?

MT: They reached the place where I'd seen it, but didn't find it. They looked and looked. When they were about to give up and come home, they decided to give it one last try. That's when they saw the creature on its way back. Apparently, after I drove off, the creature crossed into Barrio Cambalache, and was now on its way back. Miguel says it was returning to the place where I'd first come across it. Do you understand?

Lucy: Yes.

MT: Miguel says it was not walking, but floating in the air.

Lucy: Did its fins move?

MT: No, he says they didn't. He says it was defying the laws of gravity.

Lucy: At what speed was it levitating?

MT: Not a normal one. It floated slowly.

Lucy: What speed more or less?

MT: I can't tell you. You'd have to ask him.

Lucy: So then the creature walks, jumps like a kangaroo, and floats?

MT: Yes, that's how it is.

Lucy: [Looking at the sketch] Its fins start at the head, as shown here?

MT: Look, in my opinion, it doesn't start from the head, because where I saw those feathers starts from its neck downward.

Lucy: So the feathers run from its neck to its back?

MT: Yes.

Lucy: What about its head?

MT: It had less hair on it, and its face was pinched—skinny and so forth.

Lucy: Was its body thin or fat? What was the skin under the fur like? Did it look like flesh or what?

MT: It looked like rubber. It was thinner on top (chest area), but below it looked chubby. It had hips.

Lucy: Have other people seen it in this area?

MT: Yes, but they don't want to talk about it. They are asked many times, but they say nothing to avoid publicity.

Lucy: But have you been told that the descriptions are the same?

MT: Well, that boy I was telling you about earlier told his grandmother that he'd seen a monster, and his grandmother chided him. His father asked him, "Tony, tell me the truth," and the boy explained what he'd seen.

Lucy: How old is the boy?

MT: Six or seven years old. There's a girl who saw it also, and she is really in shock. The crew of the *Ocurrió Así* program came here, and the girl's father brought her over because they wanted to interview her. She was so nervous that she cried constantly. Later, some other people from the *Primer Impacto* show with Pedro Rosanales came, and the very same thing happened. The girl describes the same characteristics, agreeing in every detail.

I was affected for two weeks after seeing the creature—to the degree that, when I went to bed I thought, "That creature knows I saw it, and it's going to come back here to get me." [Laughs]. That's what I thought, because, to my mind, it was nothing of this world. It was neither animal, nor human, you know? I thought, "What if that thing has some powers and it appears inside the house even though it is locked?" You see how it affected my mind? I thought it was going to come back for me.

José: I think the smell you told us about is what the creature uses to suffocate animals and have its way with them.

MT: Yes, it's like when you suck one of those Chloraseptic® lozenges, and you feel so numb you can't even feel yourself breathing. That's similar to what I felt.

Lucy: Any other experiences?

MT: A young man complained to the police about an experience he had at the very same location where I saw it for the second time. He said he had been driving along, and hit what he thought was a child. He got out of the car and found no traces of anything, but the front of his car was badly damaged.

Lucy: Anything else?

MT: Elieser Rivera had something similar happen to him on that road, precisely where the creature was about to cross where I saw it.

Lucy: That would appear to be one of the creature's daily routes.

MT: Yes. In the Cambalache sector. Lomas del Viento is a very lonely place.

José: Elieser Rivera is the church pastor?

MT: Yes, he's a pastor. He was coming from church when it crossed his path. He thought it was a plastic dummy. He even got out of his van to take a closer look. When he approached, he says, the creature produced a long thing like a fish gig from its mouth, pulling it in and out very fast. And it had fangs. He says it was incredible.

Lucy: Was he also aware of the smell?

MT: Yes, he was.

Lucy: Did he feel pain in his throat?

MT: I haven't asked him about it. He thought, "This has got nothing to do with me. I'm getting back in the van." He told me the thing didn't even fly off...it seemed as if something jerked it straight up into the air.

Lucy: Did it rise and vanish?

MT: He claims it vanished as if a magnet had drawn it upward—without using wings. I would really like him to come forward with his story. His experience was truly terrifying, to tell you the truth.

Lucy: Were there any noises, sounds, murmurs, or whistles at the time of the sightings?

MT: He says it made a sound like, "sssssssssssssss."

Lucy: Where did the sound come from?

MT: From around the creature.

Lucy: Any other experiences?

MT: There's a gentleman named Daniel Pérez, who once ran for mayor of Canóvanas. He's a serious, well-educated man. It was around the time of the primary elections. I'm not exactly sure when. He had to go supervise the polling places when he heard that "sssssssss" sound, and saw the creature drop out of the sky onto a rock. He let out a scream. He says he was shouting to his wife: "Brunilda, a Chupacabras!"

Lucy: How did he know it was a Chupacabras?

MT: Because he had already seen the sketches, and knew what it looked like. He says the creature stood on the rock for a while, then suddenly leaped through two dense trees without damaging a single leaf.

José: Any dead animals around here?

MT: Around September, more or less, there were some dead goats on a nearby hillside. Miguel and my uncle went out to shoot some videos. Mr. Jorge Martín, of *Evidencia OVNI,* was there with the boy who had allegedly seen the creature. This boy is the brother-in-law of the man on whose property they found the dead goats.

   Mr. Martín told Miguel that he would stop by to show us a sketch of the Chupacabras, to see if it looked like what we had seen. But the sketch they brought me was the one in which they had even added vulgar genitals to the creature. I told him, "It really wasn't like that, you know." I told the boy: "You're making it look like a science-fiction character." Would you believe it even had a pointy tail like a devil?! I told the boy, "Sit down and get your mind straight, because no one is going to believe that. You've got to tell the truth about this." He said the creature was a few feet away from him, and that it chased him and everything. He says the creature had made a nest of grass, and that a tornado-like thing had been left behind. It so happens that, when the creature was here, it also left a round thing on the grass.

Lucy: In other words, it squashed the grass into a circular shape?

MT: Like it was making a nest.

José: As if turbines had done it.

MT: Yeah. Precisely. He left the same thing here.

Lucy: Does it leave these marks in the place where it takes off, or where it's pulled upward?

MT: Yeah. It seems so. Then Martín told me to draw it, but since I can't draw, I described it and they drew it. I was still very nervous at the time. Not anymore. I can discuss it normally now. We've been on shows like *Christina* in Miami.

José: Were you paid for that?

MT: Yes, our expenses were paid. We also did a show with Carmen Jovet. We also recorded *Primer Impacto*, *Paranormal Borderline*, *Strange Universe*, and *Unsolved Mysteries*.

José: Did any of them pay you for the interview?

MT: Yes, *Unsolved Mysteries* did, because they did it like a mini-series where we all had to reenact what happened. The sketch you have there is the one Martín drew here. I signed it and everything.

José: I think Chemo [José Soto—the mayor of Canóvanas] appeared on Christina's show.

MT: Yes. Chemo appeared. So did Martín and veterinarian Carlos Soto. Carlos Soto was involved in the case with the Doberman Pinscher. Did you see that program?

Lucy: Yes.

MT: Well, Soto has had experiences with this thing, and he's not covering it up. He's not like the other veterinarians, or the people from the Department of Agriculture, who claim that it's all wild dogs or monkeys without knowing what it is because they haven't really seen it.

Lucy: What do you think—is there only one, or are there many of them?

MT: I think there are many of them. I don't know. Sometimes you think so many things. Because, if there's life on Earth, and God made so many things, we don't know if there might also be life elsewhere. We would be limiting God. If God made everything, right? He created the universe and everything in it. We don't know if there's life out there. We'd be imposing our limitations on him.

Lucy: So you believe in the possibility that it is an extraterrestrial animal?

MT: Exactly. Just like we have dogs and animals here on Earth, maybe they have their own, and have left them here to reach out to humans. I've thought about this too, you know.

Lucy: Could it be a mutation?

MT: It could also be an experiment or who knows what. Look, we rented a movie called *Species*. It would be a good idea if you saw it. The movie begins here in Puerto Rico, at the Arecibo observatory. There's an experiment going on in the film. There's a girl in a glass box as a result of the experiment. They put her inside to kill her, because there was something evil within her. When they try to kill her with poisonous gases, she breaks the box with supernatural strength. What came out from inside the girl made my hair stand on end. It was a creature that looked like the Chupacabras, with the spines on its back and all. It even sticks something out of its mouth. Why did they make that movie? Why did they make it, and why in Puerto Rico? It was really impressive, you know.

Lucy: What was? The resemblance to the Chupacabras?

MT: Yes. I watched the movie and wondered, "My God! How can they make a movie like that when these things are happening in Puerto Rico?"

Lucy: In other words, does it make you think there might have been an experiment in which a being escaped and is now at large?

MT: Yes, but they manage to kill her in the movie. But before killing her, she kept on reproducing. I had the impression that there would be a sequel. Look, a journalist told me that El Yunque was allegedly closed down because of the damage caused by Hurricane Hugo. He told me that the truth was that some experiment had escaped—not monkeys or anything like that. They never found those creatures. The journalist was turned back, but he knows a lot about it, because he's been researching this for a while.

Lucy: Has Mayor Soto seen the Chupacabras?

MT: No, he hasn't. But he has taken part in numerous searches.

Lucy: What other mutilations have occurred?

MT: It killed some goats on Lomas del Viento. Their owner was Lt. Jorge Rivera, of the Carolina CIC (Center for Criminal Investigations).

Lucy: What is the government doing with the mutilated animals?

MT: I'll tell you. The Civil Defense did nothing with those goats. The Civil Defense director didn't want to take them to Dr. Soto in Vega Baja.

Lucy: So what did they do to the goats?

MT: Well, they had to bury them.

Lucy: What do they find around the mutilated animals?

MT: Slime. The creature leaves some sort of slime. It also left slime on some rabbits it killed here in this allotment. The newspaperman from *El Voc-*

ero kept it and sent it to Linda Moulton [Howe], a lady from Pennsylvania, who brought Miguel all the equipment— even a radio station. She had the slime analyzed over there, and says it's nothing from this world.

Lucy: What color was the slime?

MT: Greenish—sometimes pinkish. They say they have no idea what it belongs to, but that it's nothing from this world.

Miguel: Hello.

Lucy: Hi, I'm Lucy Plá.

Miguel: I'm Madelyne's husband, José Miguel Agosto.

Lucy: What kind of bites does the creature make?

Miguel: Surgical cuts. Perfect ones. If they were made by an animal or wild dogs, they would tear the flesh, but no, these are perfect cuts, as if made by a scalpel.

Lucy: Where on the body does it make them?

Miguel: Around the throat area or near the genitals. In many cases it has taken the animals' genitals.

Lucy: How does it remove them?

Miguel: It apparently rips them out and takes them, since they are nowhere to be found. It has taken their livers and other body parts. They once brought a rooster that had had all the inside of its head taken out. You'd look at the rooster and it was hollow. It had its head, but hollow.

Lucy: But how could it have extracted the contents of a head?

Miguel: By means of some incisions it made. There is no good explanation for it.

José: Dead animals are turning up in Miami.

Miguel: And in California.

Lucy: Have there been cases involving household animals, such as dogs?

MT: Goats, rabbits, roosters, cats...

Miguel: The cats in Juncos. We went there because she called us. The lady
called the Civil Defense, the police, the Fortaleza [governor's residence],
and nobody—nobody went.

MT: And we had to go show our faces. No one wanted to listen to her. No one.

Lucy: What became of the cats?

MT: They lived.

Lucy: What happened to them?

MT: It made some orifices beside their anuses. Excreta was coming out of the
orifices. The lady was scared.

Miguel: She noticed that the cats were [urinating and defecating] all at once.
She had two cats. There were three punctures. Some [victims] only had
one.

Lucy: What else have you seen?

Miguel: Here in Barrio Quebrada Prieta, in Canóvanas, there was also the case
of some mutilated sheep. Some TV cameramen showed up, and when
they lifted the animal's foot, it had a tiny little hole. Suddenly, the hole
sort of opened, and they could see its intestines and everything else inside. The cameraman filmed it all with his camera. It's as if its ribs were

missing.

Lucy: What was around the sheep?

Miguel: There was no blood on the wound, nor on the ground.

Jose: No blood?

Miguel: It sometimes leaves them with some blood. The strange thing is that, when it leaves them with some blood, it won't flow. The blood remains within the body.

José: It coagulates?

Miguel: No, it's not coagulated, and it doesn't flow, either. We noticed at Lt. Jorge Rivera's house, when we were checking out some goats and sheep, that the characteristics were exactly the same. In other words, three perforations—and in some cases only a single one running from one side to another. The sheep had been dead for a day or more, and were still flexible—not stiff at all. These are the things that make you think. It's as if the creature gave them a liquid that kept them entirely flexible and kept their blood from coagulating.

Jose: Did they smell?

Miguel: Yes, very strongly. A bad odor.

José: Was it the typical smell of decomposition?

Miguel: Well...yes, somewhat. But please remember that when an animal decomposes, the worms appear right away, and there were no worms, either.

Lucy: Would other animals come close?

Miguel: No. That was weird, too.

Lucy: Has anyone noticed smells or noises when the mutilations occur?

Miguel: Yes. In the Lomas del Viento sector of Campo Rico, we observed the area where the creature appeared three or four days in a row. One of those days, a girl saw it walking in the pose everyone has seen it adopt—on two legs, with its arms in an attack gesture. That day she told her husband, who doubted it because it was so hard to believe. The following day, we found the dead sheep and goat. We reported to the scene and found some Civil Defense people.

Lucy: What does the Civil Defense do in such cases?

Miguel: Frankly, some of them took notice of the case, but the cameramen from Channel 11 and others showed up looking for evidence. We had a dying goat with several perforations. We were able to check it out completely.

Lucy: Are you with the Civil Defense?

Miguel: No, like any responsible citizen and volunteer, I am interested, having had the experience of seeing the creature, and reaching a conclusion of what is going on.

José: Do you know Chemo?

Miguel: Yes. After we checked out the sheep, we found it had few perforations and little blood. We wished to speak with Dr. Carlos Soto, the veterinarian, who had told us that any dying animal or any subject suitable for his study should be taken to his office. He said he would help us out. We called, and he told us to bring it in, since it was still alive. When we spoke to Mr. Aguayo of the Civil Defense, he said no.

Lucy: Why did he say no?

Miguel: Because he wasn't authorized to leave the jurisdiction. I believe that, in an emergency situation such as this one, the Civil Defense should be able to leave their jurisdiction. I believe the situation calls for more government help in order to benefit the investigation.

Lucy: Is the government not involving itself?

Miguel: I'd say a little bit more now. If they had let us take the dying sheep to Dr. Soto at that moment, we would be closer to the truth.

Lucy: No one wanted to bring it in?

Miguel: We could have, but my Jeep was in no condition to make a long trip. We called Dr. Soto, and he came the following day. The sheep died as he arrived...he was able to take samples.

Lucy: What were the results?

Miguel: The samples showed that the attacker was no known animal. He has conducted many autopsies, and says that what is killing these animals is nothing known.

Lucy: At what time did you see the creature?

Miguel: It was around 7:00 AM. I was in my shop fixing a truck. When I turned the ignition over, it made a very loud noise. I ran down to see what was going on, and I noticed the creature coming out from under the engine. It is worth noting that the pad cover was missing between the fan and the radiator. There was a space about 12 to 18 inches wide where someone could have hidden. It ran out, gave me a look, and jumped over the fence.

Lucy: How did it jump?

Miguel: It propelled itself upward. It jumped all of a sudden.

Lucy: How did it fall?

Miguel: Frankly, the creature never hit the ground. It jumped and vanished at a spectacular speed.

Lucy: Could you measure the speed?

Miguel: It was too fast. It was like seeing a reflection.

Lucy: Were the fins on its back moving?

Miguel: I didn't get to see that, but when it came out, I noticed that it looked like a kangaroo. It was large, like a giant rabbit, but it lacked the tail and the front pouch of a kangaroo. I'm knowledgeable about animals and birds, and I've never seen anything like this creature.

Lucy: What were its skin and hair like?

Miguel: Short, but thick and well combed. When I opened the truck's hood, I saw a lot of hair and wool in the air.

Lucy: Did you take samples?

Miguel: No, because I was uncertain about what it was.

Lucy: Did you notice any smells?

Miguel: Yes. I thought it was battery acid. I thought the truck's battery was leaking. It never occurred to me that the creature was producing it.

Lucy: Did you hear noise or buzzing?

Miguel: No, none. But the second time I saw it was when my wife was coming along Route 185 in Canóvanas back home, and saw the creature for the second time. She told me what she'd seen, and I got in the van with her uncle and went to the scene. We saw nothing at first. When we left, we decided to take a look in the woods bordering the Loíza Valley development, since the creature had killed some rabbits there. When we reached the place, the creature floated right over us, suspended in the air.

Lucy: Was it flying?

Miguel: No, not flying. I know what it is to see a bird fly or balance itself. This thing was floating.

Lucy: Did it flap its fins?

Miguel: We couldn't tell if it did or not. It was already around 8:00 PM. We saw the animal's silhouette. It had human-like arms and legs. It was precisely the same creature, but suspended in the air.

Lucy: How long was it suspended?

Miguel: About a minute, at a height of 25 feet. We could see it well because of the full moon. It was a clear night, and the reflection [of city lights] helped us out.

Lucy: In other words, it levitated?

Miguel: Exactly. It was defying the laws of gravity.

Lucy: Was it looking at you?

Miguel: Apparently it was aware of us. My wife's uncle, who was with me, a 56-year-old gentleman, was very frightened.

Lucy: How old are you?

Miguel: Thirty-two. I also was shocked to see a creature suspended in midair. People are saying that it's a wild dog or ape, but no dog or ape can hang in the air like that. What is it we are dealing with? It's a completely unknown creature.

Lucy: What's your take on this creature?

Miguel: In my opinion, it could be an experiment that we are not aware of.

Lucy: You mean an experiment conducted by humans?

Miguel: Exactly.

Lucy: Have you had UFOs or extraterrestrials around these parts?

Miguel: My neighbor was close to one of them.

Lucy: What did he see?

Miguel: A large saucer with many lights, about a hundred feet wide, suspended in the air and making a loud buzzing sound.

José: How high up was it?

Miguel: Some 40 or 50 feet high. They looked at it for a good long while. After three minutes, more or less, it disappeared.
    I was looking toward El Yunque once, and I noticed a star-like thing that was shooting colored laser beams sideways. We saw it for a few minutes before it vanished.

Lucy: What is the purpose of the gear Linda Moulton [Howe] gave you?

Miguel: Infrared equipment. Originally she told us that it was from CNN or something like that. She is a reporter, and devotes herself to investigating this phenomenon. She has written books and all. She gave it to me as a gift, since we have taken it upon ourselves to continue the investigation after having had our own experience.

Lucy: In other words, you go out every day hoping to catch it?

Miguel: Almost every night. What I want to do is take its picture.

Lucy: What is that you are holding?

Miguel: It's a mock-up of the project we're conducting. [Note: The mock-up is contained in a box. It represents a field with a wire box in its middle, connected with cables to the far right, where it connects to another box. At the left is a figure of a man holding a camera.] See? This would be me holding the camera....this is a decoy, a bird or a sheep...and this is where we were going to ground a battery cable with the positive cable grounded as well, to create a magnetic field of sorts...this is a project that some scientists believed would attract the creature—but it didn't work.

Lucy: What was the name of the project, and who directed it?

Miguel: Project EPOCA. It was directed by Linda Moulton [Howe] and John Caldea.

Lucy: When was it conducted?

Miguel: From December 1995 to January 1996.

Lucy: How long did it last?

Miguel: Two months or so, almost every night.

Lucy: What else has happened?

Miguel: One night, Chemo, the mayor of Canóvanas, called me at two o'clock in the morning because some people had had a close encounter with the creature that night. We reported to the area. We checked it out, and the animals were restless.

Lucy: Who went?

Miguel: Only ourselves. Chemo didn't want to call the Civil Defense. He said they would make too much noise.

Lucy: What equipment did you carry?

Miguel: A photographic camera, since our goal was to capture it on film.

MT: Miguel, tell her about the piece of meat from Lomas del Viento.

Miguel: Oh, right! I found a piece of meat. That was in Lt. Jorge Rivera's home. It was a rather large chunk. It was stuck inside a cubbyhole he uses to store tools. That's where the piece of meat was.

Lucy: What's so special about this piece of meat?

Miguel: It was fresh and covered with slime.

Lucy: Did you have it analyzed?

Miguel: No. Quite frankly, it was unpleasant. No one dared pull it out and bring it in for analysis. In another place, we found a hair sample with the same unpleasant odor emitted by the creature.

Lucy: What did you do with it?

Miguel: I gave it to Jorge Martín. He took it to be analyzed. He later told me that the analysis proved it did not belong to any known animal.

Lucy: What else has happened?

Miguel: We went to a place in Dorado because some spaceships had allegedly deposited some creatures. We investigated, but had no results whatsoever.

Lucy: Who told you a spaceship had dropped off creatures?

Miguel: Area residents.

Lucy: What was it they saw?

Miguel: Mr. Jorge Martín, of *Evidencia OVNI* magazine, could give you a better answer. Some said they descended from the saucer. Others say they came down in single file with slightly taller beings. Some of the neighbors pointed out that the lagoons in the region would bubble up when those creatures were present. They bubbled strangely.

Lucy: So you're telling me that the mere presence of the creatures in the area caused the water to bubble?

Miguel: Yes.

Lucy: What else concerning the Chupacabras?

Miguel: The creature attacked a Chow dog at policeman Juan Collazo's home. He heard some noises in the lower part of his home. He went down with his service revolver, and he saw the creature attacking his dog. He immediately fired at it. His car was parked behind the creature. The creature took the bullet's initial impact, bounced off the wall, took off in a flash, and disappeared. He says it flew off—something truly incredible.

Lucy: Was the dog struggling with the creature?

Miguel: There was a struggle between the dog and the creature. That's what he heard.

Lucy: Did the creature hurt the dog?

Miguel: The creature had apparently shaved the place on the dog where it was going to make its incision.

Lucy: So you're telling me that the creature cleans the spot where it's going to make the incision?

Miguel: Precisely. In fact, when we visited Mr. Negrón's house in Campo

Rico, in the La Pirámide sector, we found a sheep with perforations that had a cauterized area surrounding them. There were no traces of blood on the sheep or the surrounding area.

Lucy: Is the slime a constant factor in all cases?

Miguel: No, only in some. There are others in which the animal has no blood inside. The incised area doesn't look inflamed, either.

Lucy: What are the incisions like?

Miguel: Sometimes they're perfect circles.

Lucy: What size?

Miguel: Some two or three inches, more or less. They expand, but there's no inflammation in the area.

Lucy: Are there organs missing in every case?

Miguel: In almost every case. They once brought us a rooster that was missing its brains. It almost always tears off the left ear. In other cases, it has taken bones from the trachea, the jawbones—all through tiny holes. I'm not sure if you noticed that a sheep in Miami had part of its ribcage drawn out through a tiny hole. It's incredible. Elieser Rivera and I reached the conclusion that it could be something like a spur that emerges from its mouth. It could be that the spur helps it perforate and extract the organs, fluids, and bones from the animal.

Lucy: What's the name of your friend who saw the creature produce the spur from its mouth the day Madelyne saw it?

Miguel: Mr. Elieser Rivera.

Lucy: Do you feel there's more than one creature?

Miguel: Yes, because Mr. Martín is in touch with us. He tells us where activity has been at the time.

Lucy: When was the last time the creature was reported around here?

Miguel: A month ago. There was a case while I was in Miami, and there was another in Vieques.

Lucy: Has it ever attacked anyone?

Miguel: No, I don't think so.

Lucy: Do you carry weapons on your searches?

Miguel: Elieser Rivera was armed, and he couldn't fire. Lt. Rivera carried a shotgun, and he couldn't fire. It is as if the thing controlled his mind. When Collazo fired at it, the bullet went out. The creature shed no blood, and the distance was only nine feet.

Lucy: Where was the first mutilation in Puerto Rico?

Miguel: Here, and then in Orocovis.

Lucy: Have other people seen the creature and confirmed the description?

Miguel: Yes. This thing is real.

Lucy: Is the sketch we have here the one based on your description of the creature?

Miguel: Yes. It was made by Jorge Martín. It's the right one, but the spines don't come out of its head. They start farther down.

Lucy: Well, many thanks for your cooperation and your hospitality.

Miguel: Thank you.

Chapter Six

Stalking the Beast

There are no hard and fast rules for monster hunting. Certainly crypto-zoologists can indicate the most suitable equipment to take on an expedition, but every researcher, from Heuvelmans to Lara to Chorvinsky, has his own method. Some might opt for a photo-safari approach, hoping to capture images of the elusive critter. Others might consider carrying firearms, in case there should be a replay of the Goat-man incident, during which a cornered entity began hurling tires against his pursuers with the ease of a Frisbee® thrower.[1] Certainly the method of Canóvanas' mayor, José Soto, and his unarmed cadres —using a cage built from welded iron fencing and a goat as bait—constitutes another option.

Jorge Martín, like Salvador Freixedo before him, would not be considered a monster hunter by these standards. Both have gone for documenting eyewitness testimony with a vengeance, because both realize that the human component of the phenomenon is the only facet over which we can truly say we exercise any control or claim any knowledge. It is also better than returning home empty-handed after outfitting a massive hunt.

The Martíns' files are filled with accounts that will make a fantastic, absorbing book when it is finally published. In one case, an industrial complex could not find any security guards to work the graveyard shift, because three Goatsucker-like creatures had been seen at the same time. In another, people waiting for a bus saw a Chupacabras walking down a street in broad daylight. One woman looked out a window in the midst of a hurricane and saw a Chupacabras standing at a distance, impervious to the rain, wind, and lightning. A man with a machine gun fired a hail of hot lead at one the creatures, but was afraid to report his case because his firepower was illegal.

Flashback: The Moca Vampire

During the 1975 wave, Freixedo observed that the small size of Puerto Rico allowed any investigator to hop into a car and drive to the scene of the events in an hour or two—something that would be difficult to do in his native Spain, much less in the United States. It was this closeness that enabled him to be one of the first people on the scene at Moca. Freixedo wrote:

> During an evening in which UFOs were sighted over the town of Moca, two ducks, three goats, a pair of geese, and a large hog were found slain the following morning on a small farm. The owner was going insane wondering who in the world could have visited this ruin upon him. The animals betrayed the wounds that have become typical of this kind of attack, and, of course, they were all inflicted with incredible precision. I did not doubt for one moment who could have been responsible for the crime...I got in my car and visited the area immediately, and realized what was filling the animals' owner with wonder and fear. There was no trace of blood in any of the animals, in spite of the fact that the dead geese had snow-white feathers, upon which the slightest speck of blood would have shown up immediately.
>
> Over the next few days, the newspapers continued reporting the growing number of dead animals encountered in the region.

No explanation could be found for these mysterious deaths. I visited the rural areas on various occasions, to investigate the events firsthand, and found that the farmers were as intrigued by their animals' deaths as they were by the enigmatic lights they could see in the nocturnal skies. One of them told me that the lights reminded him of the revolving lights atop a police cruiser.

During one of my forays, I was able to see a black-and-white cow spread out in the middle of the field. I got out of the car and tried to reach the cow, which was not easy. The dead beast had characteristic wounds on its neck and head. Skin had been pulled back on one side of its head, as if by a scalpel, and the opening to one of its nasal orifices was missing, although there was no indication of rending. In spite of the whiteness of its head, there was not a single drop of blood to be seen. The farmer who escorted me could not stop wondering what had caused his cow's death. He related how, that very same night, he had heard his dogs barking furiously. He said a blind, elderly woman who lived on the edge of the field had told him that the cattle's frantic, maddened running from one end of the field to the other had kept her from getting a good night's sleep.[2, 3]

The benefit of 20 years has added little to the investigator's arsenal. Researchers of the paranormal still stand over the carcasses of bloodless, mutilated animals, wondering what explanation might satisfy the pleading look on the rancher's face. Can the ufologist, cryptozoologist, Fortean investigator, or paranormalist really "level" with the animal's owner, who has just lost a valuable investment or a beloved pet, and start spouting wisdom about EBEs, killer UFOs, interdimensional beings that need blood for their sustenance, and other standbys of the occult? On the other hand, can the skeptic tell the same distressed farmer that an "archetype" or figment of the popular imagination just put a finger-sized hole through an animal's throat?

Avian Unknowns and Aliens

The Chupacabras is one of many winged weirdos—ranging from pterodactyls to Mothman-like creatures—that have populated Puerto Rico's Forte-ana over the years. Apparently the winged monsters retain a fondness for their old stomping grounds in the mountains, as exemplified by the following case.

Georgie Quiñones, a citizen of Naranjito (a community located in the island's interior), reported that his mother had run into a being she at first thought was a child, because its height and build resembled that of a three-year-old boy. The being was standing next to some hedges. Upon closer inspection of it, Mrs. Quiñones realized that she was, in fact, staring at something that she had never seen before. It had a large head, large eyes, a flattened nose, and a delicate jawbone that appeared to be connected to its body.[4]

Creature and woman held each other's gaze until the latter began feeling faint and nauseated. Taking advantage of her discomfiture, the being abandoned the area with stunning speed. The small intruder apparently belonged to the same order of beings seen earlier in Orocovis.

Mr. Quiñones' mother had witnessed a flight of gigantic birds passing over the area two weeks earlier. She said one had a hump on its back. She was familiar with eagles and the native *guaraguao* (a kind of hawk). She assured her son that the birds did not resemble either of these. One of the birds landed on the branch of a nearby tree, which bent under its weight.

Mrs. Quiñones also found 47 of her chickens dead on her property, which added a touch of horror to a strange situation. One of the dead hens had a considerable puncture mark on it, large and deep enough that a finger could be stuck into it. A neighbor of Mrs. Quiñones had an encounter with a small humanoid that allegedly "jumped him" and caused him to flee in panic.[5]

The Canóvanas Sightings

The summer brought sporadic sightings and reports of the Goatsucker, while UFO activity remained constant. The situation did not pick up again until the focus of activity had shifted from Orocovis to Canóvanas.

Canóvanas is a prosperous community that benefits from its location on Route 3, which handles the heavy traffic between San Juan and Fajardo. The majestic, mist-enshrouded peaks of El Yunque are only a stone's throw away, and the excellent beaches of Luquillo attract thousands of local and foreign tourists. Canóvanas also boasts the spectacular El Comandante, one of the finest race tracks in the entire world. It was this fortunate piece of real estate that the gargoylesque creature called the Chupacabras would select as its own.

Residents of Canóvanas' Lomas del Viento neighborhood were treated one evening to a rather spectacular UFO sighting. One of them, Victor Rodríguez, told Jorge Martín that around 11:45 PM, he became aware of a scintillating object that descended upon a group of trees. The light, described as "round and brilliant," took off from the area as if it had been spotted.

Lucy Batista, who resided in the Alturas de Campo Rico neighborhood, said the Chupacabras' inhuman screams resembled the combined sounds of a cat's yowling and a goat's bleating. The unearthly cry scared her and caused all of her animals to panic. One night she heard the sound of an animal running behind her house. At first she thought it was a horse, until the terrifying cackle filled the air, causing her to fear for the safety of the children in her household.

During her interview with Martín, Mrs. Batista expressed her belief that a link existed between the Chupacabras and bright, colored lights she and her husband and son had seen entering and leaving El Yunque, which faced her development. At first she had thought the lights belonged to National Guard helicopters on nightly maneuvers. Then she realized they were executing senseless maneuvers that even helicopters were not capable of. Curious, her husband and son drove up the tortuous mountain road to El Yunque to investigate. They proceeded on foot to avoid detection by patrols, but encountered Forestry Service workers, who turned them back, putting an end to their expedition.

Mrs. Batista now believes the lights are from flying saucers. "The creature being seen everywhere in Canóvanas must be an extraterrestrial," she told Martín. "The drawings that are going around show a combination of extraterrestrial and terrestrial animals. This is the conclusion that we've reached, and the conclusion of the people who've seen it." Other residents of her area refer to the creature jokingly as "the rabbit" because of the shape of its hind legs, or "the kangaroo," because of its ability to take prodigious leaps with its powerful legs.[6]

In the light of all the commotion the creature's antics caused in Canóvanas, many of the locals were surprised that only members of the Civil Defense had chosen to look into the matter. "The Department of Natural Resources was called, but no one was sent to investigate," one local grumbled. "Perhaps they thought this situation was something cooked up by the townsfolk."[7]

Witnesses were subjected not to the negative influence of Men-In-Black (MIBs) or hostile government agents, but to the scorn of their own peers. A young woman named Mariane, also interviewed by Martín, indicated that her husband's coworkers had taken to teasing him by calling him "Goatsucker." Other members of their family who also had expressed belief in the existence of this creature, or had seen it with their own eyes, also had been subjected to ridicule. "This creature isn't a joke," Mariane said angrily. "I didn't make it up, either. It's real."[8]

Undoubtedly, one of the foremost witnesses of the Canóvanas sightings, whose credibility was never an issue, was a pious gentleman named Daniel Pérez—a religious man who was well-regarded in his community. Pérez, whose interview Martín broadcast on his radio program, encountered the Goatsucker not once, but twice.

At about 6:45 AM, Pérez heard a moaning sound. He went to his window to investigate. He saw nothing unusual and was about to close the window when he heard a buzzing sound. Then he saw the creature. It appeared to be flying. It descended and landed on a large rock twenty feet away. It appeared to him to stand about three feet high normally, and about five feet when standing erect. It had long, powerful hind legs, short forelegs with tiny hands, large, slanted eyes, and a little belly. From the top of its head to the base of where a tail would be (had it had a tail) was a row of fins, which moved in the direction it was headed. It sprang back into the sky, clearing the trees without touching them.

The next day, at the same time of day, the witness saw the same creature, or a similar one, flying back the other direction. He said that its skin was the color of a squirrel, but covered with something other than normal fur—something that caused a strange sensation.

At first, Mr. Pérez decided not to tell anyone about his encounters, but eventually he told his wife, who repeated the story to a neighbor. Soon everyone knew about it. He thought the creature might be some kind of alien life form because it seemed to glide through the air only by virtue of the extremely rapid movement of the 6- to 8-inch-long fins on its back (which caused the buzzing sound that he had heard). He stressed that his sighting was a serious matter, not a joke. He urged others not to fear the creature, and stated that he saw no conflict between what he had experienced and the teachings of the Bible.[9]

Pérez was not the only educated, perceptive member of the population who provided a highly detailed account of an encounter with the elusive creature, but his testimony was vital for an important reason. He was privileged to have seen the "monster" twice. The second time, he was able to contain whatever fear or concern he may have had for his safety or that of his family; thus, he was able to take a long look at the entity and study its peculiar characteristics.

The excellent drawing composed by Jorge Martín, which had been featured on the first page of San Juan's *El Nuevo Día* newspaper, was revised on the basis of the Pérez testimony. The "spikes" running from the creature's head down its back were apparently fin-like appendages that vibrated so quickly as to seem like hairs to other witnesses (particularly those who did not stick around to take second look).

Pérez' testimony created an added complication. Previously it had been believed that the entity merely took prodigious jumps from one location to another by means of its powerful hind legs. Now it appeared that it was capable of wingless flight by means of these buzzing appendages. While the wings of hummingbirds and bumblebees theoretically are too small to support their weight, *eppur si muove!* (as Galileo would have said). Could this be the case with the Goatsucker? Pérez also corroborated descriptions of the creature's head, eyes (though not their color), arms, and legs.

Chapter Seven

An Incredible Month

The end of the summer of 1995 was dominated by "Roswie" (the nick-name given to the controversial, lifeless protagonist of the "Roswell Alien Autopsy" aired by the Fox Television Network in the US and by Telemundo in Latin America). Many high-ranking UFO investigators had already viewed the debatable footage earlier, but the democratic transmission allowed everyone to join the fray. The large-headed, immobile "spaceman" stole whatever head-lines were being commanded by the alive-and-kicking Chupacabras.

At this point, newspapers began to give the Goatsucker regular coverage. At least some of the latest exploits of the bloodthirsty being were recounted in the daily papers.

Puerto Rico has four newspapers serving the needs of its 2.7 million in-habitants. Foremost among them is *El Nuevo Día* (*The New Day*), which re-mains the public's choice for information. It is followed by *The San Juan Star*, a well-produced English-language paper formerly belonging to Scripps-

Howard. *The Star* has fine international and domestic coverage. The rest of the market is occupied by two radically different newspapers. The weekly *Claridad* (*Clarity*) is a government watchdog that advocates independence and espouses nationalist causes. *El Vocero* (*The Town Crier*) is a tabloid whose headlines, in bright, red, uppercase letters, often surmount a grotesque photograph of a murder or automobile accident. Unlike stateside tabloids or Mexico's *Ovaciones*, it provides little or no celebrity coverage.

The first three have traditionally handled any supernatural material gingerly. *El Vocero*, however, has always rushed in where angels fear to tread, developing consistent UFO/paranormal coverage as the situation demands. Julio Víctor Ramírez, a respected journalist, brought a degree of maturity and professionalism to the "saucer beat" throughout the early 1990s and up to the present. Rubén Darío Rodríguez covered the fanged bird, which caused a sensation in 1989. Many have chosen to disregard these facts and simply dismiss the UFO/paranormal coverage along with the sensationalistic car crashes, homicides, crimes of passion, and other matters that fill *El Vocero*'s pages. Unless stated otherwise, the following diary entries reflect events that appeared in *El Vocero*.

Tuesday, October 31, 1995

Halloween was never like this. At best, I recall the antics of my friend Toti Troia, who would take advantage of the cover of darkness to throw eggs against anything in sight—homes, cars, neighbors he disliked. But nothing ever matched the supernatural madness produced by the Chupacabras—particularly on a night like this.

Mayor José "Chemo" Soto, of Canóvanas, and his band of camouflaged hunters made it clear that not a single member of their 200-man militia had been armed during their latest foray into the tropical night in pursuit of the Goatsucker. Looking to all the world like a recon leader from the Vietnam War, Mayor Soto said that the small-arms fire heard that night had issued from weaponry in the hands of fearful citizens.

Soto was clearly pleased at the response elicited by his nocturnal patrols in search of the winged intruder. News of the Chupacabras and its nefarious deeds had made worldwide headlines. According to the mayor, one of his constituents had described the beast as a creature about three feet tall that could increase its height suddenly, and was endowed with either a crest or horns on its head. It also had large hind legs resembling those of a kangaroo. This matter, stressed Mayor Soto, was a very serious one. He said his patrols served the added purpose of calming the citizens of Canóvanas. His political opponent, Melba Rivera, who hopes to unseat Soto in next year's elections, has gone on record saying that the incumbent mayor is doing his level best to discredit the city by his ridiculous antics.

Wednesday, November 1, 1995

What a way to start the month. The Goatsucker or its peers is crisscrossing the countryside, laying waste to the small animal industry that had characterized rural Puerto Rico for decades. This time, the predatory gargoyle descended on the community of Sábana Grande, located near UFO-haunted Laguna Cartagena.

A report filed by officer Abraham Báez, of the Sábana Seca police, noted that a Nubian goat belonging to José Vega Lugo was found in a lot adjacent to Route 167, which leads to Barrio La Torre. The officer's report states that the animal was found missing an eye and displaying a curious wound on its neck. The carcass gave no indications of having been attacked by dogs, but the goat's innards were outside its body. The animal had also been rendered bloodless by its nameless attacker.

Lugo discovered, at 3:00 PM, that his goat had been slain in a lot near his property. Neighbors found several black hairs entwined in a barbed-wire fence.

Lt. Medina, the interim chief of the Sábana Grande district, noted that the wounds inflicted on the hapless goat "were precise and without any rending." Perhaps to keep at bay the more fanciful explanations for the goat's demise, he promptly added that there had been reports concerning the presence of feral monkeys in the area. Three years earlier, an unknown assailant had decimated a flock of sheep belonging to a doctor from the nearby city of Yauco. The dead animals presented the same throat punctures, and had inexplicably lost all their blood.

Mayor Soto's paramilitary antics may have been scorned by his political opponents in Canóvanas, but they were hailed as pro-active by Carlos De

Jesús, manager of "Junker Correa," an auto-salvage lot located on the main highway between Caguas and Rio Piedras. Mr. De Jesús insisted that the course of action taken by the mayor was neither foolish nor futile.

De Jesús' junkyard had just been the Chupacabras' latest lunch stop. Upon opening for business at 7:00 AM, De Jesús was puzzled that the five sheep and four geese he kept on the premises had not come out to greet him and demand their morning meal. Manuel Correa, the junkyard's proprietor, accompanied De Jesús in search of the animals, only to find they were all dead.

De Jesús declared emphatically to reporter Rubén Darío Rodríguez from *El Vocero*:

> The Chupacabras is a serious matter, not a cause for levity. The government should pay greater attention to this weird situation. Right now, only farm animals are being killed, but in the future, it could well be our own children or grandchildren.[1]

Thursday, November 2, 1995

The Chupacabras has hit the big time. No, it hasn't decided to kill circus elephants or giraffes—an Associated Press writer has apparently picked up the story and broadcast it on the news wires.

This time it was residents of Ponce who had the dubious pleasure of the visit. The Chupacabras feasted on four cats and five dogs in the Lajés and Bellavista neighborhoods of the city.[2]

Angela Lajés told the press that she woke up in the morning and found that her dog, who had been put outside in perfect health the previous evening, was dead. As well as showing a trickle of blood around its anus, the dog was described as being desiccated with a few viscera exposed.

Mrs. Lajés ran to her neighbor, her sister, Angela Santiago, who told her that two cats on her property had been found entirely dry, as if they had nothing inside them. "I heard the sounds of a fierce fight last night, but I felt afraid to come outside," she said, "but the fact of the matter is that a number of animals have been slain without any explanation whatsoever."

Other reports continue coming in from the Halloween spree embarked upon by the seemingly supernatural Chupacabras. Today's newspaper reports that 20 parakeets—hardly containing enough blood for a creature the size of the Goatsucker—had been found slain in the coastal town of Yabucoa, down the road from the prestigious Palmas del Mar resort. Not satisfied with killing the parakeets in their cage, the bloodthirsty creature topped the night off by relieving five goats of their vital fluids.

Mr. William Rodríguez's five goats were inspected by Officers Lozada and Ortiz of the Yabucoa precinct, who noted that the animals had been slain in a manner identical to the other deaths reported all over the island.

Melba Rivera, the politician who hopes to unseat Mayor Soto in the 1996 election, has asked Illeana Carlo, the Commonwealth's Controller, to look into the possible misuse of funds, personnel, and equipment by Soto during his patrols in search of the Goatsucker. Rivera's letter to the controller stated unequivocally that Soto had:

> embarked upon yet another propaganda act characteristic of his administration. Not satisfied with placing Canóvanas in ridicule, Chemo Soto also has taken advantage of the situation to squander public funds that could well be used to help our needy townspeople...the hunt for the Chupacabras resembles something lifted from old *Fantasy Island* episodes. Undoubtedly, a need for public recognition has caused the mayor to resort to the ridiculous, to the great embarrassment of his constituency."[3, 4]

Monday, November 6, 1995

So far it has only been animals, but the fear behind every single mind on the island was that the Goatsucker would get it into his head to give human hemoglobin a try. Two fishermen who had cast their hooks by the banks of the Canóvanas River almost became an entree, according to Obed Betancourt, a writer for *El Vocero:*

> The two men had been fishing for buruquenas (a sort of Caribbean shad or sunfish) in the early evening (7:30-8:30 PM) in the Barrio Palmasola section of Canóvanas, when they suddenly became aware of a sound in the vegetation behind them.

Luis Angel Guadalupe and Carlos Carrillo, his brother-in-law, were convinced that the thing that interrupted their nocturnal fishing was none other than the Chupacabras itself. Guadalupe observed that it was "horrible—like the devil himself." He proceeded to describe the creature as having large ears, oval, luminous eyes that alternated between orange and red, claws, and wings. The nightmarish intruder stood between four and five feet tall.

This close encounter prompted both men to run faster than either of them had ever run, while the Chupacabras pursued them, flying above the treetops. Upon reaching his house after the mad foot race, Guadalupe availed himself of a machete and turned around to see the Goatsucker perched on a nearby hutch, ready to pounce. But battle was not joined—the gargoyle jumped to the ground, leaving deep prints in the earth, and dashed back into the woods, tearing down the hutch, fences, and other structures in its path.

Perhaps it wasn't hungry. It was later learned that, earlier that evening, the winged terror had slaughtered fifteen peacocks and a heifer belonging to one Miguel Domínguez.

Mayor José "Chemo" Soto and thirty of his "Ramboes"—the militia-like posse of fearless Goatsucker hunters—patrolled the areas in question in search of the creature. At one point, Mayor Soto expressed a belief that the Chupacabras prowls the riverbanks to drink water after killing its prey.[5]

Tuesday, November 7, 1995

The Chupacabras strikes again: this time it has chosen to add a cat to its goat-and-lamb diet. Striking at a junkyard, it killed a cat and a sheep, and apparently swallowed an entire lamb, since the third animal being kept by the junkyard owner was never found.

The junkyard, known as "Junker Tito," is located on Route 1 between Caguas and Rio Piedras, a heavily-trafficked urban corridor. Perhaps the solitude that reigns over used-auto-parts cemeteries is perfect for the creature's depredations, since this is its second strike at a junkyard.

Victor Ortiz, owner of "Junker Tito," had this to say to the press:

> We have no idea if it all happened on Sunday night or in the early-morning hours of Monday. When we opened for business on Monday morning, we were surprised that the animals had not come looking for us, as was their custom. A short while later, we found the dead cat, two almost-dead sheep, and a missing lamb.

Ortiz went on to add that, in spite of the muddiness of the junkyard's terrain, there were no footprints to be found anywhere. However, there were signs that a fierce fight had ensued between the animals and the attacker, who vanquished them in the end. The dead animals had the characteristic, circular puncture marks around their necks.[6]

Wednesday, November 8, 1995

The Chupacabras, now believed to be merely one of many creatures, continued its killing spree throughout the island's central municipalities, this time leaving 15 guinea hens completely bloodless. The dead birds exhibited bizarre stinger marks, as if they had been attacked by a swarm of bees. This event transpired in the locality of Cidra, at a body shop owned by Juan R. Colón.

A few days earlier, a Cidra mechanic had seen a very strange creature land on a tree branch. Not willing to risk ridicule, he confided his experience to a cousin. The mechanic repeatedly stated that he had never seen anything similar in his life, and believed that he had quite possibly seen the notorious Chupacabras.

The undercurrent of fear caused by the Chupacabras spread throughout the city of Caguas and its outlying suburbs as a result of the mind-bending killing of a large horse and four goats belonging to Efraín Rojas, Jr.

The animals, kept at Mr. Rojas' property off Route 183, which links San Lorenzo to Caguas, were found with deep incisions in their chests. One incision led directly to the heart. No blood stains were found on the ground, nor was any blood left within the carcasses.

Jonathan Rojas, a high-school student, claims to have awakened from a deep sleep at 2:30 AM, after hearing the noise made by the horse kicking the door to its paddock. When he glanced through his bedroom window, he was amazed to see an odd, pyramidal object some 16 feet tall by 20 feet wide floating amid the heavy fog.

Rojas added that the object seemed to have a sort of entrance or doorway, and was hovering over a small brook 300 feet from his house, as if supplying itself with water. He fell asleep once more, and awakened at 5:00 in the morning to see the same object in place. This time he alerted his uncle, who was only able to distinguish an intense glow departing from the area as he looked out the window.[7]

Thursday, November 9, 1995

Mrs. Ada Arroyo, identified as the assistant director of the Mount Sion Nursing Home outside Barrio Turabo Arriba, in the city of Caguas, fell victim to a nervous breakdown after seeing the infamous Chupacabras. According to the story, the event took place at 7:00 PM. Mount Sion is a peaceful, inviting facility, equipped with a large, modern swimming facility.

Mrs. Arroyo was quoted as saying:

> I heard screams similar to those made by a lamb being slaughtered. I went out to the patio, and managed to see a strange, hairy figure, greyish in color, covering its body with a pair of wings. It had a flattened, vulpine face, with enormous, red eyes.

Mrs. Arroyo added that the creature held her gaze with its mesmerizing eyes before taking off into the air and vanishing from sight immediately.

It was later learned that the noises identified by the nursing-home director came from a herd of cattle downhill from the place where she spotted the winged oddity. No dead animals were discovered.

Other animals in Rio Piedras weren't so fortunate. Two sheep, a goose, and a turkey were found dead the following day. It was rumored that the Chupacabras had been active in the area only days before, when a 150-pound sheep was found dead and drained of all its blood. No footprints were found around any of the victims.[8]

Friday, November 10, 1995

Word on the streets has it that the Chupacabras is hiding out in the vast, natural cave systems that riddle Puerto Rico like a piece of Swiss cheese. Hundreds of residents of the town of Aguas Buenas, famous for being the birthplace of Luis Muñóz Marín, the Commonwealth's founder and first governor, believed that the famous, bat-infested caves of their region were providing shelter for the Chupacabras.

Mayor Carlos Aponte, taking a page from Mayor Soto's book, decided to organize a posse and go after the creature, which had already left its calling card in Aguas Buenas. The entity appeared in broad daylight. It killed a rooster and two hens at a private farm located at Barrio Camino Verde before being scared away by the screams of local residents who witnessed its deeds. Those selfsame residents allegedly saw it enter the gloomy caves. The police, members of the Civil Defense, and dozens of townsfolk headed to the cave area, but none dared venture into them for fear of cornering the creature.[9]

Saturday, November 11, 1995

Gun control is a non-issue in Puerto Rico. Not only is it a citizen's right to bear arms, but it is safe to say that one of every three island residents owns a weapon, registered or not. This freewheeling ownership of sidearms enabled farmer Elliot Feliciano to open fire on a nocturnal predator that turned out to be the hellish Goatsucker.

According to Feliciano, a large animal jumped the fence surrounding his home, prompting the armed response. While he cannot say with confidence that he scored a hit, the farmer believes that the sizable creature may well have been the Chupacabras. He described the beast as three to four feet tall, with large eyes and with what appeared to be wings.

Police report 95-5-050-15435, filed by police officers Gonzalo Tubens and José Toro, states that an animal making a noise that the complainant could not identify was shot at on the property. A search by both officers revealed no trace of the Goatsucker.

The El Rosario sector, located between Mayagüez and San German, has been gripped by fear since the first sightings of the gargoyle-like creature prompted farmers to safeguard their animals. UFO sightings over the mountainous region of Maricao (a notorious materialization point or "window area") have done nothing to assuage these concerns.

Two locals claimed to have seen a brilliant, round object fly over the Sábana Grande area. The following day, elements of the local police found an 80-pound goat, which had been killed by means of strange wounds to its throat and rendered bloodless.[10]

Monday, November 13, 1995

The possibility that the mysterious Chupacabras could well be an extraterrestrial force was reinforced by a very strange occurrence that took place in the town of Vega Baja.

Although five chickens were found entirely drained of blood in the backyard of the property owned by Julio and Julia González, the most spectacular event appears to have been the strange mark placed on the forearm of the couple's daughter this past summer.

Oralis González, five years old, was marked with a tatoo-like impression that read "OJO-10-OJO," after an alleged account with non-human entities. While the child is reluctant to discuss exactly what transpired, and her parents discouraged mention of it for fear that it would affect her studies, it is generally acknowledged that this supposed event has triggered the child's IQ, causing her father to describe her as a prodigy.

Little Oralis' experience came to light while police officer Pablo Robles interviewed Mr. Gonzalez about the dead poultry found in the backyard. The chickens were found lying in a perfect row, giving the impression that they were "sunbathing." This charming notion was soon put to rest when it was discovered that the animals were dead and drained of blood.

Tuesday, November 14, 1995

The UFO question rears its ugly head again. A resident from Aguas

Buenas claims to have seen fiery spaceships shooting "elevators" of light against the ground, primarily at sites where bloodless and mutilated animals have been found. In this anonymous witness' opinion, the dreaded Chupacabras is simply a being from another world in space. The man, age 37, insists on the need for anonymity out of concern for his wife and children. He lives near the renowned Aguas Buenas cave system.

When asked to describe the luminous elevators, he explained that they resemble cones of opaque light whose interior cannot be seen. He theorizes that some kind of suction must lift whatever is on the ground toward the unidentified object above, whose dimensions cannot be made out, due to the alternating green, red, and yellow lights surrounding it. The Aguas Buenas resident deduces that the recently slain ox and two goats found near his home could have been sucked upward to the vehicle, exsanguinated, deposited back on the ground, and discarded.

Other residents elaborated upon this theory, surmising that the Chupacabras may have been a creature lowered to earth from a spaceship, which was then unable to retrieve it, due to some technical difficulty, thus leaving it to roam the countryside in search of sustenance.[11]

Wednesday, November 15, 1995

A society raised on *Friday the 13th* movies, the exploits of Freddy Kruger, and "splatter-gore" films is usually immune to monster stories, but what happens when a creature that could well be an escapee from one of these celluloid nightmares sticks an arm through an open window?

Ask the wife of Bernardo Gómez, who saw, with her own eyes, how a clawed hand belonging to a long, thin, hairy arm entered through her bedroom window just as she was getting ready for bed. The claw seized a teddy bear sitting on a counter top and shredded it in seconds. Mrs. Gómez hurled a coffee cup at the sinister appendage, which withdrew immediately. She managed to see a single red eye and the left side of the intruder's face. The creature promptly vanished into the heavily wooded area behind the house.

These events took place in the city of Caguas, directly south of San Juan. Agents of the police, Civil Defense, and Municipal Guards responded to the emergency phone call. They found a slimy substance deposited against the torn window, as well as an unidentifiable piece of flesh that had apparently been left behind as the creature beat a retreat.

The Technical Services Division of the local CIC agency dusted the window for fingerprints, but were unable to find any. A thorough search of the nearby wilderness failed to reveal any sign of the mysterious intruder.

Thus far, city dwellers had felt safe from the attacks of this elusive creature or creatures. Yet, the same evening that Mrs. Gómez underwent her harrowing experience, two hens and their chicks had their blood drained by a Chupacabras-like entity in the heart of San Juan's Puerto Nuevo neighborhood, a heavily built-up area filled with shops, restaurants, and main avenues. The owner of the slain hens had gone to nearby Dorado for the day, and returned to find the hair-raising scene.[12]

Thursday, November 16, 1995

The long-suffering citizenry has decided to fight back. Neither monster, nor alien, nor gargoyle will ever crush the human spirit. The residents of Barrio Caín Alto, in the town of San German, chased the Chupacabras away as it was poised to kill three fighting roosters belonging to one of the neighbors.

This foiled attack took place in the afternoon, when the people of Barrio Caín Alto heard commotion taking place in the area where the cockfighting roosters were kept. Three of the neighbors encountered the nightmarish attacker, which appeared to hesitate at the sudden appearance of the humans whose fear was overcome by intense rage. They began throwing stones at the Chupacabras, which rose to its full height, sprang upward into the air, and flew away in the direction of a nearby hill.

The three rock-slinging witnesses described the intruder as greyish-brown and simian, with large, almond-shaped eyes, an oval face, and small hands protruding from its shoulders.

In his regular column on UFOs, Julio Víctor Ramírez, who reported most of the UFO incidents taking place during the 1991-92 sightings, observed that area residents did not link the Chupacabras with UFO activity. He pointed out that farmers in Western Puerto Rico linked the Goatsucker with giant vampire bats, which may have been introduced (deliberately or not) from their habitats in South America.[13]

Wednesday, November 22, 1995

Rubén Darío Rodríguez observed, in a column, that elements of the Department of Natural Resources had completed tests on a number of dead rabbits that evidenced deep puncture marks. They returned a stunning verdict: the wounds on the hapless bunnies could not have been produced by anything native to Puerto Rico.

The investigators thought it strange that the dead rabbits had been found outside their cages, which showed no signs of having been forced open. One of the rabbits had punctures in its paws, and was covered in a slimy substance (which would later be found at a number of sites). The slime also underwent analysis, but no report on the findings was ever issued.[14]

Coincidentally (but perhaps not), the rabbit killings took place in the town of Gurabo, where the vampire bird had been discovered in 1989.

Thursday, November 23, 1995

Reason enough to panic, yet no one did: The Chupacabras' depredations are coming closer to the urban sprawl of San Juan. This time it struck in Carolina, a municipality bordering the island capital. A small, mongrel dog belonging to Demetrio Rivera was found dead.

According to Mr. Rivera's testimony, his dog was tied out in the backyard, as was customary, when it suddenly began barking furiously. But the barks soon turned to pitiful moans, as if something were suffocating the small pet. This prompted Demetrio and his daughter, Ivette, to turn on the patio lights and take a look. They allegedly heard the strong fluttering of a winged thing flying away. Their dog, near death, was covered with a strange slime like that found on the Vega Baja cattle. It was reminiscent of the substance made famous by the film *Ghostbusters*. The canine was so terrified by what it had experienced that it refused to let its owners come closer. After a while, the Riveras were able to pour water on their beloved pet and remove the curious "goo" that covered it.

Maribel Arroyo, a resident of the same neighborhood as the Riveras, also had a visit. Mrs. Arroyo, who runs a chicken farm, stated that she heard the cries of large birds over her farm. The following day, she discovered that 30 of her hens had been slain and rendered bloodless. The unfortunate fowl had puncture marks in their throats and bellies.[15]

Friday, November 24, 1995

The very real possibility that witchcraft could be at the root of these mysterious killings was aired in the media for the first time, just as a UFO connection to the Chupacabras situation was reinforced by a close encounter near Toa Baja.

A resident of this town, less than half an hour from San Juan (in good traffic, that is), told the media that he had a close encounter with a small, four-foot-tall creature shortly after residents of the city of Arecibo were treated to the sight of a "saucer" crossing their skies.

A slight whiff of high strangeness accompanied this case in Toa Baja. Policeman José Matos, sent to investigate, found a number of dead heifers lying in a perfect row down the middle of a lonely road in the Hoyos sector of Toa Baja. The oddity was that no heifers of the kind slaughtered can be found anywhere for miles around the area. No one claimed the carcasses. This led to the belief that they were slain elsewhere and deposited in Toa Baja for some reason.

The eerie disposition of the carcasses was captured in a photograph taken by Baltazar Vázquez, of *El Vocero*. It led many residents of the area to speculate that a warlock or witch might be making use of the animals' blood.[16]

Saturday, November 25, 1995

It was only a matter of time before the lunatic fringe chimed in, ready to drop its two *centavos* worth on the Chupacabras scare. This time, the fringe was embodied by Brother Carmelo, a clairvoyant from Caguas, who wanted to describe the creature and the best methods to capture it.

Brother Carmelo was quick to state that the Goatsuckers (note the plural) were definitely extraterrestrial. He said:

These creatures are vampires, who nourish themselves on the fresh blood of their victims. They are purplish-grey in color, have fiery, red eyes, are equipped with a short tail, and could have two small, horn-like protuberances on their heads. These beings can come out only at night. They spend the day in places where the vegetation is extremely dense, or else in deep caves.[17]

In his infinite, supernatural wisdom, he added, "Not everyone can capture one of these beings. To do so requires the use of laser beams or a silver bullet."[18]

Need any more be said?

Monday, November 27, 1995

The Chupacabras (whether singular or plural) appeared this time in Rincón, a small, seaside town that may have been Columbus' landing site during his discovery of PR in 1493 (an honor disputed by the neighboring cities of Aguadilla and Mayagüez).

Five goats, out of a flock of 29 such animals, described as "costly" by reporter Tomás de Jesús Mangal, were found comatose. One of the goats died, but, as of today, the other four remained between life and death. A local veterinarian kept them alive with judicious injections of a coagulant known as Azium, which stanched the bleeding caused by the creature's trademark single puncture to the animals' jugular veins. The owner of the flock, Edwin Lorenzo Féneguez, was beside himself because of his considerable loss.

Things took a darker turn when elements of the pseudo-UFO research group Nova appeared on the scene. The leader of this cult-like organization declared that the remaining goats—the ones that had not been attacked by the Goatsucker—would die anyway. His explanation? They had been injected with a poisonous substance that would bring about death within a matter of days. This hardly comforted Mr. Féneguez.

An official from the Commonwealth department of agriculture, Hector López, visited the Féneguez farm and asked the distraught owner to touch neither the dead goat nor the four dying ones until his agency had had an opportunity to run a number of tests on them. [19]

On a lighter note, a young theater student from the José Julián Acosta School, Daynalee Cardona, has written a prose poem on the Goatsucker that could become the basis for a stage production on this phenomenon.[20]

Tuesday, November 28, 1995

Proof of the Goatsucker's existence? Hardly. The papers reported the discovery of a footprint or handprint—the very first found since this rash of animal mutilations began—at the site of an attack near Vega Baja. Photographs showed a splayed, six-fingered (or six-toed?) print in the clay-like ground. (The Chupacabras is usually described as three-fingered and three-toed.) More impressive was the viscous slime left around the neck of a wounded cow.

The bloodsucker was only steps away from becoming a victim itself. Police sergeant Jesús Medina Montes regretted not being able to steal a few shots at a being, shaped like a bird, which fluttered while making a loud noise with its mouth. The Chupacabras would have paid dearly for the wounds inflicted on a number of steers and a large Zebu bull.

Sergeant Medina told *El Vocero* that a local landlord, Anselmo Rodríguez, toured the property after the Goatsucker's attack, only to discover that much of his herd was bleeding from their humps. Some of the beasts were covered by a slime that could not be properly described. Irene Mercado and her nine-year-old niece allegedly saw the creature fly away from the area that night.[21]

Chapter Eight

The Infiltrators

Webster's Dictionary defines an infiltrator as one who "enters or becomes established gradually or unobtrusively." We speak of infiltrating enemy lines, of James Bond infiltrating the arch villain's stronghold, etc. The UFO community, a Hydra-like entity whose heads are always snapping against each other, has been howling in protest since the late 1950s that it has been infiltrated—like the labor movements earlier this century—by government operatives, outside agitators (shades of *The Graduate*), and agents intent on spreading disinformation. NICAP was infiltrated by these types, APRO probably was, and MUFON possibly is. From reading the vast corpus of saucer literature that has piled up over the decades like stacks of *National Geographics*, we can infer that the mission of these putative agents has been to drive ufologists mad by providing false leads, tantalizing evidence, and, above all, impressive-looking documents like the MJ-12 papers, which have the effect of splitting up an already divided community even further. The internet, the modern equivalent of the Roman Forum, contains thousands of postings that "name names" in real or imaginary efforts at unmasking the moles lurking in ufology's mainstream.

The infiltrators—whose existence is undeniable—have honed their techniques over the past thirty years, leading to the development of a bold, new technique. Rather than taking the trouble to infiltrate the UFO organizations, why not create their own cadres of UFO "researchers"?

The first of these shadow organizations in Puerto Rico surfaced in 1995. Their agents appeared at mutilation sites, places where witnesses had experienced encounters of every single kind, and at the homes of the witnesses themselves. They sported impressive ID cards, and were fully outfitted with gadgets designed to convince interviewees of their professional status. Forsaking the gas-guzzling limos and Caddys of the legendary Men-In-Black, they drove around in government-issue Fords and Chevys, which were eminently easier to drive on the tortuous back roads of the Puerto Rican interior.

These pseudo-organizations first appeared during research conducted by CEDICOP (Center for UFO and Paranormal Study and Dissemination) into the Orocovis situation. Subsequent information received by CEDICOP indicated that the members of these shadow organizations were in possession of "directories" with the names of witnesses to the mutilation phenomena and UFO activity. Their *modus operandi* consisted of interviewing these witnesses, offering them membership in their organizations, and promising to provide them with special means of identification that would allow them access to areas restricted by the police or similarly important agencies.[1]

At this point, we may well wonder if this equivalent of the all-access backstage pass is merely a delusion aimed at ensnaring the unwary. The power to cross police lines would be reserved for agencies like the FBI, the Drug Enforcement Agency, and other federal agencies. How could an allegedly civilian UFO study group acquire such clout?

Efforts to discredit serious UFO research also took a high-tech approach. Items disseminated on the internet created the impression that a UFO had crashed on the island during the month of July. This created a brief flurry of electronic messages from one researcher to another. This untruth was "substantiated" by the clever distribution, from an unknown source, of promotional materials (glossy photos) from a cable TV special depicting the bodies of dead aliens found at the Roswell, New Mexico, crash site. The special's cleverly fabricated corpses were circulated as the real thing among UFO aficionados on the island. These shenanigans prompted a response by *Evidencia OVNI* in the form of an editorial denouncing these efforts to deceive. Photos of the special-effects dummies, clearly identifying them as such, accompanied the editorial.[2]

The shadow organizations increased their visibility to parallel the rise in Chupacabras activity. One of them, calling itself Nova, operated out of the western shore of the island. Another, dubbed UFO, wore black caps with the unimaginative name of their organization stitched on them. These groups expressed an utterly unfounded theory that the bloodsucking creature was one of 20 or more beings that had descended to Earth to conduct experiments with human blood in order to produce blood viruses aimed at eliminating humanity. This effort was supposed to depopulate the earth, leaving it open for alien colonization efforts. They also claimed that the Goatsucker was "the source of the AIDS epidemic," and was unstoppable. (Perhaps they should have tried Brother Carmelo's silver bullets.)

Aside from casting a pall of ridicule upon the entire situation and discrediting any clear-headed investigations underway, the groups clearly had a dark side. They claimed to have been endowed with such broad powers as to be unstoppable by the FBI or Puerto Rico State Police. They offered membership in their ranks to a number of people, even a prominent political sience professor at the University of Puerto Rico at Río Piedras. These activities were discussed openly on Jorge Martín's radio program, *OVNIs Confidencial*, in a conference with Argentinean ufologist Guillermo Aldonati and other local researchers.[3] After their activities were denounced on the air, the phantom groups went into hiding. One of them even eliminated its trademark black outfits.

What can we make of the seemingly infantile, yet dangerous behavior displayed by the phantom groups? Only that someone is interested in keeping control of UFO information emanating from Puerto Rico at any cost.

Friday, December 1, 1995

The Chupacabras has chosen the Caguas suburb of Bairoa as its latest stomping ground, feeding off rabbits kept in outdoor hutches throughout the area. Rafael Ortiz, one of the individuals affected by these mysterious depredations, found two of his rabbits slain by means of holes in their necks. Another four were removed from their cages. Ortiz claims he heard some noises coming from the backyard area in which the hutches are located, but, much to his regret, he did not pay much attention. At daybreak, he was confronted with the sight of the dead animals and noticed the others were gone.

On the southwestern corner of the island, in the picturesque city of San Germán, a pair of ducks, a rabbit, and two chickens were added to the Chupacabras' tally of slain animals. As has happened in all the other cases reported in these diaries, the owners found their animals in the morning at feeding time.[4]

Some of San Germán's residents claim to have seen a strange, three-foot-tall being, brownish-grey in color, with slanted eyes and small hands, and equipped with what appeared to be wings. This creature was allegedly responsible for the death of a goat in Barrio Caín Alto. Nonetheless, the police and other government agencies have chosen to dismiss the matter as a joke.

The city of Guánica, site of the landing of US forces during the Spanish-American War of 1898, was also chosen by the Chupacabras for something other than its beautiful bay and fine beaches. A police report filed by Lt. Noel Quiles states that two goats and thirteen roosters were found slain with peculiar marks on their bodies at Barrio La Montalva. Officers responded to a call by an unidentified resident, who had found that all his black hens had been slain by strange perforations, while all the white hens had been shredded by the claws of a predator. Lt. Quiles was hesitant to say that the Chupacabras had been at work here. He stopped at saying that the birds had been slain by an unknown assailant.

A second complaint was filed by Reinaldo Serrano, who found two goats dead upon returning home at 6:00 AM. According to Serrano, the goats had been alive and healthy when he left for work earlier that evening. Although neighbors admitted to having heard strange noises, none saw the intruder.

Friday, December 8, 1995

Six sheep were left bloodless by a mysterious attacker, according to a police report issued by the Homicide Division of the Carolina Municipality Center for Criminal Investigation. The locale was none other than Barrio Campo Rico, the Chupacabras' regular feeding ground. The police report did not rule out the strange creature as the "perpetrator" of the incident.

At around 4:00 AM, neighbors were awakened by horrifying noises. A local man who happened to be walking by the place where the Chupacabras' attack took place was so frightened by the feral screams that he dropped his lunch box and ran away from the area. Police officers reporting to the location found five dead sheep, and a sixth one with an unusual wound on its head. It did not recover.[5]

The Chupacabras was not blamed for another bloody killing in which two dozen cockfighting roosters were torn to pieces. To the relief of local law enforcement, the crime was readily attributable to a pack of wild dogs. Edwin Velázquez, of Yabucoa, lost all of his fighting cocks, a misfortune estimated at almost four thousand dollars.[6]

Tuesday, December 12, 1995

As if the loss of the six sheep only a few days ago had not been enough, the residents of Canóvanas' Barrio Campo Rico are now being mocked by the Chupacabras, which has taken to running at a blinding speed after cattle and other animals. According to a police report, the mystery beast spent the weekend chasing frightened animals from one field to another, and even managed to steal a piece of meat that had been left out as bait.

Lt. Jorge L. Rivera, who has been in charge of police response to the citizenry's complaints about the creature, observed that the creature emits a smell resembling that of paint thinner. The local newspaper, *El Vocero,* quoted him as saying: "There is a great deal of concern here [in Canóvanas]. This is not a joke or a humorous situation."[7]

Last month, when one of Lt. Rivera's men fired at a strange animal he thought was the Chupacabras, a small sample of blood was collected and sent for analysis. An anonymous veterinarian who handled the tests declared that the samples were neither human nor canine, nor did they belong to any known species. These samples have since been consigned to a stateside laboratory, and no results will be available until after the holidays. [We broached the subject with investigator Jorge Martín during our stay. He added that the results had yielded levels of proteins and acids that did not correspond to any member of the animal kingdom, but that the blood also contained strong traces of chlorophyll!]

Wednesday, December 13, 1995

A curious vigilante movement has arisen as a result of the Chupacabras' depredations—possibly in imitation of Mayor Soto's posses. These armchair "regulators" have the distinct advantage that they merely conduct their nocturnal watches from the comfort of their own homes. They most often sit on their back patios, terraces, rooftops, and even in duck blinds located amid the branches of massive tropical trees. A respected professional from the town of Juncos explained that, around nightfall, he sits in a chair with his back to the wall, wielding a hunting rifle in the company of a German shepherd, hoping to "get lucky" one night and bag a Chupacabras.

Other armchair vigilantes have conducted their silent watches of the warm tropical night from the slopes of El Yunque to Orocovis. One of these self-appointed sentries has apparently discovered a correlation between the phases of the moon and the Chupacabras' attacks. It would seem that the elusive creature takes advantage of moonless nights and of the waning moon to pursue its hunting activities.[8]

Thursday, December 14, 1995

Seers and mystics continue to proliferate as the situation becomes more and more complex. Aside from "Brother Carmelo" and his Lon Chaney inspired silver-bullet theories, there is now "Brother Serafin" who claims to have plotted the trajectory of the Chupacabras' flights over the island. On an island 110 miles long by a scant 45 miles wide, the trajectory put forth by the seer matched many of the places where killings have occurred, such as Naguabo. Brother Serafin boasted of employing "sensory waves and vibrations" to find the Chupacabras' lair, conveniently located at the heart of El Yunque. Unlike the earlier mystic, Brother Serafin had complete confidence in his psychic gifts. He stated that he had been chosen in his youth to do good and to make predictions about the future. His ability to capture waves and vibrations like a TV set enabled him to learn that the Chupacabras comes from another world within our own galaxy, and that its kin are slowly dying out, due to genetic reasons.

Serafin's "vision" of the creature(s) describes them as hideous, with hair-covered wings and a pestilent odor about them, tall, but not very strong, and possessing the ability to "charm" their prey until they suck out their blood. He added that the creatures sleep during the day and move about at night, and that they will soon go into hibernation, perhaps in underground caverns.

A resident of Naguabo, José Luis Oyola, discovered that a number of the rabbits he owned had been bled dry by a creature leaving vampiric puncture marks on their bodies. This attack had a distinguishing feature. Many of the rabbits were missing, as if the attacker had chosen to first slake its thirst, then take other bunnies "to go." In this case, the victim believed in neither apes nor aliens —he was firmly convinced that the mysterious deaths were brought about by evil forces.[9]

Tuesday, December 19, 1995

The bloodthirsty Chupacabras struck again, after lying low for a period of time. This time residents of geographical locations as disparate as Naguabo (south of San Juan) and Guayanilla (on the island's Caribbean shores) experienced the loss of chickens and rabbits.

Undaunted by their losses, local residents have managed to find some grim humor in their predicament. A number of citizens of Caguas suggested that the Chupacabras' name be changed to that of the *Gallinejo* (a contraction of *gallina*—chicken—and *conejo*—rabbit), since, according to their tabulations, the nocturnal predator has slain a greater number of those two animals than goats or larger creatures.

Nemesio Vargas, of Guayanilla, lost a dozen chickens to the Chupacabras on the previous evening. Grimly, he estimated his losses—attributed to the Chupacabras' supper—at less than a hundred dollars, and denied that dogs of any breed could have caused the strange deaths of his birds. While he refused to say that the mystery beast had been the culprit, he observed that the punctures in the necks and backs of his fowl corresponded to the Goatsucker's *modus operandi*.

As if not to be outdone by his new rival, "Brother Carmelo" staged a return to the scene after the Chupacabras killed five rabbits at the home of Valentín Rodríguez. The alleged clairvoyant called the newsroom of *El Vocero* to explain the reason for the Chupacabras' preference for animal blood. He said the strange being has chosen to feed on the beasts of the field because their blood exhibits a greater purity than human blood, since it is free from the toxins that pollute humans. In the clairvoyants' philosophy, "the uncontrolled ingestion of fats, alcohol, and nicotine by humans have made our blood unsuitable for these creatures."[10] *I'll have French fries with my double cheeseburger, please!*

Chapter Nine

On Site

The winter holidays have a stronger hold on Puerto Rico than on any comparable location in North America. Anglo-Saxon traditions—the singing of carols, wreaths of holly, and the ubiquitous Santa Claus—blend imperceptibly with the thundering beat of Christmas *plenas*, the melodious singing of *jíbaro* holiday songs, and the serene majesty of the three kings on their way to visit the Christ child. Armies of *plena* singers beat their chimeless tambourines, singing litanies, and wearing the red caps associated with Santa Claus. This revelry continues past Christmas, past New Year's Day, for another week into the Three Kings' Day, and for yet another eight days after that as part of the *octavitas*.

Yet all this holiday fervor did not hold the Chupacabras at bay—nor did it comply with the skeptics' cherished belief that Christmas cheer would drive the phenomenon back into the dungeons of the imagination. From the moment my wife and I arrived in San Juan, the Chupacabras was foremost in everyone's mind—even if only as a figure of fun. A TV beauty leered saucily into the camera and tauntingly called out "Chupacabras!" at the viewer. Endless comedy-show sketches promptly blamed any damage done on the island on the terrifying creature. Cartoonish T-shirts depicted the intruder masquerading as a lifeguard from the *Baywatch* TV show, sipping blood out of a dead bovine through a long straw, or debating the right kind of condiment to apply to his next kill.

A fleeting hint of paranoia crossed our minds. Could the aura of hilarity bestowed upon the Chupacabras have been encouraged by officialdom in an effort to defuse a potentially critical situation? The ruling New Progressive Party (NPP) had already chastened one of its representatives, who had urged a formal investigation into the matter, and another had already lost his reelection bid. Would the gallant Chemo Soto also be unseated as a result of his participation in the Chupacabras crisis? Only the future held the answer, and our crystal ball was hazy.

The fact remained that, in spite of the initial concern caused by the Chupacabras, the bulk of the population was unconcerned with its activities, or with the doom-filled assumptions put forth by the phantom UFO groups in their statements to the newspaper. This point is certainly worth stressing: despite Puerto Rico's well-deserved reputation as the island that harbors every single kind of supernatural and ufological phenomenon, its population remain largely unaffected by the possibility that non-human entities are sharing their living space. If and when a formal announcement is ever made declaring that aliens (extraterrestrial or otherwise) are, indeed, visiting the island—or are estab- lished on it—the man on the street will not perceive any "loss of self" or enter into a panic as a result of a "shattered paradigm."

This resilience is perhaps characteristic of island dwellers around the world, who are accustomed to seeing unusual visitors pull in aboard ships or land in airplanes, silent testimony to lands beyond the horizon. Any visiting non-humans would merely be a continuation of this pattern. Jorge Martín has speculated that this tolerance toward the unusual, the spiritual, and the un- known could, in fact, be the reason that has impelled the government to use Puerto Rico as a testing ground for human reaction to the revelation that—as has been stated so dramatically over the years—we are not alone in the uni- verse.

An Early Morning Drive

Leaving San Juan on Route 3, the main traffic artery eastward, gives the visitor an idea of how congested the island really is, and how the so-called Metropolitan Area, which stretches far beyond the municipal limits of San Juan, is spreading like an ink stain on a tablecloth, growing exponentially every few years. However, the urban environment, with its garish neon signs and inescapable traffic jams, ends abruptly at a given point just short of El Yunque, giving the tourist a glimpse of what life must have been like before the onset of the industrial age. Cattle graze by the roadside where vendors sell *maví* and *guarapo*—derivatives of sugarcane—while horses roam freely with no fear of the increasing traffic. The rural bliss is already being marred by immense Wal-Marts and shopping malls popping out in the midst of the rural communities, yet there is enough vegetation to conceal an army of Chupacabras. And who can tell what lurks under El Yunque?

Canóvanas prides itself on being a growing municipality. The main entrance to the town off the highway boasts a monument depicting a Taíno chief and his spouse. Large letters spell out: *Canóvanas, Ciudad de los Indios* (Canóvanas, City of Indians). A well-paved street runs past the single-story, concrete homes which constitute the Puerto Rican equivalent of the American tract house. But bypassing the more modern part of the city, we come to the narrow, busy streets and hair-raising traffic of Canóvanas proper. The *Casa Alcaldía* (Town Hall) is finally within view. Our plans to speak with Mayor Soto, however, are thwarted when two beige-clad municipal guards inform us that the Town Hall is closed in preparation for a holiday performance to be held in the *placita* (square) directly outside the municipal building. We catch a glimpse of a platform and drive off, following a street that leads us out to the rural surroundings.

The fertile plains on both sides of the Espíritu Santo and Loíza Rivers have been prime grazing land for cattle since the Spaniards arrived in the sixteenth century. This place, where cows are allowed to sleep in the open at night, has been a magnet for the Chupacabras.

As we drive farther eastward, toward Fajardo, where bloodcurdling screams were heard coming out of the sky earlier in the year, we appear to come inexorably closer to the baleful mass of El Yunque, access to which is closed as a result of a shutdown in the Federal government. Despite the blue skies and fine sunshine, clouds cling to the mountain like cotton candy, giving it only the slightest hint of menace. With palm tree-covered Luquillo Beach on our left, the imposing bulk to the right conjures up Tolkien's descriptions of cloudy Mordor, as seen from the fair valleys outside its mountains. If a similar Dark Lord commands El Yunque's lofty, verdant heights, then there is some truth to the old Taíno legends of Yukiyú.

The next town along the road is Río Grande, and the mountain rain forest is still at hand. The Navy radio towers on Pico del Este, one of the El Yunque complex's summits, can be seen through the enshrouding fog. The inspiring sight of man's triumph over nature is promptly replaced by more immediate doubts. Is the US military using the rain forest as a laboratory to produce mutant species? What of the gigantic radar complex projected for the Lajas area on the island's southern shore, which bears more in common with Alaska's Project HAARP than with any other over-the-horizon radar?

The flow of questions is disrupted by a road sign indicating the distance remaining to Ceiba and Humacao, farther down the highway. Ceiba is the municipality containing the vast Roosevelt Roads Naval Installation—one of the foremost US naval bases. The presence is strong enough to be felt at this distance.

We finally reach Fajardo, the easternmost point on the island, a thriving community looking out to the Lesser Antilles and providing ferry service to the smaller island-municipalities of Culebra and Vieques. This area has had its own share of unusual activity. Not too long ago, UFOs were reported plunging into the ocean and emerging once more, and local fishermen and yachtsmen reported objects causing upwellings of water around their craft.

Perhaps no other incident describes Fajardo's reputation as a strange location better than the controversial *Garadiávolo*. Twenty years after a book on the subject appeared, heated discussions regarding the creature's true nature still take place. A respected professional who visited Laguna de San Juan, a large lagoon on a promontory jutting out into the sea to the north of Fajardo, discovered a most unusual amphibian during one of his trips. The diminutive creature was able to walk on spindly legs and even climb up trees. The man captured the specimen and brought it home. It soon caused a sensation in the press. Unfortunately, it was confiscated in the dark of night by men who claimed to be with the US government. It has been argued that the *Garadiávo-*

lo was simply a common sea-ray sliced in half—an old "sea monster" known as a "Jenny Haniver" to cryptozoologists. I can attest to the fact that samples of this *Garadiávolo* were sold for the affordable price of $7.95 at my mother's store in San Juan under the name "devilfish." Yet, others who saw the original creature firsthand insist that its cat-like face, eyes, and fangs could not have been the product of any hoaxing, like the "Jenny Hanivers."

The magnificent El Conquistador Hotel crowns the peaks above the fishing village of Las Croabas. Its terraced parking lot provides a spectacular view of El Yunque that cannot be fully captured by the camera. As noon approaches, the sun's heat lifts the veil of fog that conceals the rain forest from the looks of the average curious mortal. Within the halcyon environment of the hotel, we ask an employee of one of the dozen boutiques on the promenade if the Chupacabras has been seen in the area. "I think people exaggerate too much," she replied with a smile.

The Investigators

A writer for an Italian UFO magazine described Jorge Martín as having so much energy to spare that he could sell it. With a research caseload nearing 600, Jorge and his wife Marleen have covered UFO sightings, landings, bizarre creatures, and paranormal activity. It is remarkable that, in spite of the grueling amount of time devoted to one-on-one interviewing and on-site research, they still have enough breathing space to put out *Evidencia OVNI*, their magazine, and do a weekly radio program. *Evidencia OVNI*, by the way, is unique in the Spanish-speaking market because it is the only publication to deal in a sober, detailed fashion with nothing but ufology and its cadet branches. The glossier magazines have wandered down the commercial garden path of New Age mysticism, self-help, and "lite" ufology.

The Martíns' experiences with Chupacabras research have been described throughout this report, so there is no need to repeat them here. At the time of our arrival on the island, new reports were being deposited on their answering machine every day, although the media had apparently been advised to "cool down" the subject. Jorge is quite familiar with the print media's games. He once was a reporter himself, and he has seen media reactions to stories involving the unusual over the decades he has devoted to studying UFOs on the island. During the years in which activity dwindled to a handful of cases, Jorge was the only active investigator.

My wife and I had the pleasure of being invited to *OVNIs Confidencial*, the Martíns' radio program on the *Noti-uno* network, which has repeater stations throughout the island (and even, I believe, in New Jersey). Jorge had recently completed the tremendous show during which the proverbial whistle had been blown on the phantom groups described in the previous chapter—an act which led him to add, ruefully, at the end of the broadcast, that it might cause his show to be yanked off the air. To his surprise, he not only received strong support from station management, but also caused the phantom groups to tone down their activities—at least for a little while.

The best segment of any radio program is very often the call-in portion. This is certainly true of *OVNIs Confidencial*. Half an hour into the broadcast, when I had spoken about all and sundry with the host, an interesting telephone call concerning our discussion on the Chupacabras came in.

The caller, who had earlier been given the pseudonym "Julio Marín," was a former military man, whose involvement in sensitive operations had provided him with an insight on the situation. Among the items discussed up to the moment had been the Aberdeen Proving Grounds' alleged role as a harbor for strange beings, the greenish blood that had been recovered from a Bigfoot-like creature, and other instances around the world in which chartreuse-green blood had been reported. A portion of the December 21, 1995, program, including Marín's call, is transcribed below:

> J. Martín: Well, we have a caller on the line who is going to be making use of the alias "Julio Marín" in view of the information he'll be passing on tonight. The subject we're discussing this evening is rather sensitive—the strange creatures currently being seen, and the link they seem to have with the UFO situation. Therefore, let's go to Line 1. Good evening! To whom are we speaking?

> Caller: This is Julio Marín.

> J. Martín: Good evening, Don Julio.

Caller: I heard you discussing the Aberdeen Proving Grounds. I've been there—that's where weapons, including biological weapons, are tested. However, certain things cannot be tested there, which is why they have to make up wars overseas to test them out there. That so-called "peace treaty" [sic] in Bosnia includes Puerto Rican soldiers who don't even speak the local language. If you look closely at a photo of these soldiers, at their rifles—

J. Martín: Yes?

Caller: Certain weapons are designed, and since they can't be tested here, there has to be a conflict—

J. Martín: They take advantage of those opportunities?

Caller: Precisely. They take advantage of those opportunities... there are other sites in the US where aircraft are tested, such as Nevada and Utah, which are flat, and...Arizona, which is inaccessible, having mountains some nine thousand feet tall, and has valleys in spite of these mountains. It is a large state, yet among the least populated ones. There are many [Indian] reservations, and within these reservations one finds—there's no better way of putting it—other reservations. It's very hard to reach them. The roads aren't always paved...to reach these places might even jeopardize the lives of those who make the attempt.

J. Martín: Excuse me, Don Julio—What's the importance of these valleys?

Caller: The importance is that these valleys house structures in which experiments of different kinds take place...call them animals, or creatures, or whatever you like....The Indians who live on these reservations are sheep farmers.

J. Martín: Yes?

Caller: If you notice, the Indians there are sheep farmers, and suddenly we get a creature called the Chupacabras...

J. Martín: So what you're trying to tell us, in fact —

Caller: ...if you put one and one together, you understand? The climate out there is, well, slightly colder...it gets cold, but still—

J. Martín: It's a warm climate.

Caller: Yes. I remember reading that this creature seems to prefer tropical climates.

J. Martín: Don Julio, let me ask you something. Please answer only if you feel comfortable doing so, because we're aware of your position. You were once linked to an area that was dedicated to researching these strange creatures, but from the military intelligence standpoint.

Caller: Yes.

J. Martín: This is the reason you cannot use your real name tonight, correct?

Caller: Well...[unintelligible].

J. Martín: What moved you to call us tonight?

Caller: I've been hearing your show, and I've been hearing things that aren't true.

J. Martín: Such as?

Caller: Uh, well the blood...the chartreuse-green blood...just can't be. It's not ordinary blood.

J. Martín: But that's precisely the reason we're discussing it to-night on our show. There have been a number of situations and cases here in Puerto Rico which, we believe, may be related to experiments conducted in this field. You told me confidentially a few programs ago about your knowledge that creatures matching the Chupacabras' description...had been seen in the late 1950s and were known to exist by the US government, who even had some of them in captivity at the time. Is there any truth to this at all?

Caller: It's very true. These were creatures quite similar to what has been described here. If you take a kangaroo, cut off its tail and a bit off its legs, it would look similar to it, but it has spines running down the length of its back.

J. Martín: Where did you see this, Don Julio?

Caller: I saw it at a place in...in...gosh, I really can't recall...

J. Martín: What sort of facility?

Caller: I remember traveling from Kansas to a state near Texas or Mexico...

J. Martín: New Mexico?

Caller: Yes, New Mexico...

J. Martín: And where in New Mexico would this have been?

Caller: It was in New Mexico, but I can't recall now...I know that there was a [unintelligible] and we went past a town called Flag-staff.

J. Martín: And I ask you, Don Julio, why did you have to be the one to see this?

Caller: Well, because I had a Top Secret clearance at the time, and I would volunteer to do what's known as "riding shotgun." Remember the Old West? They still use the term to refer to the guarding of the merchandise.

J. Martín: Don Julio, since we don't want to reveal too many details that might give your identity away...did you, in fact, get to see one of these creatures related to the Chupacabras in that place?

Caller: Yes, but I want to add that this creature is completely harmless.

J. Martín: How so?

Caller: The creature is very intelligent, and is capable of distinguishing between a human and an animal.

J. Martín: Are you sure of that, Don Julio?

Caller: Of course.

J. Martín: Why?

Caller: Once, in Vietnam...if you go to Vietnam, you'll find the climate is...identical to Puerto Rico's. In fact, when you touch down in Vietnam you'd think you're landing in Puerto Rico. As I told you the last time, when I saw that "thing"...I forgot to tell you that a light came out from under it, and two human-like beings came down to the ground. They were humans. We saw them through the binoculars, which was hard, because the light was so brilliant

J. Martín: For the benefit of our listeners, you are now describing an incident that you and your comrades witnessed in Vietnam.

Caller: My companion and myself [saw it] during a New Year's Eve.

J. Martín: This was in Vietnam?

Caller: Yes, and he was an American whose name I can't recall. We didn't notify the authorities when the event took place because we were afraid of being ridiculed.

J. Martín: Now, Don Julio, so as not to digress: in what circumstances did you see these creatures now described as the Chupacabras in Puerto Rico at this secret US facility in New Mexico? What year?

Caller: This creature is a sort of pet, to put it that way. There's a radar currently being built in Lajas with the purpose of detecting aircraft.

J. Martín: With drugs?

Caller: This not only picks up aircraft but also any...any aircraft.

J. Martín: Including the unidentified objects seen in the area.

Caller: Anything flying five to seven feet off the ground.

J. Martín: But let's go back to the subject, because we're out of time. Under what circumstances did you see these creatures at this secret US facility in New Mexico?

Caller: They were caged.

J. Martín: Why?

Caller: I don't know...they were being studied, and evidently, their sex could be distinguished...there was a male and a female, and...

J. Martín: And what happened?

Caller: Well, she was getting bigger and bigger—her stomach was—and, and they realized she was pregnant. And they "put her to sleep," as they say, in order to study her.

J. Martín: They sacrificed her?

Caller: They opened her up and found another creature within, just like her. They procreate.

J. Martín: Did this creature at any moment try to attack you or any of the people working at that facility?

Caller: No. These creatures looked at you pleadingly with their sad eyes, and they inspire pity. They appear to be lost on an unknown world.

J. Martín: What kind of personnel was working with those creatures at the site?

Caller: They wore those outfits that cover the entire body, and changed garments from one room to another, discarding them as they returned. Decontamination room to the showers, discarding clothing once more and burning it.

After a pause, Martín continued with the program.

J. Martín: Don Julio, please forgive the interruption, but time is of the essence. Feel free to answer only if you can. I understand from what you told me during your call a few programs ago that you were alongside these creatures, which, according to you, may have been brought to Puerto Rico as part of an experiment. Is this so?

Caller: No. They brought creatures similar to the ones which appeared in an autopsy a few years ago...there were three. One of them was a female, who died from a wound to the thigh—

J. Martín: You're referring to what appeared in the [Roswell] movie.

Caller: The other creature died carbonized. No one knew what it was. The third was wounded—stayed alive. I think it died of old age. This isn't the only [vehicle] to have crashed, or to have been knocked out of the sky. It's all very secret, and right now I'm putting myself at risk by calling you.

J. Martín: Don Julio...I'm concerned about something you said earlier about your days as part of this special intelligence service, where some of these creatures seen in Puerto Rico were kept. These creatures seemed harmless to humans, contrary to what is being circulated by some groups in Puerto Rico. Are you certain of what you're saying?

Caller: Yes, I'm sure...they're harmless. The problem is that, since they're ugly and different from us, people become afraid. They are like lemurs or those sloths that dangle from trees, only they have a terrible odor and are quite ugly. Anyone would be afraid.[1]

The pseudonymous caller had played hard-to-get throughout the length of the call, wandering off to other subjects and giving out as little information as possible. Naturally, he made a few mistakes, such as placing Flagstaff in New Mexico rather than Arizona, but his completely unverifiable story had an undeniable ring of truth to it.

After the program was over, we discussed "Julio Marín" with Jorge and Marleen at a local restaurant. The caller really claimed to have been an intelligence officer during the fifties and sixties, and had been subjected to harsh treatment when he attempted to speak out about the things he had seen during his career. Throughout the conversation, his voice sounded muffled, as though he were using a handkerchief to disguise his identity. The most outstanding feature about his story, had it been a concoction of bad science fiction films, was his conviction that the creatures were harmless. We all agreed on this. It seems that anyone trying to make up a story would have gone for a flashier, more dangerous creature like those in *Alien* and *Predator*, as the phantom saucer-research groups had done. Julio's story, told in the slow, deliberate voice of a man who had experienced a great deal of suffering, remained present in our minds for a long time. But, as we accompanied the Martíns on some of their cases, we realized that tantalizing stories were, in fact, legion.

The Dog that Got Away

Three-month-old Suki the pup looked like a dog sprung from a cartoonist's pen. Her elongated black-and-white body, surmounted by a floppy-eared head with gleaming eyes, was the product of a dachshund and a hardy island mutt known as a *sato*. She did not know she was a celebrity. Among all the animals in Puerto Rico, she had held off the Chupacabras with her sharp barking, and thus had avoided getting "goatsucked." Suki's tale of canine bravery (or good luck) could not have been recounted in a better location—her owner's rural home, in Barrio Valenciano, overlooking the southern slopes of El Yunque, near the town of Juncos.

Mrs. María de Gómez, a housewife in her middle fifties, told us that, a few nights before our visit, at 7:00 PM, Suki's barking alerted her that something was wrong on the high terrace overlooking her backyard (which is, in fact, a plantation spanning several acres of lush vegetation). When she went to investigate the cause of the pet's excitement, she was startled beyond belief. An ash-grey creature, apparently weighing approximately 75 pounds and standing some four feet tall, loomed over the defiant animal in silence, as if trying to browbeat it into submission. The creature's eyes were somehow able to light the entire terrace with a clear, whitish light like that of a bulb. Mrs. Gómez had no trouble making out all the physical details that had been included in her testimony.

"It was the ugliest thing I had ever seen," she explained. "All that stood between me and it was the screen door leading to the kitchen. A baseball bat, which my husband leaves here in case a prowler should come around, was all I could have used against it."

But something as remarkable as the puppy's defiance happened next. The housewife's eyes met those of the inhuman creature and stared it down, as she thought aloud, "If you're the Chupacabras, you're a pretty sorry excuse for a creature," then promptly added the abusive word *pendejo* to her thought. The gargoylesque entity slowly covered its pointed face with its wings, as if hurt by her rebuff. It moved away from its position, slinked against a wall, and half hid behind a washing machine. Eventually, it took a few awkward steps toward the railing surrounding her terrace, jumped on it, and flew off into the dark sky.

Other strange events that had transpired on the Gómez's property were no less bizarre. A black, hairy, Bigfoot-like creature had been seen through the trees on the plantation only a few years earlier, and Mrs. Gómez had seen small, silver-suited Greys hold hands and jump over a fence to escape from a watchdog.

A local industry had dumped chemicals into a pond or small lake beyond the tree-covered plantation, she explained. Eventually it was used to dump so many different kinds of waste that it would have been impossible to sit on the terrace we were on without being nauseated by the odor. It was at this point that the strangeness began. While tending to the vegetable gardens at the far end of the property, Mrs. Gómez and her daughter had seen Greys running toward the vicinity of the contaminated pond. Interestingly, the Martíns' research has found that many cases involving supposed alien activity on the island revolve around environmental and ecological issues and a concern for how we humans seem hell-bent on polluting and destroying our own world. Could this case have followed the pattern?

The mystery birds that make Puerto Rico's cryptozoological fauna so rich had also been seen in the trees close to the Gómez property. Mrs. Gómez pointed toward a tree where a creature looking like an owl with a tremendous wingspan had rested on a branch before spreading its wings and soaring off toward El Yunque. Her personal opinion, she told us, was that every one of these creatures came from the mountain rain forest.

Hand-to-hand Combat

We took our leave from Mrs. Gómez and drove along the twisting, mountain road that leads from Barrio Valenciano down to the plains. We headed for the nearby town of Gurabo. The community came to mind immediately as the place where the fanged mystery bird of 1989 had made its debut, causing the sensation that filled newspapers locally and overseas.

The Chupacabras had also been seen in Gurabo, and many, including Mr. Jesús Sánchez, had experienced losses. Sánchez is a devout man belonging to one of the many Protestant churches that are claiming an increasing number of followers in this traditionally Catholic country. His experience with the creature could best be described as actual, hand-to-hand combat.

Our arrival at the Sánchez household coincided with a private Christmas party, so the awkwardness of discussing a questionable subject in a religious household was doubled by the reproving looks of the guests, who believed the Scriptures as far as the Chupacabras was concerned, and had no illusions at all about it.

"I'm still affected by what happened," Mr. Sánchez confessed. "I haven't been myself since the encounter. My wife and daughters can testify to that."

The bloodthirsty predator had landed in his backyard one evening and killed the rabbits Mr. Sánchez raised there by opening the cages, one by one, and leaving the characteristic puncture marks on the animals' bodies.

Fearing that the creature would stage a return (since attacks were still being reported throughout Gurabo), Sánchez decided to mount a watch. He hoped to overcome and capture the creature. His wish came true. The repeat visit came at four o'clock in the morning only days later. The homeowner apparently blinded it with a light bulb, causing it to seek shelter behind a tree. When the light was turned off, the predator raced past him out of the darkness, allowing only enough time for a terrified Sánchez to deliver two stiff blows with his machete against the creature's skin. Shuddering at the recollection, Sánchez added, "*aquello sonó como un timbal*" ("the blow sounded as if it had hit a drum").

In spite of the state his close encounter with the Chupacabras left him in, Sánchez guardedly hoped the creature would come back for more. He promised himself to capture the creature, despite a threat leveled at him by an official with the Department of Natural Resources, who warned him that this agency would prosecute him if he killed a "protected" creature. The defiant Sánchez riposted that a creature that is said not to exist cannot be protected by anyone, and that any action taken by the agency will only point to its complicity in the hundreds of animal killings that have plagued the island since the beginning of the year.

Not wanting to keep him from his guests, we said good-bye to Mr. Sánchez and headed back to San Juan. The expression on the witness' face as he recounted the frightening seconds when the creature rushed past him left no doubt in anyone's mind that he had experienced something utterly unnerving, and that the tropical twilight engulfing us housed a creature that could not possibly be dismissed as a rogue ape or dog.

Bigfoot Enters the Stage

Human nature is curious. Many of us prefer to carry out certain tasks at different times from others. So no one should be surprised by the urge to wash a car at 2:50 AM. That is exactly what Osvaldo Rosado was doing on December 23, just hours after our visits to the Gómez and Sánchez residences.

Rosado, a resident of the city of Guánica, where the Chupacabras had already made its presence felt earlier in the month, allegedly had finished hosing down his vehicle and was getting ready to disconnect the hose when a strange, hairy creature approached him from behind and gave him a bear hug so strong that wounds appeared on the victim's abdomen. Although rendered speechless by panic, Rosado finally was able to scream and struggle with the entity until he managed to break the deadly embrace. When he turned to face his assailant, he was doubly shocked to find that it was a simian creature much taller than his own six-foot height. The shaggy embracer turned and ran away from Rosado's backyard. Neighbors responded to Rosado's screams, and eventually took the badly shaken victim to a hospital in Yauco to have his wounds treated.

Conflicting stories circulated. The creature in no way matched the descriptions given of the Chupacabras. Rosado believed his assailant must have been at least eight feet tall, and it certainly did not have wings. Nevertheless, one newspaper blamed the incident on the Chupacabras. The victim claimed he never spoke to the reporter who wrote the story.

This landmark encounter may be the first time that a full-sized Bigfoot creature—similar to the kind regularly seen in the Laurel Highlands area of Pennsylvania—had been reported on Puerto Rico. Previously, the island had been known for the activities of man-sized or smaller mystery apes, jokingly dubbed "Smallfoots."[2]

Incident at the Lovers' Lane

Far from observing the holidays on the 24th and the 25th of December, the Chupacabras killed a number of small animals belonging to residents of Piñones, a scattered community between the Torrecilla and Piñones lagoons and fantastic unspoiled beaches long considered a lovers' lane.

In Rio Grande, Raymond Frías, manager of a horse farm, found that an 18-year-old horse on the property had been killed by a creature originally taken to be the Chupacabras. But the strange marks found on the dead animal's body did not correspond with the neat punctures that had become synonymous with the mystery prowler's bloodletting activities. Furthermore, the dead horse's anus had been cored and removed in the fashion typical of cattle mutilations in the American West. Was another creature at large?

The Bahía Beach Plantation and The Berwind Golf Course, 15 miles away from Piñones, in the municipality of Loíza, had also been visited by the Chupacabras, who was apparently unimpressed by the well-manicured fairways and greens. Groundskeepers had become accustomed to seeing weird creatures and UFOs over both golf courses over the years. A story circulated that the Chupacabras had chased the herons near the numerous water hazards on the course. Without skipping a beat, the pro shop at one of the courses ordered a number of pricey golf-club covers to be made in a comical likeness of the mystery creature—a sable critter with little felt bat-wings. The sheer size of both links and the density of the tropical vegetation they contained could have easily hidden an army of strange, bloodsucking animals—and were enough to discourage any player from chasing a ball into the rough.

A Public Figure Comes Forward

The last days of 1995 were not heavy in Chupacabras activity, but because Latin Americans from Mexico to Argentina consider December 27th—Day of the Holy Innocents—to be their April Fools' Day, references to the mystery prowler were too good not to use.

In the town of Cabo Rojo, a man strapped a loudspeaker to the top of his car and drove through the streets, warning townspeople to get themselves and their animals to safety, as the Chupacabras was reportedly in the neighborhood. Pandemonium ensued, and it remains unclear if the driver was ever charged with inciting a panic.

A radio announcer observed gravely that the Chupacabras had just killed several goats, mares, and other animals. Allowing the incredible tally of kills to sink in, he promptly broke into a sweet voice, informing his listeners that he had been pulling their legs.

One true story among the many humorous ones appearing at the time was that Fernando Toledo, President of the Puerto Rico Agricultural Association, had publicly expressed a belief that the Chupacabras could not be from this Earth. "I think that if we already know it's not an ape, then we must be dealing with an extraterrestrial," he said candidly during a Christmas Day radio interview on *Noti-uno*. Toledo reasoned that, if our solar system only has a dozen known planets, there must be other star systems in the galaxy with worlds capable of supporting life. This "thing" must come from one such point of origin.[3]

Toledo's statement, which did not appear in any of the major newspapers, represented a landmark moment in the Chupacabras wave. A major public figure was willing to concede that the extraterrestrial hypothesis—the butt of jokes and popular derision—was now being taken into consideration in attempting to solve the riddle posed by the creature that had caused havoc among Puerto Rican livestock.

It's in the Trees—It's Coming!

December 28th, 1995, was a significant night, for *OVNIs Confidencial*, and for local ufology. Even before the radio show began, telephones were ringing. Callers wanted to report UFO activity taking place over San Juan and recent Chupacabras encounters. A woman from the residential suburb of Guaynabo was watching a motionless object hover over power lines. A man from Cayey, where another military radar was being built, had found a number of his ducks slain by the Chupacabras, and wanted to turn the carcasses over to a reputable veterinarian. In short, the silence into which the Chupacabras reports had fallen—by official decree or not—had been circumvented by direct reports from people experiencing the sightings and situations.

Minutes into the broadcast, shortly after my wife and I had given our impressions on the Chupacabras situation, a call updating us on the Bigfoot "attack" arrived at the switchboard from Cuco Rodríguez, a UFO researcher on the southwestern corner of the island. He said the creature that had attacked Osvaldo Rosado had been seen by many other residents of Guanica. These eyewitnesses corroborated the size and description of the attacker, and were able to compare it with the smaller Chupacabras, which they had seen also. Hairy creatures, though not quite as tall, also had been seen around the aerostat installation near Laguna Cartagena, Rodríguez said.

It was obvious already that 1996 would be another busy year.

Chapter Ten

The 1996 Encounters

Reports of the attacks did, indeed, continue unabated into 1996. We recorded them in the Chupacabras diary, which, by now was growing thick:

Friday, January 5, 1996

Two goats were slain by the Chupacabras in Caguas' Barrio Cañaboncito. Police officials reported to the scene after being alerted by Wanda Rivera, who discovered her two young goats dead within their concrete-and-wire cage, which was still closed and gave no signs of forced entry.

Three sheep were also bled dry at the residence of José Ramos Aponte, in Aguas Buenas. According to the owner, he rose early on Thursday morning to find that his animals were agonizing from their puncture wounds.[1]

Tuesday, January 8, 1996

The Chupacabras attacked a farm in Canóvanas, killing a pair of sheep belonging to Monchito Colón. Police officers Orlando Marín and Rosa Santiago reported to the site. Just as they reached the area, another call was received from José Febo, who had allegedly just seen a creature with pointed ears, a strange profile, and a shaven head. Febo encountered the creature as it rested on a tamarind tree. When it noticed the human, the entity jumped off the tree and ran "like a gazelle."

Thursday, January 11, 1996

Mayor Soto made a formal request of Police Commissioner Pedro Toledo to help him obtain the resources needed to capture the creature. While the commissioner met with Mayor Soto, no allocation of police resources was made.

The creature attacked the Canóvanas area once more, killing a sheep and a rooster belonging Tomás Santiago López. The sheep was badly wounded, and was later euthanized by a local veterinarian. Mayor Soto visited the Santiago farm, located in Barrio Cambalache.[2]

Friday, January 12, 1996

The police seem unable to protect even their own. Police Colonel Agustín Cartagena, who owns a farm near Caguas, received a visit from the Chupacabras. The intruder killed an assortment of 22 ducks, chickens, and guinea hens. This incident apparently took place just days after six sheep were killed on the property of Police Lieutenant Jorge Rivera, whose farm is located in Canóvanas.[3]

Monday, January 15, 1996

Two sheep were found dead on a farm in Lajas. Wisbel Ayala, head of the Civil Defense, looked into the matter. He declared that a veterinarian, identified only as "Dr. Ruiz," had offered to analyze the carcasses, which had been "attacked by the monkeys that live in the area." The possibility that the carcasses might be frozen and shipped to the CDC in Atlanta has not been ruled out.[4]

According to *Samizdat* correspondent José Valdez, the unusually cold weather conditions Puerto Rico experienced during January 1996 may have kept Chupacabras activity to a minimum. He speculates that the creature may have gone into some sort of hibernation for a period of time. In fact, the elusive creature is back, and has even been reported on the island of Vieques, miles off the Puerto Rican mainland.

Thursday, January 18, 1996

The Chupacabras turned its thirst for blood against five ducks, slaying four and leaving one mortally injured. However, it met its match in the fierce flock of geese kept by Mrs. Luz Bonilla in her Guaynabo backyard. Even the Chupacabras meets its match now and then, it seems.

According to Mrs. Bonilla, the geese made a racket in the wee hours of the morning. Upon venturing into her backyard to see what had happened, she was faced with the sight of the dead ducks. Mrs. Bonilla added her voice to a growing number of citizens demanding a serious investigation, by the Commonwealth government, into this matter.[5]

On the other side of the island, reports came in from a number of sources describing a flurry of UFO activity. Police officials confirmed receiving distressed phone calls regarding this unusual activity. The sightings allegedly took place over the Costas, Sábana Yeguas, and Candelaria sectors of Lajas. The objects were described as triangular in shape and moving at prodigious speed across the night skies from south to west. Curiously enough, the UFO reports coincided with the arrival of several squadrons of jet fighters from the USAF. Local residents were awakened to the deafening sound of the fighters making low-level runs over their homes. The police could not speculate as to why the Air Force had chosen to embark on practice runs in the area.

Friday, January 19, 1996

A professor from the University of Puerto Rico at Mayagüez, Dr. Juan A. Rivero, has become part of the scientific task force currently investigating the puzzling deaths of animals throughout the island—deaths attributed to the Chupacabras.

Dr. Rivero expressed his support for the theory that the animal deaths caused throughout the island have been the work of rhesus monkeys that were brought to Puerto Rico's offshore islands for research purposes. A Harvard graduate and director of the Puerto Rican Zoological Society, Rivero suspects that most of the strange animal deaths that took place during 1995 were caused by the monkeys, which have been known to kill for sport.[6]

Thursday, January 25, 1996

Julio Víctor Ramírez, staff writer for *El Vocero*, described the strange disappearance of a Siberian husky and the death of a number of animals belonging to Antonia Rodríguez García, a Mayagüez housewife who notified local authorities about the incident.

According to the report filed by police officer Carlos Rivera, the victim reported the loss of a pair of rabbits and one of her dogs. One of the rabbits had curious incisions on its neck, while the other showed signs of ripped flesh. The animals gave the appearance of having been drained of blood. The mutilations appear to have taken place at 3:00 AM. The police report indicates that chunks of raw meat were discovered mixed with fur from Mrs. Rodríguez's missing dog.

The dog engaged in a fierce encounter with the intruder, which tore off a clump of the Husky's fur during the fray. The report did not speculate if the rabbits had been killed by the Chupacabras or by a more mundane creature.[7]

Friday, January 26, 1996

A dead pet is a cause for great sadness in any family, but a beloved pet found shredded by an unknown force, perhaps a supernatural one, inspires sheer terror.

Julio López and his family can attest to this. They experienced it themselves on the evening of January 23, 1996, when they returned to their home in Las Carolinas, near Caguas. The pet in question—a rabbit belonging to Mr. López's youngest daughter—was found torn to bloody shreds in its cage, which showed signs of violent destruction. Some kind of dark excrement—different from that of cows, horses, dogs, or apes—was found on the site. It was suggested that the darkness of the excrement was the result of the attacker's having ingested blood.

Mr. López was quoted, by San Juan's *El Vocero* newspaper, as saying:

> The shape in which the cage was left was incredible, it being built out of metal tubing and linked wire....they took out the rabbit, killed it, and tore out its head and other entrails....This is the work of a supernatural agency. Neither a dog, nor an ape, nor a snake could have done such a thing.[8]

Ironically, Mr. López works as a butcher for a Caguas butcher shop. He expressed his understanding of what people throughout the island have felt when they discover their beloved animals viciously slain. His twelve-year-old daughter still weeps uncontrollably over her dead rabbit.

Saturday, February 3, 1996

A turkey belonging to Herminio García, a beekeeper from the Mayagüez area, had the dubious distinction of being the first animal of its kind to be slain by the Chupacabras. The gobbler was found dead with claw marks on its neck.[9]

An interagency task force, led by Wisbel Ayala and entrusted with the task of analyzing the spate of mysterious deaths around the island, took the dead animal away for autopsy purposes. Although there were no witnesses, Ayala expressed the belief that a monkey attacked the turkey. The owner did not have time to see the assailant. By his own admission, as soon as he heard the sounds made by the attacker, he ran to grab a shotgun in hopes of defending his animal, but he arrived too late.

Of a total of nine confirmed cases in western Puerto Rico, four have been submitted to forensic analysis with inconclusive results. The cases remain officially open.

Thursday, February 8, 1996

Mayor José Nazario, of Lajas, has never seen a UFO, despite persistent sightings over his municipality in southwestern Puerto Rico. He belittles the importance of the phenomenon, but does not wish to engage in arguments with local ufologists on the matter. Mayor Nazario's position on the subject differs significantly from that held by Humberto Ramos, Mayor of Adjuntas, the mountain community where UFOs became an everyday occurrence in the early 1990s. Unlike his colleague, Ramos has seen the maneuvers of unknown lights in the skies over his municipality.

The Chupacabras returned in full force to the Quebrada Negra sector of Canóvanas, killing at least two sheep and mutilating an unspecified number of other animals. The incidents occurred at approximately 3:00 PM on a farm owned by Mr. Elías Reyes. Reyes told authorities that his dead livestock had puncture marks on their necks and bellies, as well as torn flesh on their hindquarters, through which inner organs apparently were extracted. Mr. Reyes refused to believe that apes or wild dogs could have committed such a horrifying act, and called upon Governor Pedro Roselló to show some leadership concerning this distressing situation.[10, 11]

Friday, March 8, 1996

Reports issuing from Puerto Rico in January and February expressed a belief that the Chupacabras had gone into hibernation. This concept raised the question of where such an activity would take place. Popular attention focused on the extensive cave system found in the area of the municipality of Aguas Buenas.

This lull in activity ended abruptly, when farmer Arturo Rodríguez, of Aguas Buenas' Barrio Sumidero, reported the loss of 30 fighting roosters and hens. The slain birds had puncture marks on their bodies and throats. Agents from the Department of Natural and Environmental Resources allegedly visited the site to conduct further research.[12]

Tuesday, March 12, 1996

Residents of the Barrio Maravilla section of Las Marías added to their woes the appearance of an exotic creature and the strange deaths of two rabbits. The locals are frightened to admit the possibility that the Chupacabras is behind these animal deaths.

On Saturday, March 9, a boy named Ovidio Méndez, who was in the process of burying a dead hen in his backyard, encountered a strange creature. It stood four feet high and walked on two legs. The child stated that the creature had elongated, red eyes, large fangs, claw-like hands, and a dark grey body. Young Ovidio told the police officers who reported to the scene that the thing remained motionless and made no threatening gestures during the encounter. "The pointy-eared animal ran away," he added.[13]

Officials explored the immediate area surrounding Las Marías, but were unable to come up with anything. Not all residents were sold on the idea of the Chupacabras as the source of the animal deaths. One woman expressed the belief that a dog was responsible for the death of her rabbit, but another resident felt that the marks found on her dead pet were "very strange."

The Chupacabras was allegedly foiled in one of its attacks. A mare fended off its strange assailant with powerful kicks, causing it to run away. These details were released by Lieutenant Carmelo Rodríguez of the local police precinct.

El Vocero alerted its readers to the possibility that the Chupacabras and its kind have spread throughout the world—a truly sobering thought. Journalist Julio V. Ramírez observed that animal mutilations bearing the distinctive "signature" of the Chupacabras have been reported in Brazil's Amazonia, and in Guatemala, where hundreds of sheep and chickens were killed in bizarre fashion. One Guatemalan farm woman reported that more than 100 of her chickens were found completely drained of blood and with "strange puncture marks" under their wings.

Tuesday, March 19, 1996

More fighting roosters and dogs have been lost to the Chupacabras, which has haunted the city of Aguada's Barrio Mamey over the past weekend. A local youth, José Pellot, had a terrifying close encounter with the bizarre predator. As Pellot went out to his backyard after hearing an unusual sound, he became aware of a dog-like creature. To his amazement, what he had taken to be a dog suddenly became fully erect. It stood about five feet in height. Pellot later described the creature as hairy and powerfully built. The surprise encounter with the creature coincided with the deaths of several fighting roosters and a dog belonging to Santos Pellot, José's father.[14]

Wednesday, April 3, 1996

Aguas Buenas' Barrio Sumidero, which had the unenviable distinction of being the first place visited by the Chupacabras after its "reawakening" from a purported rest period, is once again in the news. The paranormal predator made off with a large number of backyard animals over the preceding days, leaving a trail of dead chickens, geese, ducks, and sheep in the La Vega, Capilla, and La Araña sectors of Barrio Sumidero.

The ravenous intruder killed 11 chickens at the farm of Luis Fontánez, who had carefully placed his birds into individual cages. Six dead ducks, discovered by Pascual Ayala at his farm, completed the night's handiwork in this part of the island, which became famous late last year, when a cow belonging to Luis Felipe Navas, a senator, was found entirely drained of blood.

On April 1, three sheep joined the list of victims when their bloodless carcasses were found on the property of Rafael Peña. A fourth was reported missing. The animals had the same puncture marks in the throat and abdomen that have characterized a Chupacabras attack. A strong smell of sulfur filled the air in the wake of the killings, making some of the individuals on the scene feel ill. This group of 16 people included farmer Peña himself, Aguas Buenas' Mayor Victor Aponte, *El Vocero* photographer Eddie Deese Conde, and elements of the Civil Defense. Nausea and vomiting among the nocturnal expedition's members caused the search to be postponed. The mute testimony of the damage was undeniable. Whatever caused the animal deaths had torn a 16- by 14-foot, galvanized iron gate off its hinges.[15]

The potent smell of sulfur was ascribed to a hypothetical "defense mechanism" possessed by the creature known as the Chupacabras. Others have speculated that the sulfurous odor may also be used to render its prey unable to flee.

Local residents kept their own counsel, however, as to the nature and meaning of the sulfur. Many Puerto Ricans believe it is an indication that the creature is demonic.

Saturday, April 13, 1996

Accompanied by a strong smell of sulfur, the Chupacabras returned in full force to haunt the wee hours of the morning. On this occasion, it chose to feast upon animals belonging to Mrs. Amparo Vázquez, a housewife from San Lorenzo's Barrio Quebrada. The death count rose to nine chickens and one hen.

According to Mrs. Vázquez, dogs all around her neighborhood had barked incessantly the previous evening, as if trying to warn their owners about a prowler in the dark.

Residents of a nearby development, Jardines de San Lorenzo, reported seeing something that resembled an enormous bird fly over the area. Those interviewed by the local media stated that they had never seen a bird of such size before, and had certainly never heard shrieking sounds such as those it was emitting.

A groundswell of sympathy from cat owners everywhere greeted the sad news that an entire litter of kittens and their mother had been slain by the Chupacabras. Mrs. Nydia Pastrana, a farm owner from Trujillo Alto (directly south of San Juan), heard sounds in her backyard in the middle of the night, but chose not to investigate. The following day, she found that her cat and a litter of kittens had been slain by perforations in their necks. Some unknown force had broken down the gate to her backyard in order to commit the crime.[16]

Monday, April 29, 1996

If the home is in the heartland, the Chupacabras certainly returned for a visit when it committed a rash of slayings in the municipality of Cidra in Puerto Rico's mountainous interior. After almost a year's absence from this beautiful lake region, the paranormal predator chose to leave a most terrible calling card. It drained the blood of a newborn colt, attacking the hapless animal with such intensity that, for the first time ever, the nocturnal assailant actually left an impression of its claws on its victim's corpse. It also left a large amount of yellowish "goo" that gave off a fetid smell of sulfur.

Authorities reported to the home of Luis Ramos, of Cidra, to investigate his claim. According to the colt's owner, the family dog had not stopped barking all evening, and had punctuated its barks with strange howls, as if it were witnessing a terrifying sight. Bravely, Mr. Ramos went outside in the dark, but was unable to see anything amiss. The following morning, when he went to check on the colt, he was stunned to find its exsanguinated carcass.

Photographer Eddie Deese Conde, whose images of chilling Chupacabras-related deaths are quickly becoming legendary, managed to capture the ferocity of the predator's attack. Those present on the scene speculated that the Chupacabras had gripped the horse's hindquarters with excessive strength in order to extract as much blood as possible. A deep perforation was discovered under the colt's right flank.[17]

Friday, May 3, 1996

When police officers in Ponce today went on record saying that they had no explanation whatsoever for the deaths of 16 ducks, they were not being naive. Hector de Jesús Santiago, a resident of the Brisas del Caribe sector of this southern Puerto Rican city, awoke, as usual, at six o'clock in the morning to feed his pet ducks—only to find them dead. Curiously, roosters and hens, which also formed part of his backyard menagerie, were unharmed. The police officer who reported to the scene, José Pérez, expressed a belief that "the ducks could not possibly have been killed by dogs, since dogs bite and chew the body. These birds only had perforations on them." [18, 19]

Wednesday, May 8, 1996

Police officials were at a loss to explain the deaths of 20 chickens—each slain by a telltale perforation beneath one wing—on the grounds of a house in Villalba, on Puerto Rico's southern shore. Mr. Randy Alvarado visited police headquarters in person and notified the duty officer that he had encountered the dead birds first thing that morning. The birds had customarily roosted on a tree in his backyard.

Lt. Victor Santiago told reporters that he "had no explanation for what had transpired, since it is difficult to catch a chicken sleeping on a tree limb...imagine what it takes to catch twenty of them." When asked if he feared that the Chupacabras had paid his precinct a visit, he declined to comment, adding only, "This is a very strange event...a complex case."

More than a dozen slain ducks had been found a week before in nearby El Tuque. They had the same puncture marks that characterize the wave of animal mutilations that had played out for more than a year.[20]

Thursday, June 27, 1996

When the supernatural intrudes into human lives, it does so when least expected. The last thing Debra Hernández, a 32-year-old housewife from Toa Baja's Barrio Candelaria, expected when she went out to her backyard on this summer evening was to find the dreaded Chupacabras tearing its way through a coop filled with helpless chickens. "It was a horrible sight," Debra told journalists. "After seeing something like that, it's hard to go back to sleep." Hernández also told reporters that this was the second time the paranormal predator had visited her property. She described the being as "black, with pointed ears and enormous fangs."

The Hernández residence is not tucked away in the tropical woods. It borders the busy De Diego Expressway. The creature escaped through a hole in the fence separating the property from the road—presumably onto the expressway itself.[21]

During the first Chupacabras attack on June 17, the Hernándezes lost a goose, two guineas, and six hens. This time, Mrs. Hernández caught the Chupacabras "hen-handed" as it clutched a hapless bird in its claws. Startled by the human, the creature dropped its prey and ran away. "I know what I saw," adds

Mrs. Hernández. "The chickens were left bloodless, but their wounds appear to indicate that their intestines were removed. I know this could not have been done by dogs because there are no feathers anywhere—only chicken's bodies."[22]

Saturday, September 7, 1996

The Chupacabras set its sights on San Lorenzo, as if returning "home" after a prolonged absence, during which its exploits in Central America, the US, and even Spain made the pages of the world's newspapers and the ever-present internet. Forty chickens on a small farm belonging to Merced de Jesús Flores became the first victims of the creature's homecoming.

The Flores farm, located in the Quebrada Lajas section of San Lorenzo's Barrio Espino district, received its unexpected visitor in the early morning hours. According to the police report filed by the visibly upset Mr. Flores, the dead fowl—a combination of chickens and guineas—were perforated around their necks and breasts.[23]

Wednesday, September 28, 1996

The sighting of a massive UFO in the skies of landlocked Orocovis caused a great deal of consternation in this community. Many residents believed they were witnessing an airliner falling from the sky. According to reports transmitted over the *Radio Reloj* news program, residents of Barrio Saltos Cabra first became aware of a light that illuminated their entire mountainside community. Laborer Miguel Torres, interviewed by the radio station, described "a massive fireball" that cast its light on the densely wooded area. Other residents described the object as circular and enveloped by an intense white halo. Members of the local police reported to Saltos Cabra. They found nothing unusual, although the desk sergeant admittedly received a number of telephone calls describing the UFO's maneuvers over the area.[24]

As the reader now knows, Saltos Cabra had for many months been a favorite hunting ground for the Chupacabras, and the appearance of the luminous UFO seemed to corroborate many local suspicions linking the predator with the prospect of extraterrestrial involvement.

A curious aside can be made here: Ufologist Salvador Freixedo has often suggested that UFOs may thrive on chaos and destruction on Earth, feeding off the energy liberated by the destruction of matter and the suffering released by humans into their surroundings. In the wake of Hurricane Hortense, which leveled the island earlier in the month, the sightings of UFOs throughout the storm-ravaged sections of the island increased. Was the increase a coincidence?

Wednesday, October 2, 1996

Following the UFO visitations, Orocovis' Barrio Saltos Cabra was soon revisited by the Goatsucker. A number of witnesses claimed to have seen the creature walking around the La Choricera sector. They described it as about three feet tall, with a crest on its back, large wings, and three-fingered hands.

These witnesses include two policemen who were patrolling the La Choricera sector when they saw the strange creature jump out from the tree line.

Arnaldo García, a newscaster with WKAQ and Radio Cumbre, received telephone calls from local residents claiming to have seen Greys in La Choricera. Scholars of the UFO phenomenon will recognize these beings as the ubiquitous, large-headed, black-eyed beings that are the staple of modern abductee experiences. According to García, the locals are also complaining that the peaceful, uneventful days that once characterized their mountainous district appear to be gone forever.[25]

Monday, October 21, 1996

The Chupacabras reappeared in Isabela, on the Caribbean coast of the island, where it killed a number of animals and left a trio of goats gravely wounded. According to reports, the incident took place near Highway 113, in Isabela's El Cotto sector, at a property belonging to farmer Gilberto Cortes. Another Isabelan claimed to have run into a plump, hairy, three-foot-tall creature on the highway. According to this anonymous witness, the creature eluded him with great agility, in spite of its weight.[26]

Chapter Eleven

Chupacabras Universalis

Many months after the initial mutilations began in the mountainous districts of Orocovis and Morovis, Puerto Rico, the Chupacabras drama, still on stage in "the shining star of the Caribbean," began a "road show" as well, with unscheduled appearances in Florida, Texas, Arizona, Mexico, Costa Rica, Guatemala, Perú, and Brazil. *Chupacabras portorricensis* became *Chupacabras universalis*.

The Central American Debut

When a woman claimed to have been the victim of the Chupacabras, this time in the town of Bijagual de Turrubares, in the tiny Central American country of Costa Rica, her experiences were written off as the delusions of someone trying to explain natural phenomena with magical, superstitious reasoning.

Erlinda Vega, the victim in question, stated that a creature with large wings and a small face and eyes seized her by her dress and attempted to carry her off. Her husband responded to her screams of terror but "did not see anything."

Bijagual, a sleepy town even by Latin American standards, was jolted into the reality of a living nightmare. A team of researchers from the Costa Rican ministry of agriculture visited the community to interview the human victim and inspect a dead heifer that had been found in the area. According to their testimony, the bovine had been slain by a vampire bat.

Costa Rican authorities tried to explain the situation as mere local folklore. Their country has a tradition of supernatural beasts. One of them, known as *el cadejo* (a diabolical canine that attacks humans), is strongly reminiscent of England's "black shuck." Francisco Escobar, a sociologist, explained that rural poverty and desperation, combined with the accessibility of television, have created a cocktail designed to fire the imagination and foster belief in supernatural solutions to unusual problems. "The real Chupacabras," he said on Costa Rica's Channel 7, "is the poverty and lack of education that impede access to services and to the means of production."[1]

Chupacabras in the USA

The Chupacabras first introduced itself into the American consciousness by means of the virtual playground known as the internet. Postings in private services such as America On Line®, Compuserve®, and Prodigy®, as well as the internet newsgroups proper, conveyed snippets of information on this strange creature who operated on the fringes of awareness.

One series of anonymous postings superciliously dismissed the manifestations as "misidentifications of the common nocturnal bird known as the night jar" (known as *caprimulgus* in Latin). This explanation was factually far from the mark, but linguistically on the money. In 1989, a strange, fanged avian that had terrorized Puerto Rico was given the moniker *chotacabras*, corresponding to the bird with a similar name. The Chupacabras, only a few letters away, was bigger, fiercer, and more elusive. It would remain fodder for

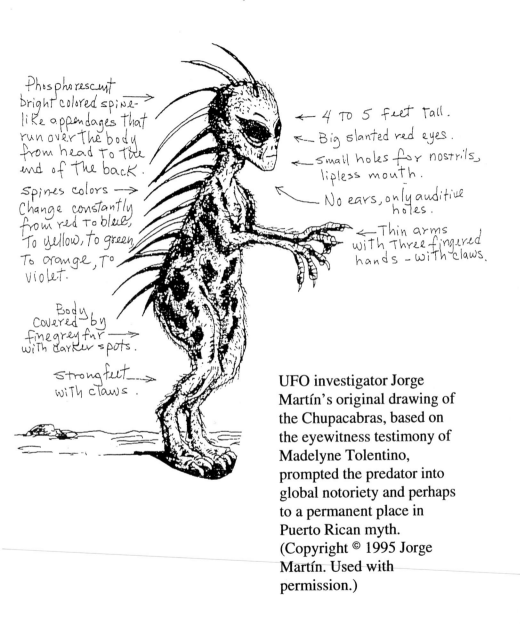

Phosphorescent bright colored spine-like appendages that run over the body from head to the end of the back.

Spines colors → Change constantly from red to blue, to yellow, to green, to orange, to violet.

Body covered by fine grey fur → with darker spots.

Strong feet → with claws.

← 4 to 5 feet tall.
← Big slanted red eyes.
← Small holes for nostrils, lipless mouth.
← No ears, only auditive holes.
← Thin arms with three-fingered hands - with claws.

UFO investigator Jorge Martín's original drawing of the Chupacabras, based on the eyewitness testimony of Madelyne Tolentino, prompted the predator into global notoriety and perhaps to a permanent place in Puerto Rican myth. (Copyright © 1995 Jorge Martín. Used with permission.)

Drawing of the Chupacabras as it appeared in the author's original, self-published manuscript.

The Canóvanas River. On 6 November 1995, Luis Angel Guadalupe and Carlos Carrillo were chased by the Chupacabras while fishing near here.

Chupacabras as seen at Mrs. Maria de Gómez's home in Barrio Valenciano, Joncos, Puerto Rico. The creature allegedly hid behind the washing machine after being scolded.

(Illustration by Jorge Martín, photomontage by Jeff Coast)

Ufologist Jorge Martín with El Yunque in the background.

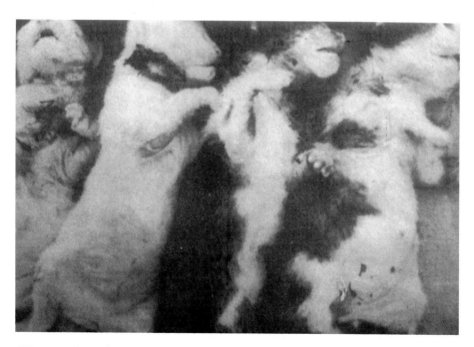

Kittens allegedly exsanguinated by the Chupacabras on 13 April 1996. The dead animals belonged to Nydia Pastrana of Trujillo Alto, Puerto Rico.

Cattle pastures like this one became the Chupacabras' "killing fields" in the Fall of 1995.

Mist-covered El Yunque, the mountain rainforest thought by many to be the Chupacabras' home.

Chupacabras as a social phenomenon. A model poses in a Chupacabras T-shirt for a Mexican Men's Magazine. (Courtesy Dr. Rafael A. Lara Palmeros, CEFP.)

Chupacabras T-shirt from 1995.

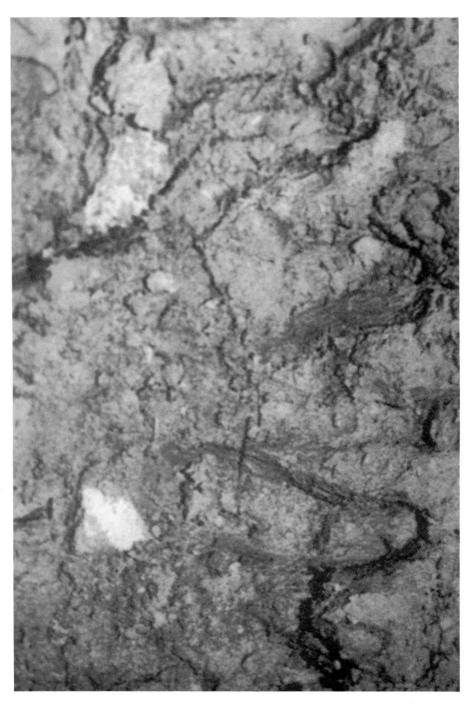

Alleged Chupacabras footprint left on the ground near Vega Baja,
Puerto Rico on 28 November 1995.

cybersurfers until its first attack on US soil.

The Chupacabras made it into the proverbial major leagues when the patrician *New York Times* deigned to include a feature on its Caribbean depredations in its January 26 edition. The article, penned by Mireya Navarro, detailed the Puerto Rican killings from a skeptical perspective. It cited medical authorities, such as Dr. Hector J. García of the Puerto Rico Department of Agriculture, who put forth the tired, straw-man explanations involving feral dogs, wild apes, and even parasites. Further recognition was lavished upon the Chupacabras in the *Wall Street Journal,* and on New York City's Spanish-language radio stations.

On March 10, 1996, Teide Carballo, a resident of Sweetwater, Florida, was stunned to see an "inhuman shape" making its way across her property. Two weeks later, Olimpia Govea, also a resident of Sweetwater, discovered that 27 chickens and 2 goats had been viciously attacked by an unknown predator that left the bloodless carcasses scattered around her backyard. Barbara Martínez, another Floridian, was even harder hit. She lost more than 40 birds, plus her pet ganders, which had apparently been slain right outside her open bedroom window.[2]

Heartbroken and enraged, Mrs. Govea railed against "experts" from the local zoo, who tried their best to assure her that her loss was attributable to canine marauders. If dogs were to blame, she challenged, why didn't they feast on their kill—and more importantly, what kind of dog leaves no blood behind at the scene of its carnage? Furthermore, Mrs. Govea's son and daughter-in-law claimed to have seen a shadow "like that of a tall man" deliberately pass by the window of the room in which they slept. Could it have been the same entity seen by Teide Carballo?

In any event, the mysterious intruder had shown a perverse attraction for the Govea household. A month later, in the middle of the night, the entire family would hear a tremendous noise, accompanied by an intermittent, orange light, as if something were trying to land on the property.[3]

On March 11, 1996, Florida's third mysterious animal mutilation occurred. The Spanish-language broadcast *Primer Impacto* reported that the attack had actually been witnessed by a woman from Miami's Little Havana district, who had found her chickens dead within the confines of their cage. The witness claimed to have seen a shadow through her window—a shadow that allegedly was neither human nor simian, but merely exhibited strange movement as it shuffled past. It disappeared into a row of banana plants.

Luis R. Shepherd, a Miami-based researcher, summed it up in his internet posting on March 13:

> We are very much afraid that this little monster is visiting us here in the Miami area. Today we got the second report that 46 domestic animals were killed in their locked pen. We think the Chupacabras is a pet of the real aliens, and that he is...a mere robot. It exists, and is being covered [up] by the authorities.

The same mercantilistic madness that had seized San Juan in the wake of the Chupacabras attacks also gripped Miami in a choke-hold. *Salsa* songs about the Chupacabras poured from radios. Video games featuring the predator made a hasty entrance. A local eatery produced the "Chupacabras Sandwich," and a restaurant proudly named itself *El Chupa Cabra*. Needless to say, the ubiquitous T-shirts also materialized.

On May 1, 1996, police in Tucson, Arizona, received a phone call from the home of José Espinoza, in West Tucson. Apparently something had broken into the house. Mr. Espinoza would later repeat his story to the media, saying that he had seen a creature with large, red eyes, a pointed nose, and shriveled features within the confines of his home. The mind-bending narration had the Chupacabras entering the home, slamming a door, and jumping on the chest of Espinoza's seven-year-old son before hopping out of the boy's bedroom window. Footprints and handprints of all sorts were allegedly left on the walls (most of them corresponded to Mr. Espinoza's three-year-old son).

On May 2, a dozen goats and a sheep were slain on a farm, belonging to Rafael Moreno, in Hialeah Gardens. In addition to the deaths, the creature had also inflicted severe wounds on a number of cows on the property. It bruised their ribs, and, in some cases, their wombs, leading the rancher and his family to believe that whatever it was had copulated with the cows. As was the case with the Govea property, the Chupacabras demonstrated an unusual interest in the Moreno ranch. It attacked there repeatedly, in spite of having been wounded by rifle fire.

The number of attacks and the repetition of the events in spite of the family's heightened vigilance led the Morenos to believe that more than one creature was at work—and that they were not dealing with feral dogs or panthers.

On one occasion, Moreno noticed a "weird bird" with a wingspan well in excess of six feet perched on a tree limb. The monster bird flew over the rancher and landed behind him, prompting him to spin around and shoot it with his rifle. The creature ran into the Everglades, and was not seen again (the reader will remember the bizarre, winged creatures which preceded the Chupacabras' appearance on the stage).

The small town of Donna, Texas, located along the Rio Grande upstream from Brownsville, was the next site to receive the unwelcome visit of the Chupacabras.

In the middle of May, Sylvia Ybarra went out to her backyard and discovered that her pet goat had been killed by three inflamed puncture wounds to its throat. The animal had been felled near its shed.

The story spread like wildfire throughout Donna (although local veterinarians assured the owner that her goat had merely been attacked by a dog, and that the puncture marks had simply become inflamed). As had occurred in Puerto Rico, the official explanation didn't wash—and this time there was a good reason for it. The Mexican-American community living along the Rio Grande in southern Texas has known for generations of eerie, giant birds that have routinely appeared in the area, many times coinciding with animal deaths in which the victim was left completely bloodless. In 1970, a Donna rancher had discovered one of his steers in such a condition.

Heading ever westward, the wave of perplexing animal mutilations eventually reached California, where a construction worker, Roberto García, claimed that a puncture wound on the back of his hand was the result of falling asleep near an open window.[4] The Orange County resident told the press that he had been awakened from a deep sleep by the sensation of something tugging on his right hand. Pulling his hand away, he saw a sizable, shadowy figure moving away very quickly. Adding to the high strangeness of this account was the fact that García's third-floor apartment opened out to nothing but an alleyway below.

Culturally, the Chupacabras phenomenon took a slightly less trashy turn along the Hispanic communities on the Mexican-American border. Rather than the proliferation of T-shirts, there was a proliferation of the impromptu songs known as *corridos*—guitar compositions, central to Mexican "ranchero" music, which put matters of public interest into song. Apparently, dozens of such *corridos* describing the exploits of the paranormal predator blossomed along the river communities, some of them even becoming popular enough to be recorded.

In the late summer, the border community of Zapata held its very first Chupacabras Festival, an event that drew thousands to the region to witness and participate in tributes to the creature. People dressed in costumes that conveyed their personal vision of the Chupacabras paraded through the streets.

By the summer of 1996, oceans of ink on three continents had recorded the exploits of this slayer of livestock and sworn enemy of the small farmer. Even skeptics felt prompted to write about this entity (albeit cynically). A political satirist in Puerto Rico, Fernando Clemente, writing about the devastation caused by Hurricane Hortense in 1996, observed:

> Hurricanes are the cause of many things, including refugees. What all of you didn't know—but will know now, thanks to my long, forked tongue—is the identity of Hurricane Hortense's first refugee. Entirely credible sources...have told me that the first refugee from the hurricane's wrath was...The Chupacabras! That's right. You heard me: the CHUPACABRAS.

The satirist went on to say that Mayor José Soto, fearing for the creature's safety, has concealed it in a closet somewhere in the town hall. He added:

> Rest assured that, as the floodwaters recede and election day draws closer, 'Chemo' will release the Chupacabras. After all, without the Chupacabras, 'Chemo' is merely another third-rate politician.[5]

The music industry took advantage of the Chupacabras' infamous notoriety, fully cognizant that its appeal would be positively lucrative. A *merengue* orchestra, dubbing itself the New York Band, took to the airwaves on Latin-oriented stations with a hit single, "Chupacabras," a bawdy ditty with few repeatable lyrics. A translated sample follows:

The classy Chupacabras
is fit for any goat
kissing their bodies and necks

inside, outside, what the heck
I'll kiss one goat, two goats
three goats, five or more
I'll never lose the taste
for a lovely little goat, mmm!

The sudden rise of Chupacabras interest in Mexico, resulting from a mind-bending string of animal mutilations and attacks upon humans, prompted the same commercial interest that had surfaced only months earlier in Puerto Rico. Taking matters to the extreme, a popular men's magazine released its own tribute to the elusive Goatsucker, featuring one of their buxom models "in the role of the Chupacabras," wearing a tattered T-shirt that left little to the imagination. The centerfold caption read, "Many have their own version, but so do we..."

Chupacabras in Spain.

The Chupacabras or its enigmatic kindred have shown no difficulty in crossing land or sea in pursuit of their prey. On May 25, 1996, on the outskirts of the village of Celadas, Spain, a bewildered shepherd notified the authorities that 163 sheep from his herd of 700 had disappeared without a trace. Spain's *Guardia Civil* conducted its own investigation, and was able to determine only that all traces of the sheep ended at a location three miles away from their original pasture.

The officer in charge of the search classified it as "the strangest [sheep] theft we've ever investigated." He pointed out that no vehicle could have approached the herd without leaving physical imprints on the ground, and that the disappearance took place in broad daylight. Journalist Bruno Cardeñosa managed to interview the local district attorney, who said that an order of secrecy had been imposed on the case. He added cryptically, "It's strange, very strange. Yes, they might well have been carried off upward."[6]

In April, when reports of the deaths of 600 sheep near the Pyrenees attracted researchers' attention, it quickly led to the belief that the Chupacabras had finally reached Spain. Insurance adjusters who visited the crime scenes issued the unanimous verdict that whatever was behind the perplexing sheep deaths was an unknown species of predator—definitely not a wolf.

Cardeñosa concluded that the Spanish version of the Chupacabras has the following traits in common with its Latin American relative: both creatures appear to exert a certain degree of control over their victims, causing both paralysis and hypnosis; all victims display two well-defined puncture marks on their necks; and the predator appears able to extract the entire blood content of its victims.

Chupacabras in Guatemala

Dr. Oscar Rafael Padilla, Guatemala's leading ufologist, found himself helplessly drawn to the depredations of an unknown animal in his country because he was among the many who lost livestock to the unseen intruder. The creature attacked the animals kept on Padilla's country estate, a ranch known as San Rafael Parga, located 20 miles from the Guatemalan capital. After having spent part of the weekend of May 18, 1996, on his property, Dr. Padilla returned to the city without incident. The following morning, however, he received an urgent telephone call from the ranch's manager, informing him that a number of his animals, including three sheep, had been slain overnight.

Dr. Padilla and a colleague, Miguel A. Aguilera, visited the ranch later that morning. They interviewed the ranch manager and scoured the area in search of any physical evidence that may have been left behind. The doctor took samples from some of the dead animals, which included chickens, dogs, and horses.

The preliminary investigation showed that the attack had been conducted by a predator capable of opening gates to the cages and coops where the smaller animals were kept. In some cases, it had twisted the highly resistant metal mesh surrounding the coops.

The animals that survived the attack also appeared to be in a curious condition—they gave the impression of being listless and sad, ostensibly in reaction to the slaughter around them, but more than likely as a result of whatever agent the predator employed to mesmerize its victims.

Unwilling to rush to judgment, Dr. Padilla considered that a wolf, a coyote, or a fierce dog may have been the cause of the carnage, but the pieces did not appear to fit the puzzle.

In subsequent days, he discussed the massacre with a number of veterinarians, who advised him that only Guatemala's DIGESPE (General Administration of Agropecuary Services) was qualified to perform the tests required to determine exactly what had transpired that night.

The veterinary report on one of the slain lambs indicated that its assailant had been neither a wolf nor a coyote. The attack had been carried out by something with claws—suggesting a jaguar—but the technicians were more inclined to believe that an eagle or some other "winged creature" was the culprit (Dr. Padilla notes, in his carefully prepared report, that neither jaguars nor eagles are common to that part of the country.) Tests showed that the attacker must have been tremendously heavy, since it handily broke the animal's neck.

A curious detail that emerged dovetailed perfectly with what had already been discovered in Puerto Rico months earlier. There were deep, sucker-like perforations on the lamb's neck, through which blood had been extracted.

Both Dr. Padilla and his assistant experienced nausea, aches, and dizziness as a result of their handling of the dead creatures. This caused the doctor to wonder if they had been exposed to some form of radiation in the area. To add to the complications, the bloodthirsty attacker returned to Dr. Padilla's ranch several times, eventually killing off the remaining rabbits.[7]

Until his own experiences occurred, Dr. Padilla had dismissed early accounts of the Chupacabras as sensational journalism. Prompted by these new developments, he visited the town of Estanzuela Zacapa on March 31, 1996, where he hoped to glean some new information on the mysterious predator, which was becoming known throughout Guatemala as the *Chupasangre*, *Mata-Chupa*, *Chupagente*, *Sacalenguas*, and other monikers. He was joined by other Guatemalan researchers.

The residents of rural Estanzuela Zacapa had suffered greatly at the hands (or fangs) of this unknown entity. Professor Alicia Fajardo already had lost a monumental 150 chickens on the night of November 11, 1995. She became one of the first of the locals to report the attacks.

Professor Fajardo stated that, while she did not hear any commotion on her property, she noticed a completely unfamiliar buzzing, flapping sound outside. Fajardo's six watchdogs were apparently no match for the intruder.

"As to the manner of attack," she told Dr. Padilla, "it carries out its deeds by sucking its victims' blood through holes punctured in their throats...." She calculated that the creature had drawn approximately five gallons of blood from her slain flock. She believed it must be a large creature to hold such an amount of fluid.

Vicente Sosa, a cattleman, informed Dr. Padilla that he had actually seen the assailant shortly after midnight in January 1996. The creature was black, resembled a dog, and had a long tail and red eyes. Other locals, such as Rolando Fajardo and Vitalino Galdámez, described it as a glossy, black bird, resembling a very large vulture or even a bat. Julio Conde, another resident, saw the creature walking erect, much like a human being.

Dr. Padilla's report indicates that the good people of Estanzuela Zacapa believe—much like those in Puerto Rico—that the monster hides out in caves—particularly those that flank a river running through their village. There is a certain periodicity to the attacks, which recur every fortnight.[8]

Speculation on the intruder's nature runs the gamut, from the possibility that a pterodactyl egg may have hatched eons later, to the possibility of mythical gargoyles being alive and well in Central America.

Chupacabras in Mexico

The Chupacabras' appearance in Mexico merits a report of its own. The wave of mutilations, human attacks, and midnight sightings do not limit themselves to encounters with a single creature, but with a "procession of the damned" that would have tickled Charles Fort to death. Reports range from werewomen who howl in the night (in the true *nagual* tradition), to horned creatures and bats with enormous wingspans.

Mexican farmers from the northern states of Sinaloa, Chihuahua, and Coahuila were affected in early April by a wave of cattle mutilations that ultimately were pinned on the Chupacabras. Mexico's ministry of agriculture dutifully reported that the drought being experienced in northern Mexico and the southern US had driven coyotes, wolves, and other predators "crazy from a lack of water," and that these animals had chosen to slake their thirst with the blood of cattle and even humans.

The animals in Mexico, unlike those in Puerto Rico, presented twin fang marks on their necks—holes through which their blood had apparently been drained. The community of Tlajomulco (Jalisco) reported 15 animals slain in this fashion. Ocotlán, 40 miles from Guadalajara, Jalisco's capital city, reported similar attacks.

Fishermen from the communities surrounding Mexico's largest inland body of water, Laguna de Chapala, claimed to have been attacked by the Chupacabras. One of them, Jose Angel Pulido, was allegedly attacked on April 14, 1996, by a "dog-sized creature covered with black hair." His testimony conflicted with that of others, who said the Chupacabras was covered in greyish or white fur.[9]

Teodora Reyes, of Sinaloa's Alfonso Genaro Calderón, was added to the list of human victims. On national television she showed what resembled lacerations or burns down her back. Hortensia Cuevas, another alleged victim, claimed that, around the same time, "a creature with gigantic wings" bit her. An unknown quantity of exsanguinated chickens was found in San Juan de los Lagos, north of Guadalajara, while 19 goats were found slain in the Jalisco town of Amacueca.

As a matter of historical interest, I should add, at this point, that vampiric attacks or human mutilations have been known to occur in Mexico. They are usually linked to UFO manifestations. Author Salvador Freixedo, whose book *Defendámonos de los Dioses* deals with many of these situations, observed:

> In 1977, when I was in the city of San Luis Potosí, some 300 kilometers north of Mexico City, the first case of this nature reached my attention. A newborn child had been found lifeless and entirely devoid of blood. The bizarre circumstances surrounding the case prompted me to investigate deeper. I immediately realized that it was not an isolated case, but one among many similar ones.
>
> The general circumstances were these: The victims were usually newborns or very young babies. Hematomas or blemishes on their skins were apparent, as if blood had been sucked through them. The common denominator in all cases was that they were entirely bloodless. In some cases it appeared as if the blood had been sucked out through their mouths, as there were no wounds or marks of any kind on their flesh. It is also common for the mothers of these children to be found in a deep, lethargic state of sleep beside their dead offspring, as if they had been drugged by someone while the bleeding of their children was being carried

out. There are also adults who claim—or suppose —that they have been attacked in their sleep, because they awaken to find themselves covered in bruises, and also feel a great lassitude.[10]

Experts from the Guadalajara Zoo made plaster casts of the impressions that the nocturnal assailant had allegedly left in the ground. Francisco Rodríguez, the zoo's director, concluded that the prints belonged to "a large dog or wolf." Mexico's president, Ernesto Zedillo, allegedly told officials in his crisis-racked administration to devise an explanation aimed at avoiding the spread of panic among the population.[11]

As of the middle of May, 1996, a sampling of the Chupacabras' alleged depredations in Mexico consisted of the following:

◆Laguna de Hermosillo, Sinaloa: The body of a drowned cat was fished from the lagoon by local farmers, given what appeared to be "wings," and paraded as the "corpse" of a slain Chupacabras.
◆Pánuco, Veracruz: Forty-five fighting cocks were found completely drained of blood. This parallels the situation in Puerto Rico almost exactly.
◆Jalapa, Veracruz: Unspecified exsanguinations took place north of the city one evening. A dog belonging to a medical specialist was found exsanguinated.
◆Mexico City: The Catholic church asked the public to remain calm, as there is no proof that "the so-called Chupacabras is demonic or extraterrestrial." Political writers for major news magazines like *Siempre!* and *Quehacer Político,* have written scathing columns, which argue that the only Goatsucker is the disgraced former president Carlos Salinas, and that the current furor concerning the mutilations is simply a means of diverting attention from the country's economic crisis.

Reports of 18 dead creatures in Texcoco caused a furor in the city, turning the Chupacabras into the subject of countless jokes, television commercials and party conversations. The director of the world-famous Chapultepec Zoo, Marielena Hoyo, declared, "Security at our institution has been reinforced, in case anyone wants to make believe they are the Chupacabras." Ms. Hoyo noted that cattle sacrifices have been performed throughout history, and made reference to a description in Leviticus that mentions the use of a perforating tool to spill animal blood for ritual purposes.[12]

Dr. Rafael A. Lara Palmeros, Director of Investigations for Mexico's Centro de Estudios de Fenómenos Paranormales (CEFP), graciously contributed the following comprehensive report about the Mexican encounters:

High Strangeness: Unexplained Animal Deaths in Mexico
A Preliminary Report

The Republic of Mexico, as never before, is utterly confused and seriously alarmed by the series of bizarre phenomena that has manifested since February of this year in a number of Mexican states.

There have been isolated reports of this aberrant phenomenon, but they were seldom taken seriously. An example of this can be found in the 1993 reports of the deaths of 30 horses in the state of Guerrero. Genitals, tongues, and viscera were removed from the animals. The blame was squarely placed on cattle rustlers. Other reports suggest that 30 sheep were slain by a mandrill-like creature in the state of Hidalgo, and nearly a year ago, the town of Iztlalmanalco (Mexico state), on the slopes of the Mt. Ajusco, reported the loss of an unspecified number of sheep, chickens, and cows, killed by "giant cats" that have remained unidentified to this very day. (The School of Veterinary Medicine and Zootechnology of the Universidad Nacional Autónoma de México looked into this case.)

The following chronicle outlines the events that have shaken the country in the past few months.

The Cases

On February 16, 1996, Professor Noé Montoya, a UFO researcher, remarked in a conversation with me that the outlying communities around the city of Puebla were reporting strange deaths among their farm animals—losses blamed on a creature resembling the Puerto Rican "Chupacabras." I did not believe this. Nevertheless, on February 24, while participating in a television program and discussing the important research being conducted in Puerto Rico by Scott Corrales and Jorge Martín, I received word that cattle mutilations were, in fact, taking place on the outskirts of Puebla. I did not know what to make of this.

Then, on March 14, 1996, I received a telephone call from Dr. Armando Gutiérrez, of Tampico, Taumalipas. He mentioned the puzzling attacks on dozens of hens, fifteen chickens, and four goats in the tiny village of Altamira, located just a mile or two from Tampico. According to Dr. Gutiérrez' testimony, the animals had wounds on their necks, and had been completely drained of blood.

I was unable to confirm this by means of the press or other media, which made me doubtful. It was not until March 29 that Dr. Jesús Benítez, a fellow doctor at the Hospital General de Zona II (which belongs to the Mexican Institute of Social Security), informed me that the *Primer Impacto* news program had mentioned the animal mutilations that had occurred in Miami, Florida, *as well as those in Mexico.* Particularly mentioned were cases from Jalisco and Veracruz, mainly in the community of Tlalixcoyan, some three hours north of Jalapa. A relevant fact was that *NotiVer*, Veracruz State's news program, informed that, since the sixth day of March, 25 bloodless sheep had been found in the Colonia 25 de Abril sector of Nayarit. The dead animals had punctures on their necks.

The first official news item concerning an unknown predator roaming the Mexican countryside appeared on April 7, 1996. The location was Tlalixcoyan, Veracruz, where local cattlemen, municipal law enforcement officers, and local authorities began a search for the enigmatic being, simultaneously issuing a list of the deaths attributed to it. Veterinarian Alfonso Hernández Pérez expressed a belief that the sheep deaths could not be attributed to bats, dogs, or felines.

On April 18th, newscaster Jacobo Zabludowsky openly mocked, "This being captured by the internet, whose means of sucking remain a mystery, is just another myth among the hundreds which surround us...." His opinion on the subject would change dramatically two days later, when he reported the unexplained deaths in the community of Las Granjas, not far from Ciudad Guzmán, Jalisco. More than 20 sheep were found dead and drained of blood, with the ubiquitous puncture marks on their bodies. Their owner, farmer Alberto Durán, could not believe what had happened.

On May 2, Víctor Barragán, a veterinarian from the Universidad Autónoma de Guadalajara, stated, "Some feline and/or wild dogs were responsible for the these massacres...." Nonetheless, Teodosio Méndez Meza, owner of the Amacueca Ranch, informed the authorities of the deaths of 16 sheep. At the same time, Bernardino Rodríguez, of La Barranca de San Miguel, experienced the loss of four sheep from their pen. Barragán remained unmoved, repeating that some natural cause (puma, feral dog, etc.) was behind these situations.

Meanwhile, Humberto Cota Gil, chief investigator for the Universidad Autónoma de Sinaloa, declared that the Chupacabras was nothing more than the *vampyrus spectrum*, a bat species originating from Brazil. The bats range from 20 to 30 inches, and they sport two-inch-long fangs and a facial lobe of 10 inches. Intermunicipal police patrolling Guasave, Los Mochis, and Bachomobanpo were sent out to find this gigantic creature.

The death list continued to rise in Tlalixcoyan. On May 3, six dead sheep were found with strange marks on their necks and in the vertebral region. The settlements of Trancas, Palo Gacho, and El Nido were also affected by the spate of activity. According to a peasant from El Nido, a dog-like creature harassed his flock. When he attempted to shoot the intruder, it crossed a barbed wire fence without wounding itself or making any noise. In Sinaloa, a brigade of specialists and policemen conducted a tour of inspection of all the affected municipalities as the death toll rose to 100 animal losses. José Luis Garibay, a pathologist with Mexico's department of livestock and agriculture, determined that the animal must be huge, since it was obviously quite capable of lifting 1,190 pounds, slaying 40 sheep simultaneously, and consuming three gallons of blood from each of them. A sheep that had been left tied at a particular place in the village of Ruiz Cortines was found some 656 feet away from where its owner left it. The animal had been decapitated and exsanguinated.

Townspeople armed with rifles and machetes took to the countryside the following day in hopes of finding the predator. According to the municipal secretary, Sergio Palencia Pérez, not a trace was found, although some claimed to have seen a kind of enormous bat flying at low altitude. In Los Mochis-Topolobampo, the supernatural predator killed 40 sheep at Rancho La Remolacha, prompting a massive mobilization of searchers outfitted with infrared lights, shotguns, electrical equipment, helmets, and riot shields.

This belligerent response did not keep the mysterious attacker from going about his appointed rounds. On May 5, Tlalixcoyan awakened to discover 20 more sheep and 12 unspecified farm animals entirely bloodless. Based on the testimony of Filogonio Jiménez, the Tlacoya *ejido* (farming cooperative) was shocked to discover 13 sheep with wounds on their throats. Six turkeys were found dead in a similar fashion at Piedras Negras, and two of Rancho El Peladero's sheep were savaged by the nocturnal attacker.

The village of La Loma, Jalisco, was not spared the bloodletting. Ten of its sheep were slain by whatever was roaming the night, while the citizenry's dogs howled pathetically. It was on this strange evening that José Angel Pulido claimed to have been attacked by the Chupacabras, which he described as a monster about 30 inches tall weighing some 66 pounds, and having ashen-dark "feathers" and sizable wings.

Juan Robles, a farmer from San Miguel Coahuila, claimed that, on May 6, 1996, four of his sheep were attacked by the alleged predator, prompting Eng. Angel Ramírez to demand a serious, formal investigation of the situation. This came about even as 12 lifeless goats were discovered in Lagunillas de Huimilpan, Querétaro. They were exsanguinated and had the trademark perforations on their bodies.

Biologists began issuing their theories at this point. Rogelio Sosa, a researcher with The Sinaloa Center for Science, expressed his opinion that serious investigation should be undertaken, since the creature was obviously very strong and equipped with formidable claws. His working hypothesis, however, was that the countryside was facing a "rabid feline." Luis Carlos Fierro, head of the Office of Rural Livestock Development, dismissed the animal deaths as "popular myths." He was confident the guilty parties were most likely coyotes, dogs, mountain lions, and cougars.

The Chupacabras made an encore in the state of Veracruz, this time at Comunidad Cruz del Milagro in Sayula de Alemán, where it dispatched seven cows in its customary manner. Hundreds of miles away, in the desert state of Chihuahua, eight goats were attacked by an enigmatic beast, according to Ricardo Oropeza Medina of the Center for Epidemiology of the state health agency.

On May 8, 1996, two sheep and six turkeys were slain in Tlalixcoyan, Veracruz. The "manhunt" scheduled by the authorities did not take place, since Atilano Martínez, the municipal president, and Armando Aguirre, the livestock farmers' representative, chose to attend a political meeting rather than comply with the wishes of the peasantry. The region is in the clutches of tension and fear.

San Miguel Coatlinchan, Texcoco (outside Mexico City), made the news when 18 birds were found dead and bloodless with marks on their necks. Residents believe that the numerous prints on the ground left by the "animal" are much larger than those of any canine, and suggest very large claws.

In the wake of all these animal killings, livestock farmers began investigating, using large hunting dogs on their almost ceaseless patrols of their ranches. The president of the Regional

Cattlemen's Association admitted that some deaths had been caused by strange animal attacks. Zootechnician David Avila Figueroa, with the University of Guadalajara, opined to the contrary. He stated that the cause of death was a kind of feline that was neither mysterious nor abnormal, and that animals, "being as sensitive as they are, die from heart attacks."

Vigilantes in the state of Nayarit fared somewhat better than those elsewhere. Six bloodless birds prompted an intense mobilization and a vigorous pursuit of the creature. According to Mr. Silva Avila, "I saw it [the creature] in profile at a distance of some 33 feet, and it stood motionless. I picked up a stone and threw it at the creature, but I missed. The animal turned toward me and moved away with hurried jumps, vaulting over a 6-foot wall. It measures some 30 inches, and has a small head with short, pointed ears, like those of a bat. Its eyes were brilliant red." He also added that the creature was covered in black fur and had legs that folded at the knees, and that two small arms, like those of a kangaroo, protruded from its torso.

The creature returned to haunt the population once again, causing the police to sally forth, fully armed, and deploy tear gas at it. Meanwhile, in Cuatichán, (Mexico state), 19 birds and 2 pigs were found dead with the characteristic marks on their necks. The natives, curiously, began painting their houses and hanging crosses made of *ocote* on their doorways. In Matamoros, on the US border, the alleged apparition of the "Son of Chupacabras" was being investigated.

On May 9, the Archbishop of Morelia, Alberto Suárez Inda, begged the public to remain serene in the face of the phenomenon sweeping the country. He publicly stated his confidence in the authorities. He declared that there exist *very strange phenomena that are complicated to investigate, and demand all the available time and means to be solved* (author's italics). Antonio Camacho Díaz, a bishop of the Orthodox Catholic Church, suggested that the creatures could be the result of some congenital deformity or a product of radiation.

According to Carlos Vega Fineda, assistant director of municipal medical services, the Chupacabras is merely a misidentification of the well-known *murciélago de las tumbas* (graveyard bat), which has simply changed its dietary habits.

As the mutilation epidemic spread, special guards, equipped with the added protection of crosses designed to scare the strange creature away, were established in the municipalities of Texcoco and Zumpango.

Much in the same manner that Canóvanas, Puerto Rico, had become the Chupacabras' favorite feeding area, its Mexican counterpart appeared to have claimed Tlalixcoyan in Veracruz for itself. The citizenry, enraged and frightened by the depredations, demanded that the authorities do something to protect them and their animals. The possibility that the creature might turn on humans next was not taken lightly.

In los Mochis, Sinaloa, one Benigno Cano claimed to have seen a strange creature, some 35 inches tall, with large, sharp fangs, red eyes, scales, and a dragon-like appearance. It allegedly caused the deaths of two ducks, a goat, and several chickens. Workers at the Abelardo L. Rodríguez dam stumbled upon the body of a dead bat, measuring 33 inches in height and almost a 40 inches wide, with gigantic fangs. Mr. Pavón Reyes, head of the Sonora special operations group (GOES), said that he would concede the *Ocurrió Así* television program the first bid at the story, since he expected a reward of $50,000 for his trouble. It was later learned that the creature was merely a dead cat that had been split open and spread out to seem larger.

León, Guanajuato, a locale famous for its UFO-related incidents, was not spared a visit from whatever was killing animals all over the country. Two boys, Jesús Barajas and Julio Bermúdez, reported having seen a strange being measuring approximately four feet tall, with black skin and bulging eyes, that later cleared a six-foot fence and flew into the air.

On May 12, a veterinarian claimed that autopsies performed on dead geese suggested that death could have been produced by a giant bat created by genetic manipulation in the US or in Mexico. This line of thought was echoed the following day by researchers from the School of Veterinary Medicine and Zoot-echnology at UNAM, who thought it likely that mutations in canines and felines could well be responsible for the deaths taking place all over the country.

On May 17, the residents of Ciudad Ayala, in the state of Morelos, had a repeat visit from the paranormal predator, which struck at their flocks of sheep. The losses were attributed to a "giant vulture." That same day, frightened peasants in El Tecomate, Sinaloa, used their machetes to kill an otter found in an irrigation ditch because they believed it was the Chupacabras.

The same homespun "experts" that had amused the Puerto Rican press turned up in Mexico. One of them believed that the Chupacabras had been brought in from Africa and was being utilized by the "Golden Lucifer" sect for their rituals. This being allegedly was able to sprinkle colored powders on his victims, put them to sleep, and later attack them. According to one "expert," the Chupacabras had a life span of between 50 and 100 years.

Human Attacks

Aside from the fact that a number of attacks on humans were confirmed throughout Mexico, it is worth mentioning the fate suffered by Mrs. Teodora Ayala Reyes, on April 29, in one of the most shocking cases of the Mexican Chupacabras wave. It took place...in the village of Alfonso Genaro Calderón, in Sinaloa. The attacker turned out to be, according to her own description, a very bizarre creature about two feet tall that gave off a strong stench and had large wings. Mrs. Ayala was attacked at night. She received bruises on her neck, back, and face. Her assailant disappeared into the night.

As reported elsewhere, José Angel Pulido, a resident of Tlajomulco de Zuñiga, was accosted by an improbable creature that inflicted hematomas and deep scratches on his arm. The images of these two victims of alleged Chupacabras mayhem caused nationwide consternation when they were broadcast on Mexican television. Attacks visited upon Juana Tizoc Montenegro and Elvira Meza were never confirmed, although they received a great deal of media coverage. Nonetheless, their descriptions of the attacker matched.

The Chiapas Case

This case is worthy of mention because it occurred in a state that is in a high level of conflict, and because certain "pseudoinvestigators" attributed it to activities of the Zapatista Liberation Army (EZLN) in an effort to direct popular attention away from what is really going on in Chiapas.

On April 1, 1996, Mrs. Julieta Calderón awoke to discover almost 20 dead, blood-covered sheep on her property, a ranch named San Antonio de los Sauces. The dead animals' throats had been ripped, which, according to the official version, proved that the attackers had been dogs. Curiously, neither the watchmen, nor the shepherd, nor the ranch's inhabitants—not even one of the hunting dogs—was alerted to the activity of the supposed pack of feral canines. According to Jesús Espinoza Ramírez, a technician with the Ministry of Agriculture, there is no doubt that the killings were perpetrated by dogs. This hypothesis is being disputed by the ranch's owner.

One of the watchmen, Víctor Manuel Samoaya, recalled seeing a naked, albino-like "person" 20 inches tall hiding among the bushes. "I thought it was a child," he stated. He and a companion went after the strange creature without much success. The president of the Asociación de Ovinocultores de Chiapas, Ernesto Sánchez Yanini, pointed out that, in the 20 years he has devoted to cattle farming, he had never known so many animals to die in a single attack—although he does not dismiss the notion that a pack of wild dogs may have been responsible.

The Other Side of The Coin: The Psychosocial Phenomena

Since it first appeared in the national media, the Chupacabras captured the attention of everyone from musicians to intellectuals. Numerous references to the creature appeared in Mexico's print media, giving us an entity that has been variously linked to Subcomandante Marcos of the EZLN, to the myth of "La Llorona," and to the poverty and lack of education afflicting the country. The real Chupacabras, it is said, is the drought and hunger afflicting the country, along with the current political crisis, unemployment, and lawlessness. Delirious minds have created their own myths and legends as a result of the penury that has engulfed Mexico as a nation. It should be noted that the newspaper *El Financiero* published, in its May 12, 1996, edition, an extensive review of the phenomenon, ascribing its existence to the oft-mentioned Mexican Crisis. It went so far as to point out that this phenomenon is a rumor that has invaded the country due to the low educational levels among the population, which needs to be better informed in order to sort truth from fiction. Paco Ignacio Taibo, a noted Mexican novelist and essayist, José Luis Cuevas, an artist, and many others have echoed similar sentiments. The Chupacabras is a rival figure to Marcos; it embodies former president Carlos Salinas de Gortari; it embodies Mexico's poverty—manipulated, extorted, and deceived by its fellow countrymen.

Faced with this "evidence," one is led to believe that all the goings-on in this world relating to this bizarre phenomenon are mere fantasies.

Yet I wonder: Are these fine gentlemen aware of what happens in cyclical rhythm in the fields of England, France, Sweden, Brazil, the US, Canada, and other countries, where mutilated, exsanguinated animals are found by the dozens? What would they think about the Exmoor Beast? The Gevaudan Beast? The recent waves of cattle mutilations in New Mexico, and the 1993 wave of mutilations in Germany? It is one thing to discuss, philosophize, and get together with cronies in a coffeehouse and find "conclusions" without ever dirtying the soles of one's shoes by investigating the scene where the events took place. In order to have grounds upon which to discuss the phenomenon, *we must investigate, visit the locations in question, interview witnesses, analyze the results gathered*, and refrain from issuing false conclusions which, in my opinion, *mislead the public*.

The Research

Upon discovering that one of the "hottest" sites in the country was Tlalixcoyan, a community located some three hours to the north of Jalapa, the state capital of Veracruz, we commenced making preparations to visit the site. Bearing in mind that the School of Veterinary Sciences and Zootechnology of the University of Veracruz might be aware of the situation already, we paid a visit to its facilities for an interview with its director, Mr. Emilio Zilli Debernardi, and academician Jesús Morales. Surprisingly, these "authorities" professed having *no knowledge whatsoever* about the events, and rather nervously informed me that I was the first civilian to approach them with an interest in this subject. To assuage their fears, I told them that I was neither an agent from the Department of State nor from National Security, but merely a medical specialist with an interest in the subject. Their response was, "We'll get in touch with you if we find anything..."

Faced with this attitude on their part, I contacted Mr. Agustín Morales, president of the Tlalixcoyan Cattle Farmers Association headquartered in Piedras Negras. He claimed not to be aware of anything in particular, but would be happy to contact me once information on the subject had been brought to his attention. To date, no further word has been received from either agency.

We visited Tlalixcoyan on May 1, 1996. The high level of apprehension among the population was clearly evident. When we spoke to a number of farmers and cattlemen, the common denominator appeared to be that *no sound was ever perceived* from the areas in which the mutilations took place. It was only on the following day that the bloodless, mutilated animals were discovered.

Mr. Pedro Hernández told us he had seen a dark, 30-inch-tall creature that resembled a large rabbit hopping along and disappearing into the vegetation. The next day, he discovered four chickens and three goats drained of blood. How it had happened, he did not know.

Another witness, Mrs. Dionisia Pérez, informed us that an animal resembling a very large dog had assaulted her sheep pen and shaken the oldest sheep "as if it were an old rag." We investigated prints in the surroundings, but did not find any traces. Possible organic remains were examined without discovering anything significant. At this point, there existed the possibility that an official investigation, which would include competent authorities as well as civilian researchers, would be launched by officials. It never took place.

Three local children—Baltazar Herrera, Ramiro Rodríguez, and Juan Hernández—said they found three dead sheep on their farm on April 6. The hapless animals had been relieved of their blood. They were unable to find any animal prints belonging to a dog, coyote, or similar creature. The boys told me that they said nothing to the authorities out of fear of reprisals.

We discovered something significant during our stay in Tlalixcoyan. The region is constantly in turmoil, since it contains marijuana and poppy fields and secret airstrips, and is a choice location for drug traffickers. In spite of this fact, the locals *were requesting the authorities' help, prompted by the growing fear of the phenomenon.* That help never arrived, because the authorities in question emitted verdicts from the safety of their desks without bothering to evaluate the real concerns of the rural population.

On May 4, television's Channel 5 transmitted a report stating that the Coatepec region (close to Jalapa) as well as Xico had been visited by the Chupacabras, which had slain six hens, four rabbits, and a goat. We visited the area the same day. We interviewed veterinarians, farmers, members of the Cattlemen's Association, and even workers at the local health-care center. The results were negative. No one was able to give any information; therefore, we cannot say with certainty if what transpired in the area was true or false.

What conclusions can be drawn from the investigation performed? None. We can only consider that *something* or *someone* killed the animals, which were found with torn throats or punctures on their bodies.

On May 11, we investigated the case in Jalapa. We visited Colonia Independencia, where we were able to see the geese that had been slain there and the puncture marks on their bodies. We interviewed Dr. Villanueva, who commented that he had been unable to find any traces of blood on the birds. Residents and animal owners told us that they heard nothing at the time the killings took place.

Analysis

As we stated before, Mexico has never faced as fascinating a phenomenon as the current one, and it is only logical to suppose that vague, silly, opportunistic, political, and pseudoscientific explanations should appear, coupled with a thorough ignorance of the real phenomenon.

It is sad to find such a lack of serious investigative criteria, backed by the scientific method, to face a situation of such proportions. It would seem that the explanations purveyed by government functionaries are efforts at convincing the population that nothing is going on in Mexico. The comments made by Juli Carabias, Secretary of the Environment, show the absence of a real awareness of the facts. The aim appears to be to lead the population into believing that it is all due to natural causes, when, to this very day, no one knows what is killing goats, sheep, chickens, etc.

As an investigator of these events, I would take the following points into consideration:

✦The cattle-mutilation phenomenon is global, since it has occurred in France, Germany, Britain, the US, Brazil, etc.

✦It is linked to a diversified phenomenology that includes the presence of large felines, winged entities, humanoid creatures, etc. (as in some of the cases presented here). To date, no UFO sightings have been linked to the phenomenon at the sites where killings have occurred (although they have been seen in others).

✦The phenomenon finishes as abruptly as it begins. (Folklorists and pseudophilosophers attribute this to the traditions and collective unconscious of all peoples.)

✦Real, objective information about the events must be made available to the population, free from bias and manipulation.

✦Scientific resources must be deployed in an effort to understand what is causing these animal deaths.

✦Brigades of veterinarians, zootechnicians, biologists, chemists, etc. should be formed and charged with investigating each particular case openly and without prejudice.

✦The government should support the individuals involved in this research endeavor with police or even military vehicles (if necessary).

✦We must keep an open mind regarding the evidence.

It is indeed fascinating that, despite the amount of research performed, both from the bibliographical and the field perspectives, the mystery still persists. It is also important to point out that some very strange reports have issued from the state of Jalisco, particularly from the Zapopan region, in which humanoid presences have been reported in connection with the mutilation epidemic. This has resulted in significant searches throughout the area. As of yet, nothing has been found. Witnesses insist that they saw a woman with wolf-like characteristics, who had already attacked a horse and two people.[13] Curiously enough, this leads us to think about events that took place in the Dominican Republic during the 1970s involving mutilated animals and the presence of humanoid creatures.

On May 14, I placed a telephone call to Dr. Bernardo Villa, in Mexico City. Dr. Villa is an investigator with the Institute of Biology of the National Autonomous University (UNAM), and is considered one of the world's foremost mastozoologists. [Dr. Villa played a critical role during the investigation of the "Teco-lutla Monster."] During our conversation he remarked:

> ...it is extremely important to conduct field research in the places that have been affected, following the scientific method: observation and an exhaustive analysis of speci-mens. This should not be dismissed lightly, particularly with the psychosis that has gripped the population.

But this is Mexico, where the words of a misguided politician carry more weight than the statements of a true scientist.

Chapter Twelve

The Hypotheses

When the Chupacabras first appeared, it amazed half the population and caused the other half to curl lips into sneers of contempt. The collected experiences of hundreds of witnesses who courageously stepped forward with their stories (and the other myriads who have kept their sightings secret, no doubt) were treated as tabloid fodder by both friends and foes of the paranormal. The friendly side was unwilling to lend credence to the sudden appearance of a Creole monster that could topple the long-established Bigfoot or Mothman from their paranormal pedestals, or felt it unworthy of interest because it lacked a clear-cut link to UFOs in these Roswell-obsessed days.

The growing evidence was ignored by major newspapers. One of them, the *San Juan Star*, went as far as reprinting only what had already appeared in the wire services concerning the story.[1] Others newspapers, such as *Claridad*, argued that the Chupacabras was merely a ploy to derail the island's bid for political independence by sinking the population into a morass of superstition and fear. This "liberal" newspaper blasted Jorge Martín, whose selfless and tireless investigation brought the story to light, as well as Salvador Freixedo, a world-class paranormal researcher, for their parts in a television program (on a state-owned educational channel) devoted to the creature.[2] It didn't help that Mayor Soto belonged to the pro-statehood political party.

Adding insult to injury, a news crew from the *Inside Edition* TV tabloid visited Puerto Rico early in December 1995 to report on the Chupacabras story. Although *Inside Edition* has covered other unusual situations remarkably well, they chose to mock the witnesses they interviewed and managed to anger Mayor Soto. Perhaps the antics of the Nova group, Brother Carmelo, and other colorful characters led them to believe that it was all a joke.

The totally unexpected furor caused by sightings of the strange entity raises serious issues for debate. What should be our response, as *commonsensical* (as opposed to prejudiced), educated individuals?

Some skeptics have dismissed these events as hallucinations or worse. People do not hallucinate the deaths of their pets or (in the case of small animal farmers) their livelihoods. The person whose income depends on a computer does not wake up one morning, arrive at the workplace, find his computer smashed to bits and say, "I'm probably hallucinating." Extensive photographic evidence is available to all who care to see it, displaying the thoroughly unnatural means of slaughter employed by this unknown being. The victims often died as the result of a single puncture mark, which apparently drained them of blood. One particularly graphic photograph shows a Siamese cat with a single puncture mark right through its skull.

Other skeptics have tried to prove their superiority by arguing that a rare avian known as the "night jar" was in fact the Chupacabras, and that it had been seen in Puerto Rico during the late eighties. Their logic is a poor substitute for their linguistic ignorance; the *chotacabras* of the eighties was in no way, shape, or form similar to the *Chupacabras* of the nineties.

Still others have reacted to the overwhelming evidence with a knee-jerk reaction, steadfastly insisting on blaming these deaths on dogs, feral monkeys, vampire bats, and other exotic beasts.

A plague of single-fanged, bloodsucking dogs is probably a more terrifying thought than a carload of Goatsuckers. Nonetheless, veterinarians have stuck to this unlikely possibility, regardless of the fact that dogs rend their prey and eat it, rather than extracting its juices.

Puerto Rico harbors a number of military, animal-research laboratories. The Caribbean Primate Research Center's La Parguera facility lost a number of rhesus monkeys in the 1970s, and these fugitive apes have allegedly been proliferating throughout the island. Jesús Rodríguez, a veterinarian interviewed by the *San Juan Star* on November 19, 1995, stated that monkeys are notoriously messy eaters, and would have left four holes and scars, rather than the single puncture that has become the Chupacabras' trademark.[3]

El Vocero echoed the possibility that giant vampire bats had infiltrated the island in cargo shipments proceeding from South America. Eyewitness reports in no way describe a bat-like creature, and normal-sized bats are fairly common in the Caribbean, so witnesses would have a good point of reference for their descriptions.

The possibility of exotic pets imported by wealthy dilettante zoologists has been dear to many skeptics on the island. However, no one can imagine what kind of reptile, simian, bovine, etc. could fit the bill of a creature answering the Chupacabras' description. Furthermore, the USDA has a very effective control of anything animal or vegetable entering or leaving the island. Tourists to Puerto Rico are familiar with obligatory USDA inspections at the airport.

Naysayers have found it convenient to blame the entire situation on Puerto Rico's particular political status. It is neither a state of the US nor a free country. Sociologists have long debated whether or not this political limbo has affected people's minds. Prominent politicians have gone on record saying that as 1998 approaches—commemorating a century of US occupation of the island—an increase in mental stress regarding this political status is bound to be experienced.

The fact is that strange creatures are not exclusive to the island. The UK experiences phantom felines and lake monsters. The northwestern US has Bigfoot. The northeastern US is home to a number of enigmatic beings, ranging from three-toed Bigfoot-like creatures to even more unusual life forms. Argentina's Lake Nahuel Huapi contains a "Nessie"-like creature seen by hundreds over the years. Clearly, no political status question affects the minds of the citizenry of these countries.

Are we dealing, in fact, with an extraterrestrial situation? Here we are venturing into truly uncharted waters—waters that have produced biased reactions in many.

Puerto Rico is famous for its myriad UFO sightings, contactees, and encounters with strange—presumably alien—beings. As Jorge Martín, of CEDI-COP, the only organization conducting responsible research on the island, has stated many times, we can only deal with the human aspect of the phenomenon—witness testimony—since the other aspects of the phenomenon are closed to us. For this reason, ufology all over the world is more properly the realm of social scientists, psychologists, and anthropologists than of physicists or chemists.

Since the descriptions given of the Chupacabras portray it as having the head and torso of one of the creatures known as Greys in UFO research, one working hypothesis has linked it to ufology. Its reputed abilities to levitate and issue beams of light from its eyes do seem otherworldly. But other working hypotheses may be just as valid.

One of these hypotheses is the possibility of a paranormal origin. A number of investigators have postulated such an origin for beings similar to the Chupacabras for decades. The word "paranormal" triggers a number of flags in people's minds, since it has been used to describe everything from Zenner card tests to poltergeists. Suffice it to say that this paranormal theory postulates entry, by means of materialization, into our "dimension" or "reality" by creatures that are not native to it .

Before dismissing this working hypothesis as science-fiction, one should consider carefully. John Keel, Dr. Jacques Vallée, and other leading investigators have been suggesting possible interdimensional origins for humanoid oddities for decades. Marc Davenport collected eyewitness accounts from Puerto Ricans who claimed to have looked through, or passed through, "doorways into other dimensions," and other researchers have documented numerous such stories from all over the world. Recent advances in physics comfortably accept the existence of other dimensions, and geometry has accepted the existence of *several million* dimensions. And, of course, many contactees say they have been told the same thing that metaphysicians have been saying for centuries—that there are many realms other than three-dimensional reality, many of which are populated.

Weird Science: Is the Chupacabras a Genetic Experiment?

It has often been said that H. G. Wells was far in advance of his time. From his nineteenth-century perspective, he predicted not only the perils of nature gone wild in *Food of the Gods*, but also the horror of tampering with genetics in *The Island of Dr. Moreau.* The fictional Dr. Moreau, a renegade scientist, turned animals into misshapen parodies of humanity as he tried to fathom secrets forbidden to mankind. The Victorian author's foresight appears particularly accurate a century later.

Genetic tampering has been a taboo subject that refuses to go away. Science has uncovered new and stunning possibilities in leaps and bounds, from "plantimals"—fusions of animal and vegetable cells—to patented animals, such as the so-called "hupigs" (pigs bred with human genes in order to minimize the danger of rejection during animal-to-human organ transplants), and even patented human organs. *Time* magazine recently featured a photo of a mouse with a human ear growing out of its back. A recent segment of Fox TV's *Encounters: The Hidden Truth* discussed the possibility of human-ape hybrids produced through gene splicing.

As we all know, technological advances in the private sector often follow those commissioned by the military by 20 or 30 years. It would not be at all unreasonable to suppose that a level of competence already has been achieved that would enable the fabrication of a hybrid being such as the Chupacabras.

Humankind's stunning inroads into the dark territory of mutations has found a curious parallel in ufology. The wave of mutilations in Puerto Rico has had the dubious distinction of featuring an unsavory array of strange creatures different from the now-classic Greys, or even the winged oddities that have often been seen on the island.

Jorge Martín described the following case in a special issue of *Evidencia OVNI*:

> A police officer investigating the mass slaughter of sheep in the town of Orocovis was startled by the presence of a "thing" standing in the darkness. The bizarre creature was roughly humanoid in shape, and had a most peculiar yellow-orange coloring, plainly visible, even at night. It scampered away into the brush before the policeman could take any action.
>
> On March 26, 1995, at 6:00 AM, Jaime Torres became aware

of a nightmarish sight in the same general area. Perched on the branch of a nearby tree was a creature with a rounded, hairless head; large, slanted, black eyes; thin, clawed hands and legs; and a tail. The skin on this chimerical entity ranged from dark grey around the eyes to brown, yellow, and purple on its back and sides. The monstrous chameleon then issued a subtle hissing sound, which made Torres feel sleepy or faint—sensations that he managed to overcome—just as the creature leaped from the tree limb onto the ground and disappeared into the tropical vegetation.[4]

These creatures would be seen by many other individuals throughout the island municipalities of Orocovis and Morovis, nestled in Puerto Rico's mountainous center. On another occasion, witnesses saw a similar creature lying on the ground, stalking a bull in a nearby field. When a light was shone on it, the creature ran quickly into the underbrush.

On April 2, 1995, a group of 15 adults and children witnessed a three-foot-tall, greyish creature endowed with the power to make the assembled onlookers nauseated. It even caused one of the children to pass out. The following day, separate witnesses encountered creatures that could best be described as "reptilian" versions of the Greys.[5]

The preceding paragraphs appear to indicate that the witnesses had encountered altered or mutated versions of the Greys. Drawings made of the creatures seen depict a specialized being of an arboreal nature, and the coarser-skinned, reptilian Greys point toward another adaptation of the classic type. The question remains: Who or what would be interested in creating such mutations, and to what end?

Proponents of an extraterrestrial perspective to the UFO phenomenon could argue that such variations represent the logical adaptation of the Greys to certain environments: an arboreal type equipped with some sort of "psionic" ability to occupy forested areas, a reptilian type for swampland, etc. These fusions could have been achieved by experimentation with terrestrial creatures.

This possibility was brought to the forefront in C. D. B. Bryan's *Close Encounters of the Fourth Kind: UFOs, Abductions, and the Conference at MIT.*

One of the abductees whose experiences are chronicled in the book reported being shown horses in a wire mesh cage aboard an alien craft. The abductee judged the animals in question to be three- to four-month-old foals with an extremely unusual characteristic. Rather than hooves, the animals were endowed with padded, toed feet (like those of prehistoric horses). When she asked the reason for this, her captors merely stated that the horses had been "changed." The same experiencer also was shown a herd of cows with sizable tubular appendages protruding from their sides. Could these adaptations, for want of a better term, constitute an effort to acclimate terrestrial animals to otherworldly environments?[6]

Whether extraterrestrial or mundane, it would appear that not all genetic tampering of this sort has been successful. Martín investigated a 1989 incident involving what could best be described as someone's experiment gone hideously awry.

One evening in November of that year, two youngsters, Ivan Cotto and his friend Luis, were playing in a field behind Ivan's house. (Martín notes that the 12 year old refused, at first, to think back on the event, which allegedly still gave him nightmares.)[7] While Ivan and his friend played, a "thing" jumped out from behind some shrubbery and landed on the ground before them. The thing was described as hairy and ugly, with sharp fangs, but no discernible nose or muzzle. The frightened boys ran under a light post, but the creature jumped once more and landed in front of them. The light from the street lamp apparently affected the monster, causing it to shudder and emit strange sounds, as if in pain. It then started oozing watery, greenish "goo" through its mouth and chest (by means of fleshy appendages in that region). The painful experience caused the being to retreat into the dense vegetation once more.

In spite of their terror, the two boys were able to give a precise description of the creature and even make a hasty sketch of its unsavory appearance. It was entirely covered in dark fur, and had a crest of fur running from its head down to its legs. It had two powerful legs resembling those of a rabbit or kangaroo, and its eyes were out of proportion with its small head. The fleshy appendages in the chest region were also a most extraordinary detail.[7]

While it could be argued that the boys were attacked by an escaped mascot from a UFO, the description is strongly reminiscent of biological experimentation being conducted in our day and age.

A 1993 issue of the Russian-language *Aura-Z* magazine delved into the experiments of a real-life Dr. Moreau. Dr. Tsian Kanchen, a Chinese physician who was imprisoned during the Cultural Revolution, later escaped to the USSR in 1971. In 1989, he became a naturalized Russian citizen. His research on the bioelectromagnetic fields linking the components of living organisms led him to discover that these fields were part of DNA. DNA is the passive component, while the bioelectromagnetic field constitutes the active component. Thus, genetic information could be transmitted and projected onto DNA, which acts much like a blank recording tape. Like all tapes, it can be overwritten.

Dr. Kanchen created a device that enabled the information in one organism's DNA to be scanned and copied onto another. His experiments with wheat and corn seeds produced a wheat-like plant with traits that were inherited by offspring. Bioelectromagnetic fields for peanuts were projected onto sunflower seeds with stunning results. The latter mutated into a peanut-like shape, and acquired some of the peanut's characteristic taste.

But Dr. Kanchen's most ominous successes involved animals. Five hundred chicken eggs exposed to the bioelectromagnetic field of a duck yielded 480 web-footed hatchlings with flattened heads, long necks, and the general characteristics of a duck. A goat's bioelectromagnetic scan was projected onto a pregnant rabbit, resulting in bunnies with camel-shaped heads and enormous, curved teeth.[9]

The ethics of weird science aside, this constitutes evidence that it is possible to create such mutations through technological intervention—and there is evidence that many of the strange creatures encountered in Puerto Rico are the products of human or non-human experimentation with terrestrial life forms.

Martín says that he was informed about a federal agency that created a task force to investigate where these nightmarish creatures were emanating from, since they appeared to be the product of mutations or some kind of sophisticated genetic experimentation. Captured species are taken to a secret laboratory, located on the island, for further study. This was the case with a strange animal captured near the town of Guayama, which could have been a mutation of an alligator or large reptile. The small "Bigfoot" variants seen in Puerto Rico could also be genetic mutations of some sort.[10]

And what about the US's Bigfoot? In 1974, California psychic Joyce Partise, holding a sealed envelope containing a photograph of a Sasquatch footprint, gave an amazing reading:

> This gorilla man...he just looks creepy but he's intelligent...It's as though they're from another civilization, long ago, and have mutated because of radiation....I'm seeing a lab with little animals in cages, and scattered around are samples of rocks, and minerals, and soils. They have one of those hairy ape-men in a big cage, and he doesn't like being trapped....it seems they are trying to control him, like a robot.[11]

The chilling detail to this paragraph is that Ms. Partise was describing the interior of a supposedly *alien* laboratory. Now 23 years have passed, and what was unlikely in 1974 seems all too possible today.

Maryland researchers Mark Chorvinsky and Mark Opsasnick also have looked into the genetic mutation aspect of the strange creature phenomenon. While they were investigating an intense flurry of big, hairy monster activity in southeastern Baltimore County between 1973 and 1976, they uncovered rumors of bizarre experiments being conducted around Poole Island, an army research center near the Aberdeen Proving Grounds. Their investigation led them to Tom Sobotka, a diver and fisherman who claimed to have knowledge of the goings-on in the offshore islands. Mr. Sobotka had been quoted by *Fate* magazine as saying:

> There are a lot of things happening over there at Edgewood we don't know about. Experiments and mutations. They keep it all a secret. But they found an orangutan dead on the railroad tracks near here two months ago. A guard told me that section in there, it's unbelievable, what they got. Human experiments...[12]

Chorvinsky and Opsasnick were told that mutations—such as a fish with the feet of a deer—could easily be found at Poole Island. The problem was that the island has been declared off-limits to civilians. The researchers were able to determine that a considerable volume of known teratogenic (mutation-producing) agents, such as perchloroethylene, tri-isopropyl phosphite, and others had been released (whether accidentally or by design) into the Aberdeen Proving Grounds area. The possibility of government experiments into human-ape hybrids, while seeming outlandish at first, was not discarded by the investigators, who mentioned that their files held at least one case in which a human-ape breeding was thwarted at the last moment.

At the end of the day, though, the genetic experiment hypothesis is just a working hypothesis, like all the rest.

Distasteful though it may seem to many—particularly those researchers who pride themselves on their strong scientific backing—there exists the widespread belief on the island that the Chupacabras and its kin are demonic creatures, heralding the "period of confusion" (*parusia*, in Greek) foretold in the Biblical book The Revelation to John. All the sophisticated arguments about one-fanged dogs, rogue apes, aliens, and genetic engineering have been unable to assuage this strong concern.

Contributing to this belief is the proliferation of pseudo-UFO research groups that appear to be trying to spread panic among the population. Members of one of these organizations, "Nova," dress in black (like the notorious Men-In-Black, a staple of early UFO stories) and spread the notion that the Chupacabras heralds the end of humanity. They ascribe to it the origin of the AIDS virus and the capacity to destroy mankind and all human works without damaging the planet (like a kind of "organic neutron bomb"), thus rendering it habitable for alien settlers. This kind of activity is irresponsible and wrongheaded. Nevertheless, to be truly scientific, we must allow the the demonic hypothesis to be thrown into the hat with all the others.

No one should feel "railroaded" into accepting any of these working hypotheses as gospel. But neither should we hold our noses and demand "proof," thus slamming the door on witnesses who would gain nothing by making up stories. Under our system of justice, thousands are convicted on eyewitness testimony. If eyewitnesses are good enough for the courts, why can their integrity not be trusted in this matter?

Alas, time permitted me neither a trip to the southwestern corner of the island, nor a fuller round of interviews with witnesses like Mrs. Gómez and Mr. Sánchez, who encountered the creature face to face. These individuals, and thousands like them, stand beside us as we turn elsewhere in search of answers.

Until those answers are forthcoming, my conclusion must remain that *real* animals belonging to *real* people *are* being slaughtered by a being not native to the Puerto Rican ecosystem. We should refrain from passing judgment on its nature until we have a better idea of what we are up against.

Chapter Thirteen

In the Thrall of Other Improbable Creatures

While he drove at dusk across the formidable Sonora Desert of northern Mexico, the last thing Ian Ingram expected to see was a creature straight out of the pages of a medieval bestiary. The strange animal had the body of a small deer, the face of a rabbit, and long ears like those of a donkey. It stood by the roadside, looking straight into his car's headlights, before vanishing into the desert twilight. Ingram reported his unusual sighting to friends and relatives upon reaching his destination. His narration was received with good-natured laughter. But a family friend in Mexico City who was well-versed in esoteric matters did not dismiss the event. "What Ian saw was a nagual—a man who can turn into an animal," he said. "Many similar cases are reported in northern Mexico, where the small towns contain an abundance of witches."

Dr. Rafael Lara Palmeros, research director for Mexico's Centro de Estudios de Fenómenos Paranormales (CEFP), is currently heading his organization's investigation into that country's own manimal. The creature, known as *Hombre Oso* (Bearman), has gone largely unnoticed, living in wilderness areas all over Mexico, ranging from the arid, desert state of Chihuahua to Veracruz on the Gulf Coast.

As early as 20,000 years ago (judging by the depiction of shamans clad in bear and deer hides in the Lascaux caverns), humans were both awed and terrified by those among their neighbors who share the ability—real or imagined —to transform themselves into animals or chimerical beings such as the one described above. It was believed that the human soul was endowed with the ability to desert the body during sleep in order to animate an animal form. More often than not, such individuals were accused of practicing the foulest kind of sorcery, and the punishment meted out by their communities for such activity ranged from expulsion to execution.

The fear of these individuals remains unabated in our postmodern, technological age. In the late 1970s, a scene from the film *Invasion of the Body Snatchers* (which featured a fleeting depiction of a human head on a dog's body) had to be edited out in certain Central American releases due to negative audience reaction.

The oldest and most popular of these transformations is, without a doubt, lycanthropy—the state in which a human turns into a wolf by art or by chance. Entire library shelves can be filled with testimonies, means of execution, and remedies for such a condition, as well as endless means by which to identify a human under such animal guise. While generally assumed to be a Nordic tradition, lycanthropy was greatly feared among the Romans and their Mediterranean neighbors, who dubbed such individuals *versipellis* (skin-changers). They believed they wore their hairy wolf skins on the inside of the body, then changed themselves inside out to go on nocturnal forays. Titus Petronius Arbiter mentions in his book *Satyricon* a character who turns into a wolf as soon as he removes his clothing. As in all shape-shifting legends, the character receives a knife wound while in wolf-shape, and that translates into a similar wound upon his body when he reverts to human form. The very term "lycanthropy" can be traced to the Greek cult of Zeus Lycaeus, whose worshippers wore wolf masks during their rituals.[1]

While European cultures lived in fear of these amazing transformations, Eastern cultures were equally frightened by metamorphoses into other animal shapes. Werefoxes and werevixens play a prominent role in Chinese and Japanese legends. A fox taking on the guise of a human female in order to marry a human male is a common motif. Upon her death, all that remains is the carcass of a fox. India is rife with tales of *raksashas* and tiger-men, just as Africa teems with wereleopards, werehyenas, and other man-beasts.

The Americas also have had their own breed of shape-shifting individuals. Algonquin legend traces this uncanny skill to the days "when animals and men were one." The Inuit of the Arctic Circle retell the legend of the bachelor who returned to his hut and found a woman tending the fire. He married her, only to learn that she was a shape shifter. One of Mexico's most powerful legends from pre-conquest times is that of La Llorona, "The Weeping One" (a spectral figure that emits banshee-like wails in the night). She is held to have been a woman endowed with the power of *nagualismo* who devoured her two children while in a bestial state, and was doomed to mourn her loss forever.

The study of shape shifting has been relegated to anthropologists and sociologists, who explain the phenomenon away as memories of tribal totemic rituals, archetypal fears, hallucinations caused by the use of hallucinogens in cultic activity, and autosuggestion. These explanations, while convincing (and, in some cases, even satisfying), do not take into account cases that have occurred in recent history.

Egyptian author Rollo Ahmed, whose *The Black Art* was among the very first modern books on the subject of black magic, mentions that his wife, during a visit to a German village in her childhood, was warned by local girls about a young washerwoman who was suspected of being a werewolf. When bringing laundry back to the house, the washerwoman tried to ingratiate herself with the children, who were repelled by "her glassy eyes, cruel mouth, and abnormally long fingernails, in spite of her profession." The author adds that the community appeared to shun her instinctively.[2]

In 1930, a farmer from the French village of Bourg-la-Reine who was known as a sorcerer to his frightened neighbors was widely accused of taking on the shape of a wolf at night. After his death, a search of his farmhouse revealed all the paraphernalia associated with black magic.

In the mid 1940s, a Navaho Indian reservation was alarmed by rumors of a werewolf attacking herds of sheep, despoiling graves, and killing and eating women.

Also in the 1940s, a woman in Havana, Cuba, who suspected her husband of marital infidelity because of his secretive behavior, followed him in secret to a desolate point far beyond the city limits. To her surprise and horror, the man took a running leap forward and changed into a four-legged, panther-like creature before disappearing into the tall, tropical grasses. She later discovered that her husband was a high priest in a secret magic sect.

In 1960, Bob Dimmock, an explorer and trader in New Guinea, made contact with the Dani tribe in order to trade tools and medicines for exotic weapons and ornaments. This fierce tribe of headhunters, who had terrorized all other jungle-dwelling tribes in New Guinea, had built thick stockades around their compounds to defend themselves against the depredations of an unknown animal they called the Adati, a boar-like creature of uncommon size and ferocity. In his search for tribal ornaments, Dimmock went into the jungle, where he was attacked by the massive Adati. Although badly wounded, he was able to fire five shots with his pistol into the beast, which ran off into the dense growth, while the explorer tried to make his way to the Dani compound. Upon recovering, he learned, to his amazement, that a war party had gone out the next day in search of the wounded Adati, only to find one of the tribal warriors dead of five distinct bullet wounds. It was decided that the fallen warrior had been a wereboar, and the tribe was now free to return to its old life in the rain forest.[3]

Haiti's secret black-magic societies allegedly carry shape shifting one step further by having the ability to change their hapless victims into animals—preferably beasts on the way to the slaughterhouse. It is often said, among the operators of these places, that many human beings have been slain under such conditions. A slaughterhouse in the Haitian capital of Port-au-Prince allegedly took precautions by administering injections to all cattle. Allegedly, one such "changed" beast cried out, "Now I am here, I remember my children!"[4]

Can it be that shape shifters are not human at all, but another form of intelligent life capable of imitating humans and animals? This theory of "mimics," proposed by renowned UFO and Fortean researcher John A. Keel, postulated that, just as there exist creatures in nature that mimic other species of animals, there may be creatures that mimic human life. This theory could be extended to account for bizarre sightings in which witnesses are uncertain whether what they have seen is an animal or a human being.

Maryland-based researcher Mark Opsasnick has collected sightings that span the history of that state from the 1900s onward. The bulk of these sightings center around "half-man/half-something-else" creatures, whose other half has been described as feline, ape-like, goat-like, or, in some cases, utterly beyond description. Could these be considered cases of "imperfect" shape shifting? More to the point, could the ease of travel exhibited by big, hairy monsters and other creatures that move unnoticed through the highly populated areas in which sightings often occur be a result of their shape shifting into an unremarkable form (human or otherwise)?

Author Brad Steiger pointed out a case in which a shocked witness looked out his patio door to see an enormous vulpine figure drinking out of his swimming pool. It had the remains of a pair of pants around one of its legs. Items of clothing were reported by witnesses in three distinct cases from different parts of the country involving Bigfoot-like creatures—checkered jackets and frayed trousers many sizes too small for the dimensions of the beings involved. Are we dealing with humans who, like TV's *The Incredible Hulk*, are caught in mid-metamorphosis with shirts and pants that cannot stretch?

This jocose notion aside, it must be observed that Bigfoot and his kin are not the only ones who have been spotted in human garb. In 1972, a Californian hiking around mysterious Mt. Shasta claimed to have seen a "reptile man" wearing a shirt and trousers making its way up the slopes.[5] In a Spanish case from 1990, documented by journalist J. J. Benítez, a group of teenagers, gathered one evening at a beach in Conil de la Frontera, near the city of Cádiz, saw two tall, luminous beings emerge from the sea, fall backward on the sand, and stand up again, transformed into a normal-looking human couple. The male was wearing jeans and shirt, the female a blouse and long skirt. The bemused group of adolescents saw the pair stroll along the sand, walk onto the streets of Conil, and disappear into the crowd. Two months later, another group of witnesses saw shape shifters matching the same description leave a trail of unusual footprints and disappear into the water. Benítez concluded his presentation of the case by saying, "I do not know by means of what formula, but these beings—perhaps only a privileged few—are endowed with the ability to mutate their original shapes, turning into ordinary humans."[6]

While Latin America has been a steady source of information on UFOs and encounters with nonhuman creatures, manimals tentatively classified as Bigfoot, Sasquatch, Yeti, and a host of other denominations are usually associated with the planet's temperate zones and even the Arctic. However, more and more reports of such creatures are emerging from the lands between Cancer and Capricorn, and providing even more eyewitness accounts concerning such entities.

Puerto Rico and Mexico have reported an increase in reports about the Sasquatch's tropical cousin, which has not yet been given a name of its own (aside from comical monikers created by the press). The tropical manimals are described as human-sized, with glowing eyes and an abundant covering of brown or black hair. Their habits are largely nocturnal, as in the case of their North American counterparts, and they also have shown a propensity toward appearing in places where UFO or paranormal events are taking place.

In 1992, as word spread of the miraculous apparition of the Blessed Virgin at Montaña Santa, a hilltop located near San Lorenzo, Puerto Rico, a number of unidentified artifacts were reported in the hill's vicinity and even captured on film. Other witnesses reported brilliant, disk-like objects flying overhead.

One of these witnesses, Delia Flores, told UFO investigator Jorge Martín that she and other worshippers were surprised to see a beige van (resembling those used by SWAT teams) parked in the area of the religious sanctuary on the hill. Its occupants wore orange fatigues with NASA insignia, and the vehicle's Spanish-speaking driver had no qualms about telling the religious pilgrims that the van contained a most unusual cargo—a simian creature captured in Carite State Forest.

According to Ms. Flores, she and the others saw a covered cage that contained something "struggling to get out." The driver added that the creature was being taken to a secret primate research laboratory located somewhere on the island, where investigation on this sort of being was being conducted. The heavy tarpaulin covering the cage was never removed, and the witnesses were distracted from showing further interest in the van and its contents by the insistent ringing of the sanctuary's bell, announcing the beginning of the morning's services. Ms. Flores' testimony is hardly unique.

An area farmer discovered one morning that a number of plantain trees on his property had been destroyed by an unknown creature that left a number of deep footprints, attesting to its massive size and weight. According to his neighbors, all the dogs in the vicinity had either barked furiously or stayed home, huddled in corners, as if frightened by something. When the farmer had gone down to gather some plantains, he discovered his crops torn to shreds, as if by powerful claws. The sad scene of destruction affected him so deeply that he refused to leave his house again for the rest of the day.

An agronomer from the Caguas office of the Puerto Rico Department of Agriculture declared that he had never seen such a sight, nor could he speculate as to the kind of beast that could cause such damage. Other residents indicated that they had seen a "hairy figure" run away from the area in the darkness, but they could not describe it in detail.

Gerardo Rosario, another resident of the Maracal sector, was weeding his property at dusk when he had a startling encounter.

> It was getting dark, and I was almost done with the weeding when I heard a noise over to the side, and I moved toward it. I looked up and noticed that it was a hairy creature climbing up the hillside. It was some five feet tall, hairy...and it was accompanied by a smaller hairy creature just like it. I couldn't make out its face, because it was climbing sideways, but I noticed that there was hair covering its features, except around the eyes and cheeks.[7]

There were other witnesses, including a 12-year-old boy on his way to school. As he walked down the road by his house, his attention was distracted by odd sounds, which he described as "a mute trying to speak." When he went over to the roadside to take a closer look, he discovered two creatures sitting on a large boulder in a mountain stream at the bottom of a ravine. The larger creature walked around the top of the boulder, as if keeping watch, while the smaller figure remained seated. The larger creature emitted the moan that had drawn his attention in the first place, causing the frightened schoolboy to flee.

Not far from the San Juan metropolitan area, the apparitions of the Blessed Virgin at Monte Santo, in the suburban location of Lomas Verdes, also involved UFOs and manimals. One night, while worshippers fervently prayed in the heavily wooded area, a five-foot-tall, muscular figure covered in brownish hair raced between the trees in a zigzag pattern. While the religious apparitions were in full swing, sightings of large-headed Greys were also reported.

El Yunque, one of the peaks located in the Luquillo Experimental Rain Forest, has been a focal point of UFO and paranormal activity since the days of the Taíno Indians, who considered the cloud-enshrouded mountain the dwelling place of their deities. Since the late 1800s, reports of strange lights flying over El Yunque have suggested that some sort of non-human activity has been taking place. Persistent rumors of an extraterrestrial base beneath the rain forest have been compounded by a number of cases that have been at the forefront of UFO research on the island.

In December 1993, a group of National Guard Reservists camping at the summit of Mt. La Mina, on the rain forest's southern end, had an encounter with a frightening creature. They described it as man-sized and hairy with glowing eyes. The reservists abandoned their camp and descended the mountain in pitch darkness, terrified by the encounter. Their superiors allegedly told them not to discuss the matter with anyone, but the guards had already told their story to local residents, who, in turn, discussed the matter with local researchers.

In all the above cases, the common element appears to be either Marian apparitions—of which there have been many over the past decade—or bona fide UFO sightings involving both craft and occupants. That a link between manimals and the latter can be established is without question—case histories from all over the Americas have often involved hairy, ape-like creatures standing outside landed vehicles, being led by ufonauts, and, in one case, seen drifting across the skies in a bright, orange ball.

The connection to religious phenomena is more tenuous. During the spectacular Puerto Rican UFO wave of the early 1970s, manimal sightings coincided with bleeding and weeping statues of the Virgin (as well as the apparition of the Virgen de Sábana Grande), Christ images seen in churches, and "Men-In-Black" activity. One of the more memorable cases involved an elderly woman who ventured into her backyard, attracted by the frantic barking of her watchdogs. To her astonishment, she saw the dogs barking at a simian figure with glowing red eyes. It had climbed to the top of a palm tree in her yard. The manimal turned into a ball of orange fire, rose upward into the skies, and disappeared from sight.

Many authors have suggested that apparitions create an "instability" of sorts, which attracts other phenomena that may not be so benign, or that may be of an entirely different nature. Mutilations—particularly the mysterious deaths of household animals such as cats and dogs—play roles in this scenario, and are often followed by sudden rises in manimal sightings.

This is best exemplified by the string of animal deaths that occurred in

Camas, Washington, in March 1974. Local police were astonished to find a decapitated dog at a local animal shelter. Its body did not betray any signs of mauling by another animal, nor had the tall fence surrounding the shelter's perimeter been breached. A few days later, four more dogs were found slain. They were also decapitated, and their brains had been surgically removed.

More recently, the incidents surrounding the Bray Road Beast, a werewolf-like entity reported in Wisconsin, have included similar canine slayings. In 1991, a man going for a walk stumbled upon the mutilated corpses of twelve dogs and seven cats less than two miles from the crossroads where the "Beast" was being sighted. Could these sacrifices have been part of a black-magic ceremony designed to "summon" parahuman entities into our reality?

Chapter Fourteen

The UFO Presence in Latin America

In the late 1950s and early 1960s, efforts of a number of scholars and researchers in the United Kingdom and the United States gradually created a greater sense of familiarity with the UFO situation in the Spanish-speaking world. A number of cases emerged to take their rightful place among the most important in the controversial discipline of ufology.

Unfortunately, many of these cases remain unknown to the contemporary UFO reader, or were forgotten after the original investigation, never to re-emerge in the chronicles of more recent investigators. Many times, the reason for this has been a either linguistic barrier or the difficulty posed by visiting the locales where these events took place. So they remain, at best, travelers' tales, or brief paragraph-sized incidents employed as fillers.

The first serious investigation of cases outside the United States was made by Jim and Coral Lorenzen of the now-defunct Aerial Phenomenon Research Organization (APRO). Much of their data were the result of collaboration with Dr. Olavo Fontes of Brazil, who gained most of it firsthand from actual visits with participants in the events. Among these events were the Villas-Boas abduction, the Saturn-shaped craft photographed over the island of Trinidade, the saucer that exploded over Ubatuba, and other cases with which the reader is probably familiar.[1]

In his very important book, *Dimensions*, Jacques Vallée remarks on the differences in the nature of contacts taking place in South America when compared with those in the US, the UK, and France.[2] The cases one encounters in the Spanish-speaking Americas tend to be much more graphic and violent than elsewhere, and the craft seem to be larger. An Argentine investigator pointed out an instance in which a UFO employed itself as a hammer to pound a car into pieces as the terrified driver ran for cover.

Such an event here would prompt general concern, to say the least. South America, with more than half of its countries languishing in what political scientists refer to as the Third World, lacks the saturation of communication to link its communities as do Europe or the US. The UFO manifestations, therefore, seem to have no need for subtlety.

The strange abduction case of Argentinean truck driver Dionisio Llanca was overshadowed by the more immediate kidnapping of two fishermen in Pascagoula, Mississippi. Though they occurred within weeks of each other, the former case remains merely another among thousands of bizarre accounts. Or is it?

Llanca, a resident of the town of Bahia Blanca (well-known for its UFO-related incidents), had embarked on a routine run in his truck. Just barely out of the city limits, in pitch darkness, he found the truck had developed a flat tire. Not having a dispatcher he could radio for help, Llanca got on with the business of changing the tire.

A light in the distance "like car headlights" appeared to be approaching him. He felt relieved. Perhaps he could take a ride back into town for help. But the light was on the horizon, rather than on the road. It changed from actinic white to brilliant blue, and bathed the darkened countryside in azure light. Llanca was transfixed. He thought of getting closer to the light to find out what it was—until he realized he could not move!

The light emanated from a domed, saucer-shaped craft, which came to hover meters away from his vehicle. To his horror, he realized that beings were standing beneath the glowing machine, observing his futile shouting.

Llanca's next memory was of lying face down on wet grass with the sound of passing traffic filling his ears. In a state of total amnesia, he stumbled around until a passing motorist offered him a lift. Seeing that he was visibly ill, the driver took him to the Bahia Blanca hospital.

Llanca recoiled when a doctor tried to examine him. The services of a hypnotist were employed to find out exactly what had happened to him. Over a period of days, two physicians, Dr. Eladio Santos and Dr. Eduardo Mata, tried to reconstruct the man's memory and pry from him the mind-bending story. They resorted to the use of Pentothal® (a so-called "truth serum") to break through Llanca's memory block and reveal his harrowing story.

The occupants of the strange craft were long-haired, oval-eyed humanoids clad in silver coveralls with gloves and boots. They held Llanca motionless. One of them, a female, approached him and placed a small, black device on his index finger. The device took a sample of his blood and appeared to have a sedative effect, but did not diminish his fear.

Next, the beings took Llanca into the glowing craft on a beam of light. They continued to perform tests on him. They conversed with him in perfect Spanish, advising him that they wished "to see if humans could withstand living" in their world.

Doctors Santos and Mata proceeded carefully with their sessions, realizing that Llanca was terrified of reliving his experience. Probing too deeply could cause the patient to snap.

After revealing detailed descriptions of the craft's interior, lighting, wall texture, and other details, Llanca fell silent. The physicians realized they had struck another—possibly impenetrable—barrier. Then, like an automaton, Llanca recited:

I have a message from the beings in the craft, but I cannot say what it is. No matter what you or other Earth scientists do, there will remain the memory lapse while I was on the ship. I was there for 45 minutes.[3]

The stunned doctors realized that it would not be possible to "unblock" the posthypnotic command without placing Llanca's mind in jeopardy. They directed their efforts instead to help the man recover from the traumatic ordeal. In the wake of the equally dramatic events at Pascagoula, Llanca's case was ignored by most investigators, but Pedro Romaniuk, the Argentinean ufologist, gathered a wealth of data on the case, as did Kevin Randle of APRO.

Recent developments in the study of electromagnetic radiation have given us new insights on the effects of the various kinds of "rays" emitted from UFOs. Low frequency microwaves can cause irreparable damage to the human nervous system. Other wavelengths have actually been proven beneficial to humans in moderate amounts. Normally, 10 to 30 milligauss of exposure is considered to be acceptable. This is the level we normally receive from computer terminals, television sets, and microwave ovens.

"Benign" rays issued from UFOs are few and far between when compared to the lethal ones that have been the topic of a dozen studies. The deaths of witnesses due to exposure to unknown radiation are discussed in Daniel Rebisso-Giese's book, *Vampiros Na Amazonia* (*Vampires of the Amazon*), in which he recounts alarming unprovoked attacks on humans in northern Brazil. At the book's core are the attacks by machine-like devices referred to as "chupa-chupas" by the natives. Rebisso leads us through nightmarish testimonies in which the protagonists—who have no exposure to a "space-minded" culture—give candid descriptions of injuries inflicted by beam and gas weapons, the deaths of friends and relatives in such attacks, and the aftereffects of the experiences.[4]

Ventura Maceira, a 73-year-old man living on the outskirts of a rural town in Argentina, was calmly sipping tea one evening when a brilliantly illuminated object appeared out of nowhere in a nearby clearing. Maceira could make out the forms of two beings clearly within the coruscant object, and, with the rustic courtesy of the gaucho, proffered his cup of *mate* to the new arrivals. His cat, which had just had a litter of kittens, bolted into the darkness away from the unnatural light, forsaking her young.

Events following the apparition of the alien craft proceeded quickly. Maceira saw the beings depart in a flash of light. He immediately began to feel ill. He experienced vomiting and incontinence. Strange tendrils of fine, thread-like material streamed from his eyes, and his blood cell count dropped.

Investigators discovered that fish in an adjacent pond had died of unknown causes. Maceira's cat returned to its kittens, but displayed patches of burnt fur, as if it had been exposed to extreme heat.

Maceira began to acquire thoughts foreign to his experience and meager education. He was able to discuss the finer points of history, philosophy, medicine, and astronomy with experts who came from the capitol to see him. And, to the amazement of his attending physicians, Maceira was growing a new set of teeth!

Investigators, scholars, and mere curiosity seekers bombarded Maceira incessantly in hopes of finding out what made him tick. In the end, the old man was taken to an undisclosed location to keep him from dying of exhaustion.

Maceira's case was first discussed in Ralph and Judy Blum's *Beyond Earth* and by Pedro Romaniuk, who met repeatedly with Maceira in a hospital and after the incident had occurred.[5]

Exposure to UFO beams in other cases has caused illnesses to be cured, hair to grow, and height to increase.

Cases involving the landing of unknown craft and sightings or actual contact of their occupants always receive the greatest attention by the media (if only to sneer) and ufologists. Meriting special attention are those events in which humans are able to observe the activities of UFO crews from concealed, undetected vantage points. Details about the entities, their vehicles, and their activities are often more precise in such cases. Perhaps this is because the witnesses are not running for their lives.

A young man in the mountainous Mexican region of Querétaro observed the landing of a brightly lit, discoidal craft in a gully next to his house. He stealthily approached the site, concealing himself behind boulders. He was rewarded with the sight of three diminutive beings jumping around, playing, and cutting down tall weeds and plants with a beam of light. After a while the creatures boarded their vehicle and shot up skyward. The young man returned to the gully the following morning and collected samples of a strange powder that smelled like sulfur. He later presented the powder to Spanish researcher Salvador Freixedo.[6]

The Azogues case constitutes another close observation of ufonaut activity by humans. On a night in the summer of 1965, Ecuadoran civil engineer Hector Crespo, his son Urgenio, and laborer Francisco López were approaching the town of Zullengo, halfway between the county seats of Cuenca and Azogues. They saw two shafts of light pointing vertically into the sky behind the bend of the road they were on. Believing there was an accident, they turned back to offer assistance.

Instead of an overturned car, they were faced by a disk-shaped machine. Two shafts of light projected into the night sky from a transparent dome at its top. The three men cautiously approached the device. They crawled behind a raised levee to within 100 feet of it.

Mr. Crespo noticed that a compartment appeared to be open. A crimson glow poured out from within the craft, and complex instrumentation could be seen inside. The vehicle itself rested on telescoping legs with plate-like landing pads (similar to the lunar excursion module from the Apollo missions), and gave the impression of tremendous weight.

Most impressive was the fact that they could see the device's "crew." Three silent humanoid shapes stood outside the craft. One of them appeared to work on the light-beam projector. The other two looked on, and at one point handed their compatriot a tool. The witnesses, frightened though they were, were riveted by the scene.

The two beings standing idly by turned their attention toward the levee, as if aware of the presence of the humans, but unconcerned. They were clad in re-splendent silver coveralls with white belts at the waist. The helmets on their heads betrayed no breathing accessories.

An amber light that revolved around the edge of the craft was considered dangerous by the witnesses. At one point, Urgenio Crespo became sick. Re-turning to the car, fearful of having been exposed to some form of radiation, Mr. Crespo was able to observe the departure of the UFO, which took off "in a flash" after wobbling up to a height.

Crespo, who had a good knowledge of drafting, produced renderings of what he witnessed that evening. The sighting was corroborated by others who had seen a particularly bright object in the dark sky that same night. One couple reported that the object landed near their house and provided enough light for them to see the trees, rocks, creeks, and trails in astonishing detail. The headaches and fatigue experienced by the younger Crespo were attributed to fear more than any sort of exposure to harmful radiation.[7]

Although rare in the United States or Europe, reports of genuine malevo-lent action by UFOs against humans emanate from many countries throughout the world. Some of these cases may be pure exaggerations or even hoaxes. But when one is dealing with such a subject, one should not dismiss anything out of hand.

In the mid 1970s, a farm in a remote area of Colombia was besieged by UFOs that fired incessant volleys of rays against its inhabitants. The witnesses bravely defended themselves with rustic shotguns. Several people were wounded, and a small child was killed during the incident.[8]

The famous Hopkinsville, Kentucky, case of 1958 pitted the Kelly family against diminutive green creatures that emerged from a landed saucer. Shots fired at the mini-monsters would cause them to fall back into the darkness, only to reappear again. This early American case would find an even more dramatic South American corollary.

At around 9:30 PM on October 21, 1963, Don Antonio Moreno, a successful cattle rancher, was brusquely awakened by shouts. One of his farm hands called out that an accident had occurred on railroad tracks less than a mile from the ranch house. Not pleased at being disturbed by the obviously excited young man, Don Antonio nevertheless humored him and took a look out of his bedroom window, from which the tracks were plainly visible. To his amazement, a most unusual light floated above the tracks, illuminating the shapes of men who seemed to be examining them.

By that time, Don Antonio's wife, Teresa Moreno, was awake. While the men looked at the unusual activity, she declared that she would take a walk down to the rails and find out from the men what was going on. She stepped out of the ranch house when a 50-foot disk swept out of nowhere toward her. She screamed in terror and retreated into the house. The device hovered at treetop level and aimed a beam of light at the house, "scanning" the interior.

Needless to say, panic seized the inhabitants of the ranch house. The children were moved from their bedrooms to a place away from the scanning UFO beams.

Four more saucers joined the first in beleaguering the Moreno's home, piercing the darkness with weird beams of light. Barricaded behind furniture, the residents did their best to keep still and silent. Any movement, however involuntary, caused one of the alien beams to strike. At one point Moreno noticed that one of the flying disks was emitting a vermilion ray toward the house.

The temperature within the house soon became intolerable. The witnesses believed the disks clearly intended to flush them out and pick them off, one by one. This attempt "to smoke them out like beasts," as Mrs. Moreno would later tell a reporter, only strengthened the family's resolve. After half an hour of living hell, the young farm hand noticed that the beings on the railroad tracks were boarding the scintillating light that hovered over them. The disks broke away, cutting off the deadly rays.[9]

A journalist from the Argentine office of the Brazilian newspaper *O Clarim* reported that a heavy smell of sulfur still hung over the ranch when he conducted his interview of the badly shaken family. Reports appeared in other regional newspapers as well.

Corroboration for the terrifying and entrancing story came from a man who had been just a mile away from the ranch after the attack had ceased. He reported six flying disks traveling across the night sky in tight formation. He did not know of the Morenos' ordeal until he read about it days later in a newspaper. No trace of anything unusual was found at the railroad tracks when railroad authorities conducted an inspection.

Although these cases are among the most prominent, each Latin American nation has its own story to tell.

Mexico

Our neighbor to the south has produced a dramatic number of UFO cases, and certainly Mexico has always exerted a fascination on ufologists and enthusiasts. The first photographic impression of anomalous aerial phenomena was made more than a century ago by Mexican astronomer José Arbol y Bonilla, who observed more than 200 spindle-shaped vehicles through his telescope in August 1883.

In January 1975, five residents of the city of San Luis Potosí, in north-central Mexico, witnessed the evolutions of an orange-red UFO flying north to south over the city late at night. Their description of this phenomenon characterizes the physical description given of most UFOs seen over this part of the country. The object resembled a ball, and gave off an intense shine that resembled fire, as if it were burning up.

Two such fireballs were seen by Jesús Aguiar in Baja California. While the young shepherd looked after some burros on a ranch called El Guayabo, he noticed two fiery, red balls heading toward him nearly at treetop level, maneuvering as if to avoid hitting trees. Aguiar said an intense burning smell filled the air after the objects went past him.

A case that caused great consternation among researchers was the strange death, in April 1977, of 14-year-old Sergio Bayardi Porta, who committed suicide on orders from a small "cloud" that apparently engaged him in conversation. His heartrending suicide note informed his mother that aliens from the planet Sonolcuclo, "three light centuries away from our galaxy," had requested his help on their world. Unfortunately, the only way to reach this improbable destination was by committing suicide. The Bayardi letter was employed by investigators as proof of the perils involved with contacteeism.[10] Coincidentally, the incident occurred almost exactly 20 years before the "Heaven's Gate" mass suicide in the United States.

On February 29, 1976, a family was on its way to inspect a recent snowfall (a rare occurrence in Mexico) at a location close to the community of El Chico in the state of Hidalgo. Parking their car by the roadside, the group entered the woods and headed toward an area used for picnics in warmer weather. At around 8:30 AM, one of the children shouted that a strange object was suspended in midair. Having brought along photographic equipment to take snapshots of the elusive snow, the boy's father swung his camera heavenward to take an impressive sequence of photographs, just as the saucer-shaped craft began to exhibit the classic swinging motion that has characterized these vehicles. The photographs remain among the most important documents ever collected on the UFO phenomenon.

Activity of this nature has always been common in this part of Mexico, perhaps owing to the fact that a number of large, active mining endeavors exist in the region. The connection between UFOs and mines has also been observed in Puerto Rico, where the test pits dug for copper near the town of Adjuntas seem to attract their interest.

In July 1977, hundreds of awed witnesses beheld a number of falling unidentified flying objects, some of which were even captured on film. The mobilization of the Mexican Army over the course of the following days made many realize that something significant had indeed transpired, and rumors spread about a UFO that had crashed in the mountains.[11]

The town of Jopala, east of Puebla in the vicinity of the Gulf of Mexico, became the target of serious research, mainly by an enterprising Mexican ufologist named Pablo Latapí. The townspeople had allegedly seen a solid craft explode into thousands of sparks. Witnesses included not only the local mayor, but also a number of schoolteachers, who had been able to retrieve pieces of a rough metal.

The most curious detail to the townspeople's story was that a group of Americans had arrived by helicopter and beaten them to recover the pieces of the unusual material. The news media would later report, as they often do, that "NASA scientists" had visited the area. More likely than not, these were members of the Air Force's secretive Moon Dust/Blue Fly recovery teams.

Upon analysis, one of the recovered pieces of UFO debris proved to be an unusually pure alloy, unavailable to earthly technology at the time. US researchers also believed that a subsequent collision had occurred in Tabasco, and that two dead alien pilots had been recovered from the wreckage. Mexican researchers were greatly annoyed because foreign investigators obtained access to the available data before their own research teams.

The mining city of Charcas, in the state of San Luis Potosí, has also attracted its fair share of UFO sightings. In 1978, a colossal, blue-white ball made a leisurely fly-over of the community, bathing it in eerie light. While driving along the road leading from Cárdenas to San Luis Potosí, Octavio Rangel was treated to a bewildering spectacle near midnight on October 16, 1977. On the stretch of road close to the Tamasopo mountains, he noticed that the dark countryside, the mountains, and the road ahead of him were suddenly bathed in an intense light as bright as day. Rangel tried to find the source of the uncanny illumination, and suddenly became aware of a tremendous fireball moving horizontally toward Charcas.[12]

Perhaps terrestrial magnetism generated by iron mines has caused many UFOs to crash. On December 15, 1978 a thirty-foot-wide, saucer-shaped craft plummeted to the ground in the Sierra Madre, not far from the northern Mexican city of Monterrey, in the state of Nuevo León. The crash—described as a "muffled explosion" heard for miles around—took place near a community known as El Potosí. The mountainous region was momentarily bathed in light, and a tall plume of smoke rose into the air, marking the site of the impact. The crash of the purportedly extraterrestrial craft caused a great deal of consternation among residents throughout Nuevo León, who had witnessed the vehicle flying over their skies and changing colors.[13]

Police and emergency rescue crews were dispatched to the remote area by the authorities. Their efforts, according to rumor, were in vain. The Mexican Army had cordoned off access to the area a few miles from the site, only allowing the entry of a medical and scientific team two days later. Their findings, if any, were never made public.

The late Leonard Stringfield, who zealously pursued UFO crash/retrieval stories, researched a 1974 incident in which an unknown object was tracked by the US military as it flew over the Gulf of Mexico and passed 40 miles to the south of Corpus Christi, Texas. Traveling at a speed calculated at nearly 2,000 miles per hour, the object began a descent into Mexican airspace, and vanished from radar screens near the town of Coyame, Chihuahua.

According to Stringfield, who published this account in his *Status Report VII: Search for Proof in a Hall of Mirrors* (1994), the Mexican military initiated a recovery effort prompted by stories of a "missing airplane" in the vicinity. He reported that the Mexican team found the wreckage of the missing plane a few miles from the mystery object, which was circular and appeared to be intact, aside from superficial damage. On August 26, 1974, a CIA-sponsored recovery team consisting of specialists flying unmarked, sand-colored helicopters, was dispatched south of the border to recover the saucer with or without the consent of Mexican authorities. Meanwhile, aerial surveillance photographs had revealed an alarming situation: the Mexican convoy with the recovered saucer had stopped in mid-desert. Two dead human bodies were seen lying on the ground next to the vehicles. The American team proceeded with its own recovery effort. They successfully ferried the 16-foot disk back to the US. Its whereabouts remain a mystery.[14]

UFOs have not limited themselves to buzzing small villages and shanty-towns in the desert. Thousands of witnesses in Guadalajara were treated to the aerobatics of a zig-zagging UFO in January 1979. The entire city was paralyzed by the uncanny spectacle, as onlookers were transfixed by the glowing, orange object. The sighting heralded the outbreak of Mexico's UFO wave in the spring of that year. Sightings were recorded every day throughout the states of Jalisco and San Luis Potosí, notably in Ciudad Valles, Cárdenas, Cerritos, Charcas, and Matehuala.

In late March 1979, two boys from Cárdenas reported a close encounter of the third kind involving more than two dozen small figures less than three feet tall, "flying" through the air enveloped in a bluish-green haze. According to the boys' uncorroborated testimony, the small creatures "were spinning like tops."

In an article written for *Samizdat* titled "The UFO Phenomenon in Mexico: The 1991 Wave in Hidalgo," Dr. Rafael A. Lara Palmeros presented a number of stunning sightings and close encounters. The article was originally translated verbatim from the Spanish; the following is a synopsis of it, edited for ease of reading:

- ✦April 22, 1991: Ms. Adriana Velázquez Montes claimed to have witnessed, along with her brothers Pedro and Miguel, "a fireball" in Monte de las Cruces, near the site known as Tepeji del Río. According to the witness, they observed two "midgets" four feet tall, who signaled to them with a powerful, red light.
- ✦May 12, 1991: Three elongated, silvery vehicles appeared over Huejutla, Hidalgo.
- ✦May 15, 1991: A flashing, oval object was seen over Real del Monte.
- ✦May 22, 1991: A small UFO fired a beam of red light over Real del Monte. No damage was apparent.
- ✦May 29, 1991: Hundreds of witnesses saw a nocturnal "parade" of twelve shining, elongated objects over Pachuca, Hidalgo. They were very similar to the ones observed by the Velazquez family at Tepejí del Río.
- ✦June 2, 1991: A sighting was made over the Tula colossi. One of the alleged UFOs came to within 50 feet of the colossi's heads.
- ✦June 4, 1991: A nocturnal sighting was made by dozens of residents of Pachuca. Some 15 triangular lights were counted. Videos of them indicate that they resemble the ones seen frequently in Belgium during 1990.
- ✦June 8, 1991: An elongated object was seen by dozens of Pachuca residents. It emitted a reddish glow.
- ✦June 20, 1991: Three oval craft were seen.
- ✦June 25, 1991: Six unidentified flying objects were seen over Huejutla, Hidalgo.
- ✦July 2, 1991: A flotilla of 10 to 15 triangular lights was seen over Jasso, Tepejí, Tula, and other cities in Hidalgo.
- ✦July 10 1991: A very fast, oval vehicle appeared in the skies over Tepejí del Río. It was seen by scores of drivers from the Pachuca - Mexico City Expressway around 3:00 PM. A day later, a UFO similar to the one seen in Hidalgo turned up over Mexico City.
- ✦July 14, 1991: Sr. Antonio Pulido Obregón managed to capture on videotape two alleged UFOs moving at high speed from east to west in Jas-

so, Hidalgo.

Dr. Lara echoed the claim that supposed "NASA" personnel visited the area of the sightings:

> ...during the first few days of June, agents allegedly from the US National Aeronautics and Space Administration visited Pachuca to inspect and gather information from the population. According to a civil engineer, an agent named Brown filled two notebooks with data provided by alleged witnesses to the sightings. We were unable to corroborate this fact with the pertinent authorities.[15]

Argentina

As noted earlier, Argentina has played unwilling host to a vast array of UFO-related phenomena throughout the length and breadth of its territory, from the vast expanses of Patagonia to the largely unpopulated Gran Chaco. Ufologists have known for years of two notorious and highly active "windows" of paranormal activity—one near the city of Salta, and the other near Bahía Blanca, on the Atlantic Ocean. The infamous BAVIC line (an imaginary line devised by the late French UFO researcher Aimé Michel) runs right through the country.

Second only to Brazil in UFO events, Argentina has been a hotbed of UFO activity since late last century, when the survivors of the catastrophic earthquake that rattled the provincial city of Mendoza in 1866 (a quake of such magnitude that the ground shook for a month afterward) witnessed "a glowing meteor...perfectly visible despite the bright sunlight, leaving smoke in its wake."[16]

The Burgos family, from the town of Neuquen, in northern Argentina, looked on bemusedly as a disk-shaped UFO emitted a succession of colors ranging from orange to blue to yellow as it flew over their community in August 1978. Some of the witnesses experienced unusual physical symptoms after the sighting. This was unusual because the sightings took place at a considerable distance. The symptoms disappeared after the experience.

A few days later, a Buenos Aires newspaper reported the discovery of "star-shaped indentations" in a field in the town of Saldungaray (Buenos Aires province). Although local residents had noticed the strange markings long before the press was alerted, the impressions remained undisturbed. It was also noted that adjacent shrubbery had been crushed flat, as if something had landed on it.

The residents of the peaceful rural district of General Ocampo, in Concordia, Argentina, came face to face with the unknown one evening in December 1978. A fleet of unidentified flying objects moved through the sky at a leisurely pace, leaving an incandescent wake. They dispersed after one of them executed a sudden maneuver, then dropped out of formation and crashed to the ground, exploding. Fragments of metal of all sizes littered the fields. Farm workers and even journalists from a local newspaper collected them. Reportedly, the metal resembled very hard steel plate, slightly burned at the edges, as if by a blowtorch. When struck by a hammer, the metal did not ring as a normal terrestrial metal would.[17] Photographs of one of these most unusual fragments were featured in Argentina's *El Heraldo* newspaper.

In 1982, two state troopers, Andrés Soria and Ramón Carpio, observed the nocturnal maneuvers of a UFO. It eventually issued a long tongue of flame, igniting a brush fire that damaged a dozen homes and wounded scores of residents of Catamarca. Gale-force winds that appeared in the wake of the glowing vehicle's departure spread the blaze.

In January 1994, a number of tourists on a camping trip in Santa María de Punilla, near Cosquín, Argentina, witnessed a remarkable aerial spectacle. Two lights changed color from blue to red, and flew over the area, crisscrossing the skies at odd angles for more than a quarter of an hour before disappearing beyond the eastern horizon.

An earlier case occurred in the Sierra de Córdoba. It involved a cabdriver who was transporting a family of vacationers from El Chaco to the Molino de Oro region. The witness related how the peaceful afternoon was abruptly transformed by the sudden extraterrestrial apparition. At 6:30 PM, according to the story, a UFO emerged from a clear, blue sky and spread panic among the vacationers before vanishing behind the mountains. A photograph, hastily taken by the tourists, proved sufficient to catapult the case to the airwaves.

Argentinean investigators, while little-known in the United States, have distinguished themselves for their scholarship in Latin American ufology.

Guillermo Roncoroni, for instance, conducted the first statistical analysis of the myriad cases that have made Argentina famous. He compiled ARGENCAT, which aided in proving that the BAVIC line had as much influence over Argentina as over Spain or France. He went on to publish *UFO Express*, for years considered one of the most important Spanish-language journals available on the subject.

Dr. Antonio Las Heras, a parapsychologist, is well known throughout South America for his *Control Mental* self-help disciplines, as well as his exhaustive UFO research and often "revisionist" conclusions. His theories about the famous case involving Chilean corporal Armando Valdés differ greatly from those of many other researchers. However, he has forwarded exciting new theories concerning the disturbing phenomenon of mysterious disappearances.

In his book *Respuestas al Triángulo de las Bermudas* (*Solutions to the Bermuda Triangle*), he posits the parapsychological phenomenon of *telergy*, the power emanating from a person's untapped psychic resources. One of the effects of this telergy is teletransportation of objects or people in open areas, produced by the complete and utter blinding of the five senses by fear, prompting the psychic state of paragnosia (awareness of the paranormal), which causes the subject to levitate and/or disappear into some unreachable place.[18]

Dr. Ricardo César Calderón investigates more terrestrial (but not less elusive) matters, such as the vast folklore concerning dwarfish beings and subterranean cities under Argentine soil. He points to the overwhelming number of South American traditions that speak of the existence of such eldritch realms, some of them as recent as 1971, when former Swissair pilot Ferdinand Schmidt ran into a compatriot in the city of Manaús (on the Brazilian Amazon). The man, Karl Brugger, related the amazing story of the subterranean kingdom of Akakor, which has been the object of countless searches since his stunning revelation. The existence of other underground cities, such as those in the region of Argentina's Sacred Mount of Uritorco, have also been the subject of a book by another Argentinean scientist, Guillermo Terrera.[19]

Other phenomena abound along the inaccessible reaches of Argentina's Andean border with Chile. The ski-resort city of Bariloche has been the site of an intense UFO flap since 1992, and sightings of "Nahuelito," a monster in nearby Lake Nahuel Huapí, have been on the rise. Reports of the Ucumari—large, hairy "manimals"—are also common to the Argentinean Andes, particularly around the vicinity of Mount Umahuaca, in the Salta Province.

But Bariloche is hardly alone. According to a news item gleaned from the Spanish EFE news agency, the community of Victoria, in eastern Argentina, experienced a flurry of UFO activity in 1992 of such magnitude that specialists from NASA allegedly paid the area a visit. The NASA investigators were lodged at the Niño de Dios de Victoria abbey, located some 516 miles north of Buenos Aires. They joined the local residents in nightly sky watches. King Juan Carlos, of Spain, whose traveling retinue has often included ufologist/journalist J. J. Benítez, allegedly requested reports on the UFO flap from Victoria's municipal authorities. A Japanese investigative group was also reportedly on hand, proving beyond a doubt that there exists a renewed interest among the international UFO community regarding the oft-unsung apparitions taking place in Argentina.[20, 21]

Bolivia

If the gods—or extraterrestrial visitors, their reasonable facsimiles—ever came to the unearthly shores of Lake Titicaca to rear the colossal ancient city of Tiahuanaco, they left no clues as to their identities. According to ancient traditions collected by folklorist Beltrán García, the "gods" dropped a strange substance from the skies that created Lake Titicaca in the shape of a man reclining. Oddly, things continue to fall from the sky in an age as far removed from the mythic past as our own.

The "altiplano," at the dizzying elevation of nearly 13,000 feet, is a landscape pilfered from the pages of H. P. Lovecraft. More mysterious than Egypt at its most inscrutable, it must have indeed resembled another world to another alien group, the Spanish invaders, who exploited its hidden wealth to depletion and made El Alto Perú (Upper Perú), as Bolivia was then known, one of the wealthiest lands in the world. And it was in these desert lands that the saga of UFOs in Bolivia began.

Enrico Martínez, a Spanish cosmographer, recorded a strange sighting on August 13, 1553. Two moons, one silvery and another blood-red, were seen at seven o'clock in the morning over the settlements of Porco and Potosí. This caused alarm among the natives and concern among the Spanish garrison, who feared the "portent" could incite an uprising among the enslaved Incas. The sighting repeated itself every day for a week, causing further astonishment. Both settlements were a stone's throw away from Tiahuanaco.[22]

Have the architects of lost Tiahuanaco returned? The increase of UFO sightings in the landlocked Bolivian republic seems to point in that direction, and strange things have continued to fall out of cloudless, blue skies.

Pedro Serrate was walking along the banks of the Mamoré River in 1953, when he became aware of a discoidal object some 150 feet away from him. The strange vehicle appeared to be fashioned of an azure, vitreous material. Curious, Serrate got closer to the craft. He was able to catch a glimpse of its human-looking crew. When the uniformed humanoids, caught off-guard, became aware of Serrate's presence, the vehicle rose silently into the air and disappeared in a matter of seconds.

In July 1962, while men from the US and USSR where taking their first steps into Earth's orbit, a "space capsule" landed in the Bolivian town of Ayo-Ayo, 30 miles from the city of La Paz. The object fell into a deep ravine not far from the town. Its fall from the heavens was followed by the remarkable appearance of a feline never seen in Bolivia—a puma. The cat was assumed to have been disgorged by the object. The hapless feline was bludgeoned to death by the townspeople and its pelt sold to the US Air Attaché, Col. Wymer. This would not be the last time that the US would play a significant role.

On August 20, 1979, the American embassy in La Paz was informed of the crash of another small artificial vehicle on Bolivian soil. The unknown device had fallen on a large private hacienda near the village of Buen Retiro. Gonzalo Menacho, a local farmer, attested to having seen "a fireball falling from the sky" in the early hours of August 19. After sunrise, Menacho was surprised to see a small military airplane circling the area, as if looking for something. Menacho and a friend discovered a lightweight sphere, roughly three times the size of a basketball, made of some unknown metal. When the men tried to retrieve the object, they were prevented from doing so by government authorities. A Bolivian Air Force colonel stated that the object was not extra-terrestrial, but merely "a fuel cell from a satellite." A film on the recovery effort was presented to the US Air Force.

The AFP News Service reported that a luminous device "the size and shape of a metal suitcase" fell from the sky in January 1991, not far from Tiahuanaco. The unconfirmed report went on to say that the odd apparatus landed on the slopes of Cerro Guarayo, five miles from the megalithic ruins, and was still emitting a strange light that terrified the local villagers and peasants. This report was echoed by Radio Panamericana in its regular broadcast from the Bolivian capital of La Paz, some 38 miles from where the event took place.

Investigator Antonio Las Heras visited the Quebrada de Humahuaca, on the border between Argentina and Bolivia, to study the beliefs of the native Coyas, who have lived in the inhospitable Andean valleys since Inca times. Strange vehicles are routinely seen flying over, and landing on, the inaccessible snow-capped peaks. This fact has led many South Americans to believe in the existence of a UFO base or materialization point somewhere in the Bolivian highlands.[23]

On September 30, 1996, the EFE news agency reported a singular case in which alleged extraterrestrials helped mountain-rescue experts find a lost explorer. Roberto Suárez Molina, an architect, became lost on a steep ridge in southern Bolivia while on a recreational expedition to the mountains dividing the Chiquisaca and Tarija districts of the landlocked South American republic.

Apparently, the forlorn Suárez had camped for the night in a desolate mountain valley. He became aware of a strange light, which hovered at a distance over him, changing color from white to a red beam of light before vanishing. Unbeknownst to him, the search-and-rescue team and another team composed by his friends had camped elsewhere in the area. They witnessed the same phenomenon, and were prompted to head for the destination marked by the red beam.

Chile

No chronicle of UFO activity in South America would be complete without the ample and dramatic case histories that have emerged from Chile. The clear nights of its vast northern salt deserts have provided an array of memorable sightings, causing some Latin American investigators to vote it "the country most visited by UFOs" during the 1970s.

The all-time Chilean classic case is the previously mentioned hair-raising (and beard-growing) experience suffered by army corporal Armando Valdés Garrido, whose story has been exhaustively documented by researcher Antonio Huneeus.

In the bitterly cold early morning of April 25, 1977, a military patrol of the Rancagua regiment, led by Corporal Valdés and composed of soldiers Julio Rosas, Ivan Rojas, Pedro Rosales, Humberto Rojas, Germán Valle, and Raúl Salinas, decided to camp in a rocky, desolate area in the Andean foothills a few miles east of the city of Putre. One of the soldiers, who had been assigned sentry duty, rushed back to the corporal to inform him that a red light was hovering above a nearby peak. Suspecting that smugglers might be at work, Valdés ordered his platoon to ready weapons and extinguish the campfire—their only source of warmth in the near-zero weather.

The soldiers moved out toward the source of the purplish-red light. They realized in a matter of seconds that they were not dealing with illegal activity or lost mountaineers. The light was moving down the hillside, but not on its surface. Having complained earlier about the frigid temperature, the soldiers were stunned to discover that it was actually getting warmer as the light grew closer, turning into a large, oval-shaped object and bathing them in a purplish-red glow.

The object landed some 50 feet away, swathed in a violet fog that stood out in stark contrast to the surrounding darkness. This was enough to cause panic among the young conscripts, but they found themselves unable to move. Weapon in hand, the corporal ventured forward alone into the unearthly fog. (He later stated that he felt attracted by something within the luminosity.) He was standing no farther than nine feet from his men when the purplish light engulfed him. The corporal stated for the record that his only recollection of the event was a dreamlike vision of falling down a deep well or chasm. He was also left with a feeling that he would meet again with the strange presence.

The truly amazing part of the story follows: The leaderless platoon witnessed the corporal's unexplained reappearance some 15 minutes later, when they heard him calling for help. Valdés gave the appearance of having been drugged. His normally clean-shaven face showed dense beard, and his calendar wristwatch indicated that the time was 6:30 AM on the 30th of April, when it was still, in fact, 4:25 AM on the 25th. By all indications, the hapless military man had undergone a five-day sojourn in an unknown region of time and space in just 15 minutes!

Hypnotic regression, which would ordinarily have been the procedure of choice in unlocking the "missing time," was expressly forbidden by the Chilean military. Medical specialists agreed that Valdés' panic at the ordeal, as well as the unknown radiation he had been subjected to, could have accelerated the growth of his facial hair, but no explanation was forthcoming about what had happened to his wristwatch.

Argentinean parapsychologist Antonio Las Heras, mentioned earlier, conducted further research into the Valdés case following a Santiago television appearance, during which he formed part of a panel with an aeronautical engineer and an astrophysicist who supported the corporal's claim. A few days prior to Las Heras' arrival in Chile, the Chilean Army had issued a communiqué confirming that Corporal Valdés and his platoon had come face to face with an unidentified phenomenon. The communiqué also added that the protagonists of the case had been forbidden to comment on the incident until military authorities had issued a final verdict. After conducting his own research, Las Heras felt that a solution to the mystery was in hand.[24]

According to the parapsychologist, both the media and amateur investigators alike mistakenly suggested that the corporal had spent five days within a UFO while only fifteen minutes had elapsed for the terrified onlookers. Las Heras posited that the corporal's digital timepiece "went crazy" upon entering the purple haze, probably as a result of electromagnetic fields emanating from the object. The digital watch was affected for a given period of time, finally stopping at a random time. In short, Valdés disappeared for only fifteen minutes, since his wristwatch had stopped shortly before his disappearance.

Las Heras challenged the theory that a space-time alteration took place, since exactly the opposite to what would be expected of any travel at relativistic speed is what happened. Valdés, the subject of the ordeal, was the one who aged, whereas the onlookers remained the same. According to the theory of relativity, the soldiers should have aged at least fifteen minutes, while the corporal should not have aged at all. On the other hand, Las Heras entirely agreed with the somatic explanation for the sudden growth of the corporal's beard.

A flood of sensationalistic information followed the Valdés Case. It was alleged that the corporal had shouted at the UFO, "Go! In the name of God, leave this place!" as if he were a country bumpkin facing a ghost. The local UFO press claimed that the corporal had been given a "message" by the vehicle's occupants. These details proved untrue.

After crisscrossing Chilean skies for decades, UFO activity dwindled down to a few unimportant sightings. According to an article from the EFE news agency, more than 400 confirmed sightings took place in the years before 1990. However, the period from 1990 through 1994 remained quiet. Not even the truck drivers who cross the Atacama Desert—the driest in the world, with a unique topography that resembles that of the moon on a starry night—witnessed any sightings worthy of public attention.

In November 1990, a woman from a small community 280 miles north of Santiago was violently awakened by a loud noise while a light as bright as the sun poured into her bedroom. She was filled with dread when she noticed a figure no more than 45 inches tall standing at the door. It had very large eyes and ears, and its skin was illuminated by a strong, violet light (perhaps the same "purple haze" that engulfed Armando Valdés Garrido in 1977?).

One of the most spectacular of the cases was reported by Chilean Gaspar H. H. In August 1990, he revealed that, 12 years earlier, in the middle of the antipodal winter, while traveling in his old car some 625 miles south of Santiago, he had had sexual relations with an extraterrestrial female.

Gaspar, who was 66 years old at the time of his revelation, attained global notoriety when he told a major newspaper in the Chilean capital that he had been inside a spaceship for four hours and managed to establish telepathic communication with its occupants. Later on, he was placed on a bed that adapted to the contour of his body, while skin samples were taken. The ufonauts threw water on him to "decontaminate" him, after which sex with an extraterrestrial woman took place.

On October 8, 1994, a forest ranger in the Torres del Paine National Park, located in the sub-polar Magallanes region, was allegedly chased by an immense UFO that hovered in the sky. The ranger, who had spent 18 years in the park, was conducting a routine inspection when he was surprised by an enigmatic, spherical object that gave off a powerful beam of light. Upset, he began a frantic race back to the Paso de la Muerte Shelter, some ten miles away. He was pursued the entire distance by the object, which emitted flashes of light. After gaining the shelter's safety, he was able to alert some comrades, who observed the UFO moving away at high speed.

A driver identified as Arturo Cofre corroborated the forest ranger's testimony. He stated that he also had witnessed the giant sphere over the so-called Cuernos del Paine. Carmen Salvat, an employee of the Hotel Explora, claimed to have seen a large, luminous sphere moving in a northerly direction as it gave out potent red and violet flashes. As a final note, a tourist, who, like the forest ranger, wishes to remain anonymous, said that the device landed and turned off all its lights before taking to the skies once more.

In June 1996, three Chilean citizens related stories of "close encounters of the third kind" to the Spanish-language news agency EFE. The stories of Newton de Oliveira, an English professor; Vivian Figueroa, a housewife; and Juan Venegas, a businessman, were later published in the newspaper *La Tercera*.

De Oliveira said that his encounter took place on August 23, 1990, while he was with friends in the Cajón de Maipo, in the Andean foothills close to the Chilean capital. He said he had split from the group to do some sky watching when he suddenly became unconscious for about 15 minutes. After he regained consciousness, his companions noticed changes in his personality. Because of this, and due to continued physical complaints, De Oliveira finally underwent hypnotic regression. The sessions indicated that a close encounter had, indeed, taken place.

Vivian Figueroa underwent a similar experience. On February 23, 1983, she felt the urge to go to a small city square in the city of Rancagua, 50 miles south of Santiago. A strange light gradually approached her, causing her to faint. When she regained consciousness, she was back home in her garden. By means of hypnotic regression, investigators were able to demonstrate that Vivian had also experienced a close encounter, and that the date coincided with the day on which one of her brothers had witnessed a UFO over Rancagua.

The most spectacular account remains that of Juan Venegas, whose encounter took place the evening June 23, 1991, as he drove his vintage truck along a road linking Santiago to Valparaíso. He said he was happily driving along with his brother-in-law when a light approached them. The truck's lights went out, and within a few seconds the engine stopped. The vehicle "flew through the air," and turned 180 degrees before coming to a halt facing the opposite direction. Five years later, the case is still under investigation by Chilean ufologists, while Venegas continues to drive along the same road, hoping for a repeat performance of the spectacular phenomenon.

Colombia

This major Andean republic has certainly provided its share of sightings. The problem, echoed by many researchers both in the US and in the rest of Latin America, is that the vast majority of UFO reports come from disreputable journalistic sources that present bogus UFO stories to boost circulations.

Such tales are dubbed *noticias de verano* ("summer tales"), and are quickly forgotten.

Perhaps the most dramatic case involved a highly unusual "firefighting" UFO, a considerable break from the case histories involving fire-starting saucers. This particular case transpired in 1976, and was researched by Spanish investigator Salvador Freixedo, who was told of the incident by one of the witnesses involved.

Inés de Montaña, a well-known journalist for Bogotá's *El Espectador*, described how a UFO had saved the *hacienda* that had been in her family for generations. The country estate, located in Tolima, a valley deep in the Andean range, was besieged by the flames of a nocturnal forest fire, which illuminated the night sky with its angry flames, devouring vegetation and croplands. Farm hands ran in search of axes and sand with which to create a fire break, since there was no water that could be used to extinguish the blaze. Their valiant efforts were in vain, because the dryness of the foliage made the flames burn with great intensity.[25]

While the journalist looked on at the advancing line of fire from her bedroom window, an effulgent blue light in the smoke-filled sky caught her attention. It moved slowly and deliberately, at a low altitude, toward the imperiled area. De Montaña described it as "a helicopter of light."

The strange object appeared to be coming in for a landing, but, upon reaching the height of the tallest palm trees, it rose again and departed with the same deliberate slowness that characterized its approach. It left in its wake a luminous, comet-like tail of such intense coldness that it extinguished the forest fire almost immediately, and caused the bemused onlookers to find warmer clothing. The UFO paused for a few seconds, then immediately began to move very slowly across the flames. As it moved, the "fire died down, as if doused with tons of water." The farm hands, who had been doing their best to contain the spreading blaze, were awestruck by the miraculous event.[26]

In January 1977, a Boeing 727 airliner, belonging to Colombia's Avianca airline and piloted by Gustavo Ferreira, was approaching Ibagué, a community west of Bogotá, when the crew suddenly became aware of a strong, white light. Believing that another airliner had strayed into their path, Captain Ferreira promptly radioed the air-traffic controllers at Bogotá International Airport. They assured him that they had picked up the intruder on their radar and were tracking it.

The Avianca crew could do little as the intense light source made a bee-line toward their jet. In seconds, the mysterious light stopped in midair. Passengers and crew were treated to the sight of an unidentified flying object three times the size of the airliner they were in. Captain Ferreira flashed his landing lights at the vehicle, which responded by changing color from white to red. A second flash of the landing lights prompted the UFO to turn green. Three minutes later, the strange object sped off out of sight. Air-traffic controllers estimated the UFO's speed to be some 20,000 miles an hour at a 90-degree angle before it vanished off their screens.

A flurry of UFO sightings filled the Colombian summer months of 1977. On July 6 of that year, residents of the community of El Socorro witnessed the flight of a six-UFO "squadron" across the night sky over their town. The UFOs flew fast and low amid heavy rainfall, emitting bursts of red and white light.

On July 20, shortly after 4:00 PM, attorney Carlos Rangel, who was looking out the window of a doctor's office in downtown Bogotá, saw five UFOs engaging in maneuvers over the city. He promptly drew the attention of the nurses in the office and people walking on the street. The number of onlookers staring skyward, including those who got out of their cars to take a better look, caused a traffic jam that lasted more than an hour. Bogotá's *El Liberal* newspaper published a photograph taken by a staff photographer, depicting one of the UFOs in question. The photograph was accompanied by eyewitness testimony.

Dominican Republic

The Dominican Republic, occupying the eastern half of the Caribbean island of Hispaniola, has been facing an increasing number of UFO sightings over the past decade, possibly in conjunction with the very same "flap" that has been active in Puerto Rico since 1987. Its UFO crisis has included a number of paranormal events, cattle mutilations, close encounters, and abductions.

Prehistoric evidence of UFO activity in both the Dominican Republic and neighboring Puerto Rico (across the UFO-haunted Mona Passage) is abundant. Petroglyphs found in the caves of the province of Sanamá show strange artifacts giving off light, objects with ladders leading up to them, and strange occupants, some of them endowed with helmets and breathing equipment.

Since the sixteenth century, controversy has raged over whether the island was discovered by Columbus during his second voyage to the "New World," or by Alfonso Sánchez, master of the hapless caravelle *Atlante*, in 1480. (Sánchez left detailed records of his exploration of the island, along with a map, which may have come into the Genoese mariner's possession.) But not even this controversy has come close to the contemporary furor over the strange objects reported in the skies, seas, and land of the Dominican Republic.

In the late 1960s, UFO researcher Sebastián Robiou looked into a number of Dominican cases. One was the April 1969 sighting of a triangular object seen in the skies over La Romana. It was pursued by jet fighters that had initiated the chase two hours earlier over Puerto Rico.[27]

Surprising encounters with humanoids were soon to follow. In September 1972, a truck driver on a nocturnal run in the vicinity of the town of Palenque encountered what could only be described as a "roadblock" consisting of a glowing, oval-shaped UFO and three humanoid entities in green uniforms. As if the sight were not sufficiently overwhelming, one of the humanoids told the truck driver that he had been as human as he, once upon a time. The being claimed to be Freddy Miller, a Dominican fisherman who had disappeared during a fishing trip almost twelve years previously. He had drowned when his boat capsized, was rescued by a UFO, and was taken, by its crew, to another world to live among them.[28]

The UFO wave first began in earnest around March 1977. It was concentrated around a number of cases investigated by the Dominican group GOFOS (Grupo Observador de Fenómenos y Objetos Siderales). These cases took place in San Francisco Macorís, a farming community in the southern part of the country.

In one particular instance, a couple was awakened at 3:30 AM by their baby's crying. When the mother went to check on her, she noticed that the entire house was bathed in a hot, greenish-blue light. The mother described it as "a buzzing lightning bolt that won't go away." The woman's husband went outside to find the source of the mysterious light. He was stunned by what he saw. Hovering above the palm trees at a height of 50 feet was a disk with a large number of "grates." The grates emitted an array of colors—mainly red, white, blue, and green. He ran back into his house as the buzzing sound increased. The heat became unbearable as the vehicle zoomed out of sight. The couple was left with irritated eyes and a dryness of the throat that persisted for a week.

On the night of June 24, 1977, an anonymous witness reported seeing an enigmatic light descend slowly from the night sky to remain motionless over the sea. A tube-like structure emerged from the vehicle's "hull" and appeared to absorb sea water for a protracted period of time. The unidentified object then rose again to hover above the witness, who noticed two beings staring at him through a porthole. A larger vehicle absorbed this smaller craft and became lost among the stars.

The stage for the sightings moved from the Dominican Republic's eastern tip to its western border with Haiti, near the sugar-producing region on the Bay of Ocoa, in late 1977 and early 1978. Events took a grislier turn. Mutilations, accompanied by strange lights and bizarre creatures, tormented the cane cutters of the town of Barahona, who reported that a "gigantic dog" was slaying and eating domestic animals in the dead of night. This monstrous canine possessed above-average intelligence, as it was able to open pens and cages. It extracted the last drop of blood from its hapless victims, which consisted largely of cats, hens, and rabbits. Local authorities dismissed any supernatural suggestions, stating that it was merely "a joke in the poorest of taste" executed by the inhabitants of this agricultural area. The fact that the locals could ill afford sacrificing their animals for the sake of a prank was deemed irrelevant.[29]

The mutilations were closely followed by a number of "occupant" sightings as the flap reached its peak. Cone-shaped beings were seen in November 1978 by five women in Santo Domingo, the island-nation's capital. Three creatures twice the height of the tallest human, carrying lanterns on their abdomens, descended a steep hillside to surround an automobile that braked to a screeching halt. The car's headlights died as the witnesses heard sounds that they assumed were blows being inflicted upon the vehicle by the conical trio. Their terrified screams attracted the attention of neighbors, who came to their aid. No traces were found of the beings, and there were no marks on the car.

In 1980 José Antonio Pagán vanished while flying in his private plane between Santo Domingo and Puerto Rico. His frantic mayday in the middle of the night was picked up by a Spanish airliner, which relayed to the control tower of the international airport in San Juan his frightened description of being pursued by a "weird light." Contact was lost soon thereafter, and Pagán was never heard from again.

In the 1980s and 1990s, the Dominican Republic's UFO activity has become closely linked with the incidents being reported by commercial and recreational mariners along the Mona Passage, the turbulent channel separating Hispaniola from Puerto Rico. Many illegal immigrants, braving the passage's fierce seas in order to land on Puerto Rico's western shore, have reported seeing bizarre lights perform spectacular aerial maneuvers before plunging noiselessly into the black waters. An anonymous ship's captain in the illegal immigrant trade claimed that his fishing boat, along with its human cargo, was almost capsized by the sudden emergence of a glowing craft from beneath the waves.

Honduras

A great many UFO-sighting reports from this Central American country have been picked up on the world's wire services and later forgotten. This small country, wedged between Guatemala and Nicaragua, sustained its highest level of UFO activity during October 1978, when it fell prey to the same kind of blackout-producing vehicles that would affect Venezuela later that same year.

On October 14, at 6:10 PM, a nationwide blackout left communities helpless for twenty minutes as reports of strange objects in the twilit skies flooded radio stations and the newsrooms of Honduran dailies. The advertising manager of one newspaper, Rogelio Bercián, happened to be among the witnesses to the unusual phenomena. At precisely 6:06 PM, he declared in an article for Tegucigalpa's *La Tribuna* that he was working on his car on the vantage point of El Picacho hill when he became aware of a strange object moving from south to north at considerable speed. It headed for a populated area at high velocity. Fearing it was a conventional airplane, he paid close attention to its maneuvers. The object suddenly executed a suicidal figure-eight maneuver. Bercián then realized he was a looking at a colossal, boomerang-shaped object with a brilliant light at its center. As it flew over Tocontin Airport, electrical current died over the city. Bercián saw the streetlights grow dim before blacking out altogether. Other witnesses directly under the flight path of the triangular UFO were able to confirm Bercián's statement.[30]

City officials preferred to find a more down-to-earth explanation for the blackout. They sought an answer from the power utility, the state-owned agency ENEE (National Electric Energy Company). Reports of "unexplained anomalies" at El Cañaveral, a power station quite far from Tegucigalpa, stated that this installation crashed after "a mysterious glow had been seen in the sky."

A hundred miles away from the Honduran capital, other power stations reported similar collapses of the energy grid. Engineers were at a loss to explain how localized blackouts in their areas could have affected the distant capital city. Martin Baide, Public Relations Officer for ENEE, was bold enough to suggest:

> I do not personally discard the possibility that technologies greater than man's could be the cause of these anomalies, since we have been unable to offer a satisfactory explanation as to the true reason for the blackouts.[31]

The massive power failure that occurred on October 27, 1978, involved an even greater UFO component. Aida Zúñiga, a secretarial school director in the town of Choluteca, to the south of Tegucigalpa, observed that, shortly after 6:00 PM, her students became aware of a light-emitting object concealed behind the clouds of a recent rainstorm. The cloud-swathed vehicle was described by one student as reminiscent of the "mother ship" from *Close Encounters of the Third Kind*. Ms. Zúñiga declared that the object remained stationary and gave off lightning-like flashes just as the lights began to brown out and then disappear entirely throughout Choluteca. The UFO changed color from a yellowish-red to a pale shade of pink before disappearing. After it had gone, the drizzle came to an end and the power came back on.

Two hours after the uncanny events over Choluteca, a strange vehicle was seen over Tegucigalpa's La Leona substation. Miguel Herrero, a technician on duty at the substation, was watching television when a sudden, blue glow was followed by an explosion among the transformers. He saw a blinding light rise up and away from the transformers. Witnesses on the streets reported seeing a circular, red light more or less hovering over the substation. Roberto Aguiar, a cabdriver, described the disk as having tendrils that moved around it in a circular motion.

The events of October 1978 may be considered unspectacular in the light of later developments in ufology, such as the rise in encounters with UFO occupants and the abduction epidemic, but it showcased the control that these objects have over our cities—and, indeed, over our way of life.[32]

Perú

The former realm of the Incas has a close relationship to the UFO pheomenon, perhaps over the course of millennia. Paleoufologists—researchers into the possibility of extraterrestrial visitation in the distant past—have been fascinated by the Nazca lines in the Peruvian desert, and have linked them and other mysterious features with ancient-astronaut activity in this country. The Peruvian navy has had a number of maritime encounters in its territorial waters with USOs (unidentified submarine objects) able to outdistance the fastest destroyer. Proponents of the extraterrestrial hypothesis have argued the existence of an underwater base in the deep waters of the Pacific off Perú.

Juan José Benítez, a journalist with Spain's now-defunct *La Gaceta del Norte*, who would later go on to become one of his country's most important (and controversial) ufologists, visited Perú in 1975 to report on the contactee phenomena surrounding a group of college students calling themselves the Peruvian Institute of Interplanetary Relations (IPRI). The group availed itself of automatic writing techniques to make contact with purported alien beings from a variety of planets. Benítez also had the opportunity to inspect echograms taken by fishing-boat pilots in 1969, showing the sonar outlines of two gigantic UFOs.[33]

The putative aliens contacted by the IPRI members foretold the destruction of our world in a not-too-remote future. They said they intended to save certain elements of the human race before such a cataclysm occurred. They were the "kind space brothers" that have become the trademark of UFO cults worldwide, like the Aetherius Society and the many defunct cults once to be found in this country. Before such associations make us dismiss the matter out of hand, it is worthwhile to note that some very interesting information has come out of such contacts—items that tie in with the argument that UFOs are not as much vehicles from other worlds as "windows" into another existence.

Among the information revealed to the members of IPRI by their improbable contacts was the existence of what they termed "xendras." These were orbs of intense light that could be entered physically. Once inside them, humans could have conversations with aliens without ever leaving the ground.

Many photos of xendras allegedly exist, but have been repeatedly misidentified by UFO analysts. These objects can project the image of the person entering them anywhere in the universe, which ties in with suggestions that many of the nonhuman beings or the vehicles themselves behave more like projections from a camera than anything else. A special type of vehicle, the contactees were told, is needed to project the xendra—a sausage-shaped UFO that lands directly on the ground, rather than hovers above it. Three of the IPRI members, Carlos Paz Wells, his brother Sixto, and Juan Acervo, allegedly entered these tunnels of light and were able to observe life on other worlds.[34]

In spite of sounding like wide-eyed cultists, the members of IPRI have serious qualifications, and their organization is chartered with the Peruvian education ministry, the Paris-based International Aeronautics Federation, and other agencies. Their leader at the time of the 1970s contacts, Carlos Paz García, was a high-ranking government functionary, and astronomers, geologists, and other professionals ranked among its membership.

Contact with the alleged extraterrestrials took place on August 22, 1974, and was a prominently featured event in the national media. A curious detail was that the contact site was the Marcahuasi Plain, which has long been considered by cryptoarchaeologists to be the site of a lost civilization. Forty members of the group had been advised, by a being calling itself "Oxalc," to report to the desert location, which is 180 miles from Lima and at the dizzying height of 13,000 feet. They witnessed the maneuvers of six disks in the night skies.[35]
The bulk of the contact, however, was achieved, as stated earlier, through telepathic means and automatic writing.

The Apuan messages included descriptions of life on Apu; descriptions of colonies on Ganymede, Mars, and the ocean floor off the Peruvian coast; predictions of the Earth's imminent destruction; and what could be described as "religious instruction" concerning the universe, spirit, and the concept of God. Scientific data was restricted to the location of Apu in space (4.3 light years from Earth, orbiting Beta Centauri), and a cursory explanation of the "ion drive" that propels their space vehicles. When pressed for more information of a technical nature, the Apuans replied that such requests were not necessary for the completion of "Operation Rama." The spiritualist aspect of these contacts was highlighted by the presence of discarnate "guides" with names like Oxalc, Senyan, and Gexo. These entities dictated the information, and not infrequently provided spurious anecdotes about their presence on the moons of Jupiter and about human space voyages. One spurious item was that the Soviet Union had, in fact, beaten the US to the Moon, but upon landing on the lunar far side, cosmonauts discovered an automated Apuan depot and fled back home in terror after a cosmonaut fired upon a robot sentry and died as a result.

The physical description of these beings corresponds with that of other sightings in South America. They had silvery-white hair, human facial structure, and large stature (six to seven feet tall). Part of their mission, as told to the IPRI contactees, is to evacuate large numbers of humans for "resettlement" in another world. Ominously, this ties in with the large number of unexplained disappearances every year—although the entire premise of the Apuans and their works is highly questionable.[36]

What can we conclude from these experiences? Only that documented contact between humans and nonhumans has been taking place in Peru for a very long time and quite openly. In one of the communication sessions, the beings from Apu warned against the presence of the small, large-headed beings that were also visiting the Earth, as they were "not part of the confederation." Such a statement has great implications if the reader believes that these aliens belong to a reality coequal to our own and not a physical world in the galaxy. It sheds light on the Biblical accounts of angels and demons, and the global folklore about other beings that occupy the world with humans and are either positive or decidedly hostile toward us.

Uruguay

Sandwiched between Brazil and Argentina, tiny Uruguay boasts a modest UFO history of its own. A number of noted investigators of the phenomenon brought cases to the attention of ufology worldwide during the sixties and seventies. However, a major UFO flap may have taken place as recently as 1994, according to some anonymous documentation forwarded to Mexican ufologist Dr. Rafael Lara Palmeros. These papers provided information (largely from journalistic sources) on a mind-bending cross section of "ufologica," ranging from mere lights in the sky to interaction between humans and UFO occupants.[37]

In 1978, a considerable number of residents in the town of Rivera, Uruguay, saw a UFO fly over this locality during the early hours of the morning.

The witnesses were workers at a refrigeration plant who were on their way to work. The object was moving at a moderate, constant speed at a height of 1,600 feet and making circular movements.

Ernesto Fagúndez, the manager of a local radio station, saw the object in the sky. Fagúndez was able to distinguish several portholes, through which he could see crew members. "They were beings with enormous heads," he said. Later the object was seen executing an odd maneuver. It dived over a bus. Terrified of an imminent collision, the passengers leaped out of the bus and ran for their lives. Instead of colliding with the bus, the object rose skyward and disappeared.

A gigantic, cigar-shaped UFO was allegedly seen in April 1994 in Rivera, on the Brazilian border. According to witnesses, the object was 160 feet long, and emitted bright, orange flashes as it flew in a straight line toward the northeast. Suddenly the intensity of the light diminished, and the object became invisible. Several witnesses claimed to have seen three subdivisions in the object's stern. These could have been several objects that escorted the larger one. According to the witnesses, a total of four compartments could be seen in the object. This led many to believe it could be a "mother ship."

Residents of Florida, Uruguay, reported seeing a UFO fly across the sky for 18 minutes on the night of May 21, 1994. While the object was still visible in the sky, a surprise blackout plunged the city into darkness. According to one witness, journalist Luis del Castillo, it was a spherical object with white, red, and green lights on its sides, which moved off to the west. The official story on the power failure was "a sudden overload of the supply system, which overrode safety systems." The manager of the Miguel Castro Ferreira Power Station, unable to come up with an explanation, dismissed it as "a coincidence."

In the city of Artigas, some 437 miles from Montevideo, a family claimed to have seen small, extraterrestrial beings on at least three occasions. Wilson Eli Da Costa, 17, was in his garden when he noticed small footprints that appeared to have been made by a child. The following day he noticed more footprints. This news was shared with the rest of the family, who decided to keep it a secret. On the following day, Wilson's sister, Marta Elena Ari Da Costa, 16, saw a little man "with a very white complexion" looking into the house.

Later in the summer, five adults and a ten-year-old child in the city of Maldonado, 88 miles from Montevideo, had a terrifying experience as they returned from Laguna del Sauce. At the 72-mile mark of the road leading to Punta del Este, the people traveling in the rear of the vehicle saw "an enormous fireball" rise from a nearby field and head for their bus. They warned the driver, who saw the fiery object. An impressive chase ensued. The witnesses stated that the fireball was so bright that it illuminated the entire area as if it were daylight. It moved in an east-west trajectory, following the same route as the bus. It finally broke off its pursuit and disappeared close to a naval base.

Villa Cebollati, a town in Rocha Province located some 156 miles from Montevideo, became the unwilling locale for contact with nonhumans. Julio César Cabrera, 45, was awakened in the early morning hours by the sound of a loud horn, which he took to be that of his own car. When he opened the car's door, a powerful electric discharge riveted him to the ground, as a strange, white-faced, green-skinned being with slanted eyes and blond hair appeared out of thin air, accompanied by a beautiful female. According to Cabrera, both creatures began measuring his body while he remained paralyzed. Within minutes, the creatures had disappeared amid whitish smoke. No physical harm was inflicted upon the witness, and it appears that he enjoyed the creatures' visit.

On September 13, 1994, five residents of Paso de las Velas, Florida Department (94 miles from Montevideo), claimed to have witnessed the collision of a UFO with the ground. The event took place after a lengthy storm. The witnesses became aware of a solid, orange, rectangular object crossing the sky noiselessly. It suddenly plummeted to the ground, setting off an explosion that was heard for miles. Large plumes of smoke filled the air, but not a trace of the object was found where the explosion took place.

Faced with all this information, the Uruguayan Air Force decided to accept all UFO-related information and investigate each case directly. This initiative was undertaken by the Receiving and Investigating Commission, affiliated to the Uruguayan Air Force, which created a special file destined to collect all known cases occurring in the country. The new commission is to be headed by Lt. Col. Eduardo Aguirre, who requested that the national media forward any UFO information to his attention.

Venezuela

During the 1960s, many UFO sightings occurred in South America's largest producer of crude oil, but spectacular cases—investigated by distinguished ufologist Francisco D'Amico, founder of the Extraterrestrial Phenomena Investigative Group (GIFE)—took place during the years that followed.

In October 1976, a huge UFO with pulsating, multicolored lights moved slowly over the community of Plan de Manzano, pausing its immense bulk silently over a drum farm containing highly flammable liquids. To terrified onlookers, it appeared as if the alien monstrosity was about to land on top of the depot, but it headed off into the night sky at a prodigious speed.

On New Years Day, 1977, a UFO moved silently across the skies of Barquisimeto, on Venezuela's Caribbean coast, beginning a significant wave of sightings.

Two weeks later, on January 23, a circular UFO giving off intense flashes of blue, green, yellow, and red landed in the community of Santa Rosa, in the state of Lara. Witnesses reported seeing the silhouettes of two diminutive, humanoid occupants move in a robotic, controlled manner. The unknown craft emitted tremendous waves of heat. It left a 12-foot-wide burn mark on the grass, and singed nearby shrubs and trees. Seven witnesses interviewed by GIFE agreed that the landed vehicle made a slight noise, but closer investigation was impossible due to the intense heat. Armando Loyo, one of the witnesses, said he employed a flashlight to look at the UFO's interior. Before he could come any closer, the vehicle took off, nearly blinding him with intense light. Venezuelan scientists visited the area but refused to issue a statement as to what had transpired that evening.[38]

The summer months of 1977 were punctuated by repeated sightings of UFOs over the village of Duaca, 15 miles south of Barquisimeto. The townspeople mounted their own nocturnal sky watch, setting up "observation posts" on a number of rooftops scattered throughout the village. This enabled them to see UFOs from different angles, thus allowing for comparisons later on. At 9:50 PM on August 22, an orange-red vehicle, calculated to be 50 feet in diameter and flying at an altitude of 4,000 feet, was sighted over the community and recorded by the members of the GIFE research team. Two more vehicles were seen that same evening.[39]

As dramatic as these sky watches might have been, Venezuela would soon face a less pleasant aspect of the UFO phenomenon: the sudden appearance of unknown craft causing widespread failures of the power grid. Caracas, the nation's capital, and dozens of outlying cities were plunged into darkness on the night of December 31, 1978—almost two years to the day after the initial sighting. The blackout occurred shortly after midnight, and prompted the cancellation of all official New Years celebrations. Radio stations had alerted the city to a flurry of UFO sightings that had taken place shortly before the blackout. The Caracas power utility was at a loss to explain the probable cause of the power failure, which extended as far as the city of Maracay, 50 miles away.

Chapter Fifteen

A History UFO Abductions

It is curious that, while instances of alleged abduction by UFO aliens are rife in North America, they are considerably less widespread in the Spanish-speaking regions of the world. This is made all the more curious by the fact that one of the earliest cases—and without question the one most readily memorable—is the Antonio Villas-Boas abduction, which took place in Brazil in 1952. The oft-mentioned sexual interlude with a space "siren" and the severe physiological aftereffects suffered by Villas-Boas rocked the nascent discipline of ufology to its core. But that was long ago, when UFO abductions involved physical interference in a deserted location, usually a rural highway, a desert, or a forest. It was long before the ubiquitous "Greys" were reported transporting helpless experiencers through their bedroom walls, inducing pregnancies, and apparently involving them in genetic studies.

Comparative analyst T. E. Bullard has pointed out that the abduction phenomenon is largely an American one, with one of every two cases coming out of the US and Canada. Half of all abduction experiences are "made in the USA." The other half are distributed around the rest of the planet, and the Spanish-speaking regions of the world certainly have their fair share. What is the modus operandi of the abductors in these locations? Are Greys, Nordics, or other non-humans involved? Is hypnosis a tool of choice as it is here?

Puerto Rico boasts a considerable number of UFO abduction cases, most of them dutifully investigated by the island's foremost researcher, Jorge Martín. One of these cases stands out among the others, due to the possibility that the experiencer's efforts at meditation "opened up" a path for abducting Greys to enter her life.[1]

Delia V., a housewife with two children, had no idea that her interest in yoga would turn her into an abductee when she and a friend visited a yoga temple in October 1991 to practice meditative techniques. At 7:30 PM, Delia decided to withdraw from the meditation circle and go to bed early. Once in bed, she felt a hand covering her face. She was unable to see who her potential assailant was due to the darkness in the bedroom. It was then that she became aware of the fact that she was flying in midair! Buildings, streets, and automobiles remained far below Delia as she drifted upward. Far from feeling elated at the sight, she was paralyzed by fear.

The next thing she remembered was being back in bed at the yoga temple at five o'clock in the morning, feeling sick to her stomach and wracked by excruciating pain. Stumbling out of her room, she told the meditation instructor what had happened. He advised her simply to go back to sleep, which she did. When she reawakened, at noon, not only did she feel physically better, but her entire outlook on life had been changed. During the following months, physical changes came about. Her menstrual cycle now lengthened to 50 days or so, and her stomach became slightly enlarged.

A subsequent encounter revealed the UFO connection to her experiences. Shortly after seeing a brilliant craft in the sky, she found herself standing in a metallic chamber occupied by a dozen or so very small, non-human beings clad in grey. Delia remembers lying on a bed, screaming and crying, telling one of the bizarre figures that she could not give normal birth to the child she was carrying because her other children had been born by cesarean section.

Delia said,

> When I woke up, I saw one of the extraterrestrials with a child in
> his arms. When I saw this child, something deep inside me told
> me that he was my child, but I also remember being afraid. I re-
> member telling one of the extraterrestrials that I considered this
> child strange, because he was half human and half extraterres-
> trial.[2]

Delia was then given the child to hold, and was told by the creatures that it
could not live among humans because it could not eat human food.

Delia's case echoes hundreds of abduction experiences collected by US
investigators. But ufologist Jorge Martín has observed that Puerto Rican abduction cases tend to have a stronger environmental content to them than those
on the mainland. Experiencers are imparted messages of ecological importance
and cases involving hybridization are few.

Mexican experiencer Rolando Quiroga Valero, 51, told his story of repeated alien abduction to a spellbound audience in a segment of a Miami-
based talk show. "There are daily sightings over my hometown," Quiroga observed laconically, "but no one cares."[3]

Quiroga's first contact took place in 1950. He was with a group of friends
in Monterrey when he saw a discoid craft hovering 160 feet over his head. He
was partially paralyzed by the vehicle, which emitted a soft orange light and a
faint whistling sound. He perceived beings watching him from the disk. His
friends ran away.

The following year he had another contact experience. He saw a UFO
cross the sky over Allende.

Twenty-four years later, he began to have strange, unbidden thoughts,
which led him to fear for his state of mental health. He began to hear a powerful male voice instructing him to "love all human beings." (It is curious to observe that the standard 1950s contactee message of peace and love continues to
play a prominent role in these Latin American cases.)

Quiroga believes that he was chosen because of his Mayan heritage. His
alien contacts have hinted that the key to the UFO mystery lies in man's deci-
phering of the Mayan hieroglyphs. His first physical encounter came about in
1972, when he was "sanitized" by a ray of light and allowed into the presence

of his hosts, who were "paranoid" about terrestrial viruses. These putative aliens died of heart complications, and had a 130-year life span, although they did not physically age beyond 40 human years. The message entrusted to this Mexican contactee is a simple one, and it has been the cornerstone of all the messages given to contactees in the Spanish-speaking world: Earth is changing, whether we like it or not. There will be a natural, not a man-made, disaster in the future, which will change the tilt of the planet's axis. Humans must evolve in order to survive. Ominously, he was also told that, of the many "alien races" that are visiting our world, only six are friendly toward the human race.[4]

Quiroga claims he was taken aboard a vehicle, where he underwent prostate and heart surgery. The contactee's physician was amazed at the improvement in his patient's condition, and was turned from skeptic into believer by what his eyes and instruments told him. Communications with the ufonauts have not ceased. Quiroga was warned, two years ahead of time, of the earthquake that rocked Mexico City in 1985. "Their predictions," he says, "are usually of a negative nature."

Abduction experiences in Mexico tend to get blurred by contactee experiences. There has recently been a revival of contacteeism due to the successful "missionary activity" of Italian contactee Giorgio Bongiovanni, whose millennialist prophecies have found fertile ground in the crisis-torn land of the Aztecs.

Not all experiencers find their hosts as benevolent as Mr. Valero's. The casebooks of Latin American researchers are filled with incidents in which malice and hostility played a significant role in the abduction. Dr. Rafael A. Lara Palmeros, director of Mexico's Centro de Estudios de Fenómenos Paranormales (CEFP), includes in his organization's newsletter the experiences of Adriana Martínez, a woman who has experienced meddling in her life by forces purportedly linked with the UFO phenomenon.

Ms. Martínez' experiences began when she was only a teenager. A large ball of red light would materialize in her bedroom at night. Due to her strict Catholic upbringing, she believed that such displays were associated with unwholesome forces. The "fireballs," as she termed them, seemed to herald the awakening of her own psychic abilities, and the distressing phenomenon disappeared as she became older.

Years later, while she was living in McAllen, Texas, a friend told her to run outside to see a UFO. Although she was not the least bit curious about such things, she complied with the request. She saw the strange, glowing light. Soon afterward she began to experience auditory communication with an entity that claimed to be her father. A luminous being appeared in a dream and told her that she would get to see this paternal figure if she went to a location in a small Mexican town—Tepoztlán, now a center of New Age interest—where a UFO display would be staged for her benefit.

On September 7, 1983, at 10 PM, a light started to appear. Ms. Martínez stated:

> I leaped to the hotel window. Above the hill was a hamburger-shaped UFO. It was perfectly motionless, and remained so for two hours. The power was going on and off all over town. I later thought to make a triangle shape with my hands to communicate with the UFO, and they responded, since three red lights on the UFO assumed a triangular shape momentarily, while green, yellow, and red navigation lights flew around the craft. Sounds like dull explosions could be heard coming from within the UFO while its lights became brighter. I went to the bathroom and told my friend that they were going to send her a light, and that she should not be frightened. A bright beam issued from the UFO, aimed directly at the hotel window, right next to my friend. It was so powerful that all the lights went out in Tepoztlán.

The entity with whom she had engaged in mental communication began to make demands upon her. He said she must divorce her husband or become a widow. He informed her that he had no qualms about eliminating anyone that stood in his path. While Ms. Martínez considered what to do, her husband had a terrible accident on the highway. Allegedly, the entity asked her if that demonstration of his power sufficed, or if further proof was necessary.

She stated bitterly:

> Contact is mere manipulation toward an end known only to them. They have given me no help whatsoever, and what they have done for me, according to them, has been very unpleasant....I see that many contactees allow themselves to be manipulated without ever knowing where they're going or allow themselves to be

dazzled by small manifestations...of course, once the contactee is "hooked," there is no escape, and you accept your fate by hook or crook. I have rebelled terribly, but there is no escape but to fulfill their plans.[5]

In landlocked Bolivia, a young TV and radio technician named Orlando Calizaya was abducted by a UFO in 1980 while taking a break from work. As he bicycled his way to the town of Capachos, he suddenly noticed that his small transistor radio went dead. Upon getting off the bike, Calizaya was struck with an orange-colored beam that left him paralyzed.

Calizaya subsequently remembered that "a Christ-like voice" addressed him reassuringly, saying that no harm would be done to him. The stunned technician and his bike were raised up by the light into a spaceship "like those seen in films." Not one to give up without a struggle, Calizaya tried to resist and somehow escape from his captors, three-eyed, large-eared humanoids who wished to know "the role oxygen played in the human body." The unsightly ufonauts wore lilac-hued tunics and green trousers.

The young Bolivian became his country's first space traveler, if his account is to be believed, having spent five days on the aliens' homeworld—a sojourn of which he had not the least recollection. Calizaya found himself once more back in Bolivia at the very same spot from which he was forcibly abducted. A group of highway workers picked him up and took him to a medical center. The aftermath of the experience left the 23-year-old technician with a nervous disorder and unable to work. Once gregarious, he turned furtive. Dr. Rubén Martínez, the attending physician, diagnosed his patient as being "in a state of psychomotor excitation."[6]

Some manage to avoid abduction. "Lydia," a housewife from Cabo Rojo, Puerto Rico, was in the middle of doing housework one evening in March 1993, when she saw a "brilliant cone" descend from the sky to a location a few feet away from her home. Intrigued by the phenomenon, she stepped into her backyard. She saw an intensely white beam of light issue from a hovering UFO. She claimed that, when she tried to turn around to reenter her home, she felt "something like a beam drawing me toward the UFO."

"As soon as she managed to scream," observed a police officer who took the report, "the object rose into the air quickly and without any noise whatsoever."

Abductions are common not only in Latin America, but in Spain as well.

"Fernando Martínez" (an alias), an electrician from the city of La Coruña in Galicia, never would have believed that a weekend of motocross on his freshly overhauled dirt bike would end in an abduction experience. One day in late October 1986, Martínez drove his bike to an abandoned stone quarry near the locale of Culleredo. Suddenly, at approximately 9 PM, he became aware of a "star moving in the sky." The light became larger and larger, until it appeared to be the size of a full moon. The astonished electrician noticed that the sphere disgorged a number of smaller, orange, triangular craft, one of which initiated a rapid descent toward the abandoned quarry.

Realizing his predicament in a flash, Fernando tried to kick-start his dirt bike. His efforts were in vain, even though the bike had been functioning perfectly earlier. The UFO was now a large object, some 30 feet wide, hovering over the surface. In the face of the phenomenon, the electrician dismounted and sat on the ground, waiting to see what would happen next.

Fernando remembers a powerful beam of light emanating from the orange triangle, and two beings descending along the trail of light. The creatures were small and large-headed. They approached Fernando silently, and guided him toward the base of the hovering triangle. He felt no fear. His captors made no effort to communicate with him.

His next memory was of standing in a large chamber. A third being, identical to the other two, came out to meet him, projecting reassuring telepathic messages. He remembers being placed in a horizontal position and feeling pain in one of his arms.

His first conscious memory was of lying on the gravel of the quarry in Culleredo. Confused, the electrician made his way home on the dirt bike, which now worked perfectly. Two hours of his life were inexplicably unaccounted for.[7]

Fernando Martínez' UFO experience had unfortunate consequences in his earthly experience. A Spanish magazine published his story, causing his employer to dismiss him. But he may be considered fortunate indeed in comparison to another Spanish experiencer.

In 1989, researcher Manuel Carballal met "Mariví" and her husband at a UFO conference in the city of Castellón, on Spain's Mediterranean coast. Mariví was afflicted by large-headed "bedroom visitors," who paralyzed her husband and abducted her straight out of her bed.

Once aboard what she considered to be a spacecraft, Mariví was made to comply with her captors' wishes by sheer physical violence. In her case, the large-headed Greys were merely robots of some sort at the service of tall, blond humanoids, who, despite their charismatic presence, were by no means angelic. In her interview with Carballal, the abductee stated that she could not tolerate many more of these experiences, and was resigned to the fact that "she would die young."[8]

The overtly sexual component of UFO-abduction cases is strongly present in this sampling of cases from the Hispanic world. A young Colombian woman, Mónica María Ortega, recounted her experiences of nocturnal sexual experiences with supposedly alien entities on a nationally syndicated television talk show in November 1991. Her experiences did not involve the ever-present Greys, but rather one of the intriguing humanoids known to researchers variously as "Blondes" or "Nordics."

Ms. Ortega was twelve years old and living in New York City when this tall, blond, green-eyed entity suddenly materialized in her bedroom. She recalled:

At first I saw two lights. I felt a presence, and naturally felt scared. One light was red in color and the other was green.

The lights told her not to fear for her safety. She began to fall asleep, and felt caresses and kisses all over her body as her nightclothes were removed.

I felt something spread my legs open, and a sharp pain soon after. I woke up, terrified, and saw a being in a tight-fitting outfit in bed with me. His eyes were so green that it made me dizzy to look at them. I found him very handsome, was attracted to him, and fell in love.[9]

Mónica's lover and his silent companion, a luminous globe that never manifested itself in human form, told her that they traveled around the world. Curiosity, they advised her, was the motivation for their sexual contacts.

After two years, Mónica moved back to Colombia, and was overjoyed at seeing her otherworldly lover again. At the end of their encounter, Mónica expressed a desire to go with him to "his world," but the being turned her down.

Nineteen years old at the time of the interview, the young woman had still not had sex with a human male. "They have the advantage of not making you pregnant," she explained.

Age does not appear to be an impediment in these affairs. During March 1993, Ernesto Cabán, a golden-ager from the town of Adjuntas, in Puerto Rico's central region, claimed that a large object emitting multicolored lights made a soft landing on a hillside close to his home. This did not surprise Cabán, who was quite used to seeing UFOs over Adjuntas for decades, until he noticed three beings—two males and a female—heading toward his house. The bemused Earthling described his unexpected guests as tall and fair-skinned, with long, blond hair and blue eyes.

Cabán claims that the aliens spoke "a somewhat strange" form of Spanish, but made themselves clearly understood. He was to mate with their female companion, and had no choice about it! The tall, blond female pointed out that it would be necessary "as part of an experiment taking place on their home world." In true gentlemanly fashion, Cabán declined to describe the particulars of the encounter, adding only that he hoped to live long enough to see the lovely alien and perhaps be presented with a "little ET"—his otherworldly offspring.

While the abductions of humans by superhuman forces of varying descriptions appear to obey the same mechanisms worldwide, there has been little support for abductees in Latin America or Spain. A growing number of medical and scientific figures have emerged as champions for the cause, but abduction experiences, as opposed to UFO cases, are met with perhaps greater skepticism in the Spanish-speaking countries than in the US or the UK. During a convention of health-care professionals held in Spain in 1990, a psychiatrist was asked to give his expert opinion on perfectly normal individuals who insisted on having experienced contact with alien creatures. "They're psychotic," the man declared cuttingly. "Anyone who sees things that don't exist is psychotic."[10]

In a report prepared on the case for alien abductions in Spain, analyzing a dozen cases from 1947 to 1979 in which abduction by aliens was an issue, veteran researcher Vicente Juan Ballester Olmos pointed out:

This systematic review of abduction reports has disclosed that all cases can be reasonably explained in terms that do not defy

present-day knowledge...it should be emphasized that the reso-
lution of these cases in terms of hoax, delusion, or psychosis has
been proposed by dedicated UFO researchers, not by debunkers
or dogmatic skeptics; consequently, it is unrealistic to suggest that
the interpretations are biased.

Antonio Ribera's *Secuestrados por Extraterrestres* (*Abducted by Extraterrestrials*) and Manuel Carballal's *Secuestrados por los OVNIs* (*Abduction by
UFOs*) are both very important books, but neither has had the success of Budd
Hopkins' *Missing Time* or any one of Whitley Strieber's works. Few Latin
American or Spanish psychiatrists have expressed a willingness to handle pa-
tients who claim to have been victims of alien abductions. (There are notable
exceptions, such as Puerto Rico's Manuel Méndez del Toro.) Consequently,
percipients are reluctant to come forward with their experiences.

In predominantly Catholic countries, experiencers might sooner choose to
confide in a priest, believing that they are the victims of demonic obsession.
Abduction cases in the Hispanic world appear to have a strong tendency toward contacteeism, complete with dire warnings about pollution, warfare, etc.,
and the urging of humans to take a greater "evolutionary step."

Chapter Sixteen

Out of Darkest Antiquity

A branch of UFO research called "paleoufology" was born in the 1970s, when authors like Otto Binder (*Unsolved Mysteries of the Past*), Richard E. Mooney (*Gods of Air and Darkness*), and Erich Von Daniken (*Chariots of the Gods?*) wrote extensively on human/alien interaction at the dawn of recorded history and even earlier. Proof of the existence of "gods" or "ancient astronauts" could be found everywhere, and to judge by the conclusions found in the books of the time, it seemed that every major engineering project in antiquity had been "farmed out" to alien contractors! Paleoufology lost its appeal and languished in obscurity until the works of Zechariah Sitchin thrust it into prominence once again. Clearly there is still a great deal to learn about this aspect of the phenomenon.

Guatemalan researcher Oscar Rafael Padilla, an attorney and Ph.D. who has dedicated 30 of his 51 years to the research of the UFO phenomenon, is also the compiler of an extraordinary taxonomy of extraterrestrial creatures, composed by taking into consideration such characteristics as the existence or lack of hair, eye type, body shape, and similarities to the human body. One of the species portrayed in *Clasificación Exobiológica de Entidades Extraterrestres* (*Exobiological Classification of Extraterrestrial Entities*) is characterized by its large head and eyes in relation to the thinness of its body. The being has been classified as belonging to the family Hominidae (due to its resemblance to humans), order Primates (due to its walking on two extremities), subclass Eutheria (since it is allegedly a placental mammal). Padilla also believes that this particular variety of non-human entity played a significant role in ancient times.[1]

Dr. Padilla recalls a very curious stele that was on display in Guatemala's Museum of Anthropology and Archaeology until its removal in 1990, when it was transferred to Japan for scientific study. The stele portrayed the figure of a being with enormous ears, three-fingered hands, elongated legs, no feet, and two strange filaments on its head, which, in Padilla's opinion, constitute "antennae."

Scientists dismissed Dr. Padilla's alleged alien as a colorful, primitive depiction of an imaginary monster—very much like our own science-fiction beasts —and left the matter at that. But there is growing evidence throughout South America that ancient artisans depicted certain things we now know to be fact much too clearly.

Brazilian UFO researcher Jean Alencar has noted that the mythology of this country is replete with descriptions and statuettes of beings endowed with the power of flight. The legends of Brazilian natives, like those of other countries, detail experiences of gods or travelers from the sky who descended to earth to instruct humans (who were then little more that animals) in the arts of agriculture, astronomy, medicine, and other disciplines. Alencar points out one figure in particular, Bep-Kororoti, a space warrior worshipped by the tribes of the upper reaches of the Xingú River. Not unlike the heroes of India's *Mahabarata*, Bep-Kororoti possessed a flying vehicle capable of destroying anything in its path. His aspect terrified the primitive natives until he stepped out of his "raiment" and revealed himself to be fair-skinned, handsome, and kind. He amused the natives with his "magic" until he grew restless for his land in the sky and returned there.[2]

The *Popol Vuh*, sacred to the Mayans, unequivocally states, "...Men came from the stars, knowing everything, and they examined the four corners of the sky and the earth's round surface." Yet another book, the *Chilam Balaam*, is even more explicit. It states, "Beings descended from the sky in flying vessels...white men in flying rings, who can touch the sky."

There are indications that something very strange took place on our very own continent hundreds of thousands of years ago, before humans arrived on this continent. Santa María Canyon holds evidence pointing toward the existence of a culture of intelligent beings who raised cattle, built weapons, and practiced funeral rites a million years ago. If we decide to stick with what academia has to say, in no way could these beings have been humans. Were they survivors of an "Elder Race"? Marooned spacemen, or colonists trying to tame a new planet? During the Prehistory Conference held during 1962 in Rome, Dr. W. Matthes presented the oldest carvings known to exist. They were created by a forgotten artist 200,000 years ago, when humans had allegedly just discovered the use of fire.

Curious details suggesting the visit of extraterrestrial travelers can be found in the presence of technological items far too advanced for the cultures in which they are discovered. Sandal-and-loincloth cultures in the Americas and the Middle East appear to have mastered the creation of aluminum (which is refined from bauxite using a highly complex process) and platinum (the smelting of which requires temperatures of thousands of degrees). Yet these very same civilizations clearly had no knowledge of more elemental technology, such as the wheel. Was specialized information "imparted" by non-terrestrial creatures to a "priesthood" of primitive humans, who surrounded the information (and perhaps the non-terrestrial devices needed to apply it) with a panoply of esoteric knowledge and mystery cults?

Perhaps some of the alien teachers stayed behind on Earth, out of sight, in an advisory capacity. Peru's Cuzco Museum holds a most interesting exhibit that has attracted much anthropological interest, but little in the way of answers. It is a high-domed skull with impossibly large eye-sockets, found at a Peruvian archaeological site. Experts affirm that the cranial deformation was not artificial (cranial deformation was widely practiced by Mesoamerican and South American cultures), nor does it appear to be that of an abnormal human.[3] Could a Peruvian museum hold the only tangible proof of alien visitation on

Earth?

The Sahara, a warm, subtropical desert, occupies almost three million square miles. Its relative humidity can go as low as twenty percent and strong, dry winds, like the *harmattan,* contribute to evaporation. Such inhospitable conditions make survival an almost insuperable barrier for animals such as gazelles, antelope, jackals, and the varieties of reptiles and insects that can be found there. Yet humans have clung tenaciously to life in this environment, and appear to have done so far back in history, when the climate wasn't so harsh. These human cultures, now lost to us, left behind a number of beautiful and disturbing drawings that have created controversy since their discovery.

Almost 9,000 years ago, one of these cultures flourished on Djebel Zenkekra in the Tassili-n-Ajjer Massif, a natural, fortress-shaped mountain formation that provided relief from the unforgiving desert sun during the day and shelter against the animals that roamed the Neolithic swamps (which would later turn to desert).

The Tassili culture bequeathed to posterity a collection of 4,000 images, painted in a variety of colors unavailable to their counterparts in the Altamira and Lascaux caves. They used flints for brushes. Dark reds, yellows, and even shades of green supplemented the basic reds and whites available to the prehistoric cave artists. Everyday life was their subject matter. The endless cycle of hunting, battle, and domestic life was captured in stone, along with a gallery of figures that stand out in stark contrast to humans in their workaday poses. While there are many such examples of cave art in other rock shelters and ledges throughout the upper reaches of the Sahara, the ones on Djebel Zenkekra hold a special fascination.

Discovered by the nineteenth-century French explorer Henri Lhote, these figures were so unusual that he dubbed them "Martians," explaining "their contour is simple, inartistic, and with rounded heads; their only detail is the double oval at the figure's center, which evokes the image we currently have of Martians."

Lhote's round-headed denizens of the red planet were depicted by the primitive cave artists as wearing suits strongly reminiscent of those worn by our own astronauts on the moon, down to the detail of the boots. Several hundred such drawings exist, scattered over many miles of desert—strange helmeted and antennaed figures, often floating in weightlessness, as if the artist had been able to witness one of our modern space walks. Other images are of a technological bent, showing what could be taken as solar panels, space stations, and floating spheres containing humanoid figures.

Unwilling to be caught up in the ancient astronaut craze, anthropologists have suggested that the Tassili "roundheads" are merely ceremonial dancers or priests wearing empty gourds over their heads. The problem with this rational approach is that the agricultural know-how and resources to grow pumpkins were nonexistent in North Africa at the time the Tassili drawings were created, and would probably not have been available for another thousand years.

Could extraterrestrial visitors have included the then-lush Tassili region among their forays in ancient human history? Dozens of books in an equal number of languages have provided circumstantial evidence of non-human intervention in earthly affairs. Biblical texts speak of the "sons of God" attracted by the "daughters of men," Mayan bas-reliefs depict what could be a space traveler, and so on.

In 1976, braving desert sands, Polisario terrorists, and suspicious Algerian security forces, Spanish researchers Jorge Blaschke, Rafael Brancas, and Julio Martínez reached the Tassili Massif to conduct a systematic study of the enigmatic cave drawings. In the course of their research, they were stunned to find a clear depiction of a helmeted and suited figure, linked by a tether to the interior of a large, spherical object, leading three human females toward it. Dr. Martínez noticed that the artist had taken great care in showing the women. One of them was an adolescent, another a mother carrying a child, and the third a visibly pregnant woman. Could this be representative of the genetic experiments allegedly still being conducted in our days by large-headed Greys?[4]

UFOs still make their presence felt in the modern Sahara. Aimé Michel mentioned a sighting made at Ouallen, some 250 miles west of the Tassili-n-Ajjer, in 1942. A group of meteorologists spotted an object at an altitude of 18,000 feet. They described it as a revolving "planet." The object remained above them for two days before disappearing. Cigar-shaped objects were reported on numerous occasions throughout Algeria in the 1950s. Personnel at the French air base at Tessalit, Algeria, mistook a low-flying UFO for a DC-3 about to land. The mysterious light made a characteristic 90-degree turn and climbed into the night sky, vanishing from sight. Even the 1976 Spanish expedition was treated to a UFO sighting near the desert airstrip of In Salah while on its way to Tassili.[5]

The examples of cave art found in the Spanish caverns of Ojo Guareña and Altamira, and the French ones at Lascaux and Font de Gaume, prove that our distant ancestors were able to represent what they saw with a clarity and simplicity that is stunning to twentieth-century eyes. This skill extends to depictions of things that anthropologists and archaeologists often find troublesome—namely, equally faithful representations of domed objects, some of them in threes, others with legs or antennae.[6]

The small French village of Le Cabrerets lies next to the impressive Pech Merle Cavern—a colossal labyrinthine complex almost a mile long. Using a red pigment, Cro-Magnon artists depicted on one of its walls a being that would fall perfectly into Dr. Padilla's taxonomy. It has an enormous bald head, an unusually pointed chin, and no ears. Its eyes are represented as elongated slits that taper toward its temples. The straight lines crossing the figure appear to indicate that it was wounded or slain by caveman spears. A drawing of a hat-shaped object appears floating over the creature's head.

Pech Merle is not an oddity. Twenty miles away, another cave, Cougnac, contains a similar representation of a wounded or slain creature. Lest we think that Cro-Magnon artists lacked a flair for depicting the human form, it should be noted that other French caves, such as Rouffignac, contain clearly recognizable human figures, including what seem to be mask-wearing humans. The Pech Merle and Cougnac "dead men" are clearly something else. Archaeologists tell us that these ancient images were drawn at the beginning of the Magdalenian Period—some 20,000 years ago.[7]

The Ojo Guareña complex, weaving its way for miles into the earth, poses an indecipherable riddle. In his book *En Busca de la Historia Perdida* (*In Search of Forgotten History*), Spanish author and filmmaker Juan G. Atienza states that some of the cave system's many entrances are considered "evil," and the local farmers will not till the soil near them or come close to them. Contained precisely within one of these "evil" points of access is an ancient petroglyph of what could only be—astounding though it might seem—a representation of the helical structure of DNA.

But the Old World certainly does not have a monopoly on these Paleolithic enigmas. North America has also provided its share of enigmatic prehistoric drawings. A particularly impressive one can be found at Canyonlands National Park in Utah. There, a duo of unusual creatures (remarkably similar to those depicted at Tassili) is engaged in strange activity. One of them appears to be pointing an item at the ground—a flashlight? Farther south, an artist of Mexico's Tlatilco culture drew a perfect image of a little man who gives the impression of wearing boots and a square helmet.

Petroglyphs found in caves on Hispaniola and Puerto Rico often represent highly unusual images, such as hirsute, bearded, male figures; hooded faces; beings with what appear to be hoses connecting their heads to their backs; and even more disturbing depictions. One of the petroglyphs found at Cueva de Las Maravillas, on the island of Hispaniola (Santo Domingo), depicts a bearded figure together with an artifact that appears to be suspended in midair. Images found in Taíno caves on other parts of the island represent flying objects with dangling ladders.

When even steadfast UFO naysayers like Dr. Carl Sagan are willing to concede that alien visitations in the remote past cannot be dismissed out of hand, can we still believe that this evidence, which is there for anyone to see, is simply a misinterpretation of conventional events seen from a primitive human perspective? Or can we lend credence to the ancient Sumerian and Babylonian stories of divine beings coming down to Earth to teach humans the rudiments of civilization? The subject will remain open to endless debate, unfortunately, for the foreseeable future.

One thing we can be sure of is that we will never solve all the riddles. Since the first human being left toe prints in the mud of Earth, incredibly strange, wonderful, frightening, inexplicable events have been happening, and they continue to happen today. Throughout the millennia, creatures of unimaginable origins have been swooping down upon our planet, wreaking their peculiar handiwork, and departing just as mysteriously as they came. Some have been intelligent (even superintelligent) beings with advanced technologies; some have been nothing more than animals. It appears that some of them have taught us techniques of agriculture and other accoutrements of civilization, some have sucked the life from our livestock in the dead of night, and others have simply made cameo appearances. Until we can capture them, put them in jars, label them, and display them on museum shelves, they must remain in that dimly-lit limbo that the late Rod Serling so eloquently referred to as "The Twilight Zone." Meanwhile, we must be ever watchful, and ever truthful to ourselves. When we encounter these denizens, we must cast aside fear and shout our experiences from the rooftops. We must have the integrity to be truthful to ourselves, regardless of the slings and arrows of skeptics and government agents. Because knowledge is our only weapon, and our only hope.

Notes

Preface

[1] John A. Keel, *The Mothman Prophecies* (New York: Signet, 1975).

Introduction

[1] Marc Davenport, *Visitors From Time: The Secret of the UFOs*, 2nd ed. (Murfreesboro, Tennessee: Greenleaf Publications, 1994).
[2] Leah A. Haley, *Lost Was the Key* (Murfreesboro, Tennessee: Greenleaf Publications, 1993).
[3] Scott Corrales, *The Chupacabras Diaries: An Unofficial Chronicle of Puerto Rico's Paranormal Predator* (Bradford, Pennsylnania: Samizdat Press,

1996), p. 9.

Chapter One

[1] Julio Víctor Ramírez, "Buscan insolito pajaro," *El Vocero*, 12 Mar. 1989, n. pag.
[2] Willie Durand Urbina, *Brightlights*, 1, No. 2 (1996), 22.
[3] Jorge J. Martín, "Cadaver Extraterrestre Hallado en Salinas," *Evidencia Ovni,* No. 3, p. 4.

Chapter Two

[1] Jorge J. Martín, "Orocovis!" *Evidencia Ovni*, No. 6, p. 2.
[2] M. Del Amo-Freixedo, "Un monstruo causa terror en Puerto Rico," *Enigmas,* No. 7 (1996), p. 46.
[3] Jorge J. Martín, "Orocovis!" *Evidencia Ovni*, No. 6, p. 2.
[4] Jorge J. Martín, "Es todo un experimento de agencias de inteligencia de los EE.UU.?"
[5] Víctor Ramírez, "Avistan OVNI sobre área montañosa de Patillas," *El Vocero*, 19 May 1995, n. pag.
[6] Ramírez, "Avistan OVNI...", n. pag.

Chapter Three

[1] Harold T. Wilkins, *Strange Creatures from Time and Space* (New York: Citadel Press, 1959), n. pag.
[2] Wilkins, n. pag.
[3] Rafael A. Lara Palmeros, unpublished article for *Terra Incognita*, Mexico, 1995.
[4] David Perkins, "Heart of Weirdness," *Spirit—The Magazine of the Rocky Mountain Southwest,* Fall/Winter 1994-95, p. 24.
[5] Conference given by Stan Gordon, Greensburg, Pennsylvania, Aug.

1994.

[6] Stan Gordon, "UFOs in Relation To Creature Sightings in Pennsylvania." MUFON UFO Symposium, 1974.

[7] Jerome Clark and Loren Coleman, *Creatures of the Goblin World,* (Highland Park: Clark Publishing, 1978), p. 2.

[8] Jorge J. Martín, *Enigma!,* No. 23, p. 31.

[9] Jorge J. Martín, "Tambien Animales Imposibles ¿Que Ocurre en Puerto Rico?" *Evidencia OVNI,* No. 6, pp. 32-33.

[10] *OVNIs Confidiencial,* WSKN AM, San Juan, Puerto Rico, Aug. 1994.

Chapter Four

[1] "Ovnis—Tema Para Una Conferencia," *El Vocero,* 2 Jun. 1995, n. pag.

[2] *Senderos,* WUNO-AM, San Juan, Puerto Rico, 2 June 1995.

Chapter Five

Chapter Six

[1] Mark Chorvinsky, "Our Strange World," *Fate,* Oct. 1992, p. 32.

[2] Salvador Freixedo, *Defendámonos de los Dioses* (Madrid: Quinta, 1985), pp. 107-108.

[3] Freixedo, *Defendámonos,* n. pag.

[4] Jorge J. Martín, "Orocovis!" *Evidencia Ovni,* No. 6., n. pag.

[5] Jorge J. Martín, "¿Que son las extrañas criaturas vistas en Orocovis?" *Evidencia Ovni,* No. 6, p. 16.

[6] Martín, "¿Que son las extrañas criaturas...," p. 16.

[7] Martín, "Orocovis!" p. 17.

[8] Martín, "Orocovis!" p. 17.

[9] "Interview With Daniel Perez," *OVNIs Confidencial,* WUNO-AM, San Juan, Puerto Rico, 6 Oct. 1995.

Chapter Seven

[1] Rubén Darío Rodríguez, "Chupacabras desangra 9 ovejas y gansos," *El Vocero*, 1 Nov. 1995, p. 4.

[2] José Rivera Renta, "Chupacabras se desquita con 4 gatos y 5 perros," *El Vocero,* n.d., n. pag.

[3] Rubén Darío Rodríguez, "20 periquitos víctimas Chupacabras," *El Vocero*, 2 Nov. 1995, p. 4.

[4] Rubén Darío Rodríguez, "Piden Contralora pesquisa la cacería," *El Vocero*, 2 Nov. 1995, p. 4.

[5] Obed Betancourt, "Chupacabras acosa a dos sujetos," *El Vocero*, 6 Nov. 1995, p. 12.

[6] Rubén Darío Rodríguez, "Reaparece la bestia en otro "junker," *El Vocero*, 7 Nov. 1995, p. 5.

[7] Rubén Darío Rodríguez, "Extraña nave en área Chupacabras," *El Vocero*, 8 Nov. 1995, p. 4.

[8] Rubén Darío Rodríguez, "Avistan Chupacabras patio hogar ancianos," *El Vocero*, 9 Nov. 1995, p. 8.

[9] Rubén Darío Rodríguez, "Chupacabras se oculta en cavernas," *El Vocero*, 10 Nov. 1995, p. 6.

[10] Víctor Ramírez, "Encuentro cercano con Chupacabras," *El Vocero*, 11 Nov. 1995, p. 39.

[11] Clarence Beardsley, "Asocia OVNI con Chupacabras," *El Vocero*, 14 Nov. 1995, p. 4.

[12] Rubén Darío Rodríguez, "Chupacabras mete brazo en casa," *El Vocero*, 15 Nov. 1995, p. 4.

[13] Víctor Ramírez, "Chupacabras asusta gallos pelea," *El Vocero*, 16 Nov. 1995, p. 11.

[14] Rubén Darío Rodríguez, "Examina DRN víctimas Chupacabras," *El Vocero*, 22 Nov. 1995, p. 6.

[15] Rubén Darío Rodríguez, "Un perrito, 30 gallinas se suman a víctimas raro ser," *El Vocero*, 23 Nov. 1995, p. 4.

[16] Rubén Darío Rodríguez, "Vinculan a brujería matanza novillos," *El Vocero*, 24 Nov. 1995, p. 2.

[17] Rubén Darío Rodríguez, "Clarividente dice es especie de vampiro

asentado en El Yunque," *El Vocero*, 6 Dec. 1995, p. 8.

[18] Rubén Darío Rodríguez, "Clarividente describe y dice cómo capturar al Chupacabras," *El Vocero*, 25 Nov. 1995, p. 4.

[19] Tomás de Jesús Mangual, "Chupacabras ataca manada Rincón," *El Vocero*, 27 Nov. 1995, p. 7.

[20] Clarence Beardsley, "Chupacabras inspira a jóven estudiante teatro," *El Vocero*, 27 Nov. 1995, p. 31.

[21] Tomás de Jesús Mangual, "Chupacabras deja marcadas huellas," *El Vocero*, 28 Nov. 1995, p. 8.

Chapter Eight

[1] Telephone conversation with Jorge Martín, Nov. 1995.

[2] Jorge J. Martín, "El fenómeno Chupacabras está ligado a estrellamientos de OVNIs en Roswell, Nuevo México, EE.UU," *Evidencia OVNI*, No. 10, p. 18.

[3] *OVNIs Confidiencial*, WUNO-AM, San Juan, Puerto Rico, Nov. 1995.

[4] Rubén Darío Rodríguez, "Chupacabras vuelve dieta conejos," *El Vocero*, 1 Dec. 1995, p. 8.

[5] Miguel Rivera Puig, "6 ovejas víctimas Chupacabras," *El Vocero*, 8 Dec. 1995, p. 11.

[6] Rubén Darío Rodríguez, "Eximen de culpa al Chupacabras," *El Vocero*, 8 Dec. 1995, p. 18.

[7] Miguel Rivera Puig, "Extraña criatura ataca ganado," *El Vocero*, 12 Dec. 1995, p. 6.

[8] Rubén Darío Rodríguez, "Montan vigilancia para ver Chupacabras," *El Vocero*, 13 Dec. 1995, p. 6.

[9] Rubén Darío Rodríguez, "Chupacabras ataca animales en Naguabo," *El Vocero*, 14 Dec. 1995, p. 4.

[10] Rubén Darío Rodríguez, "Quieren rebautizar al Chupacabras," *El Vocero*, 19 Dec. 1995, p. 5.

Chapter Nine

[1] *OVNIs Confidencial,* WUMO-AM, San Juan, Puerto Rico, 21 Dec. 1995, 10:30-11:30 PM.

[2] Miguel Rivera Puig, "Chupacabras ataca a un mecánico," *El Vocero,* 23 Dec. 1995, p. 3.

[3] Rubén Darío Rodríguez, "Ve posible Chupacabras sea un ser extraterrestre," *El Vocero,* 27 Dec. 1995, p. 12.

Chapter Ten

[1] Rubén Darío Rodríguez, "Chupacabras activo en dos pueblos," *El Vocero,* 5 Jan. 1996.

[2] Miguel Rivera Puig, "Clama por captura Chupacabras," *El Vocero,* 11 Jan. 1996, p. 6.

[3] Miguel Rivera Puig, "Chupacabras mata patos Coronel," *El Vocero,* 12 Jan. 1996, p. 6.

[4] Associated Press, "Analizarán víctimas del Chupacabras," *El Vocero,* 15 Jan. 1996, p. 4.

[5] Miguel Rivera Puig, "4 patos víctimas del Chupacabras," *El Vocero,* 18 Jan. 1996, p. 28.

[6] Laura Candelas, "Nada inexplicable muerte de animales," *El Vocero,* 17 Jan. 1996, p. 12.

[7] Víctor Ramírez, "Conejos y perro en dieta Chupacabras," *El Vocero,* 25 Jan. 1996, p. 79.

[8] Rubén Darío Rodríguez, "Chupacabras mata mascota niña," *El Vocero,* 26 Jan. 1996, p. 5.

[9] Rafael Suárez, "Añaden pavo a lista muertes misteriosas," *El Vocero,* 3 Feb. 1996, n.p.

[10] Clarence Beardsley, "Pocos misterios han fomentado tanto interes como esta terrible criatura," *El Vocero,* 8 Feb. 1996.

[11] Víctor Ramírez, "Alcalde declina opinar sobre avistamientos OVNI," *El Vocero,* 8 Feb. 1996, p. 20.

[12] Rubén Darío Rodríguez, "Chupacabras vuelve a sus andadas," *El Vocero,* 8 Mar. 1996, p. 14.

[13] Víctor Ramírez, "Chupacabras de ronda por Maravillas," *El Vocero,*

12 Mar. 1996, p. 4.

[14] Víctor Ramírez, "Chupacabras ataca gallos y perros," *El Vocero*, 19 Mar. 1996, p. 4.

[15] Rubén Darío Rodríguez, "Chupacabras deja fuerte olor azufre," *El Vocero*, 3 Apr. 1996, p. 5.

[16] Rubén Darío Rodríguez, "Chupacabras se apunta 10 gallinas," *El Vocero*, 13 Apr. 1996, p. 4.

[17] Rubén Darío Rodríguez, "Reaparece el Chupacabras," *El Vocero*, 29 Apr. 1996, p. 4.

[18] Javier Maymí, "Chupacabras cambia dieta a patos," *El Vocero*, 19 Jun. 1996, p. 4.

[19] Associated Press, "Chupacabras incursiona en el Sur; mata 16 patos," *El Vocero*, 4 May 1996, p. 4.

[20] Associated Press, "Chupacabras limpia pico 20 gallinas," *El Vocero*, 10 May 1996, p. 10.

[21] Javier Maymí, "Ama casa se topa con Chupacabras," *El Vocero*, 1 Jul. 1996, p. 4.

[22] Rafael Suárez, "Sigue pesquisa víctima Chupacabras," *El Vocero*, 26 Jun. 1996, p. 16.

[23] Rubén Darío Rodríguez, "Reaparece Chupacabras en San Lorenzo," *El Vocero*, 7 Sep. 1996, p. 5.

[24] Víctor Ramírez, "Enorme OVNI ilumina montañas," *El Vocero*, 28 Sep. 1996, p. 8.

[25] Julio Víctor Ramírez, "Reaparecen extraños seres y Chupacabras," *El Vocero*, 2 Oct. 1996, p. 8.

[26] Julio Víctor Ramírez, "Reaparece Chupacabras en Isabela (Chupacabras Reappears in Isabela)," *El Vocero*, 23 Oct. 1996, n. pag.

Chapter Eleven

[1] Manuel Figueroa, "¿Seres extraterrestres o engendros genéticos?" *Año Cero*, No. 6 (1996), p. 52.

[2] Figueroa, p. 52.

[3] Figueroa, p. 54.

[4] Jim Steinberg, "Mendota Rooster's Demise Stirs Talk of Chupacabras,"

Fresno Bee, May 18, 1996, n. pag.

[5] Correspondence with Bruno Cardeñosa.

[6] Correspondence with Bruno Cardeñosa.

[7] Dr. Oscar Rafael Padilla, "La huella radiactiva," *Año Cero*, No. 6 (1996), p. 59.

[8] Correspondence with Dr. Oscar R. Padilla.

[9] Juan Chía, "Los seres humanos, nuevas víctimas," *Año Cero*, No. 6 (1996), p. 56.

[10] Salvador Freixedo, *Defendámonos de los Dioses* (Madrid, Spain: Quinta, 1985), n. pag.

[11] Arturo Cano, "En el climax de un mito," *El Norte*, 11 M ay 1996, p. 23.

[12] Marco Rodriguez, "Aumenta por Chupacabras vigilancia en Chapultepec," *Excelsior*, 11 May 1996, n. pag.

[13] *Crónica Policiaca*, No. 4, 7 May 1996, p. 19.

Chapter Twelve

[1] "Stories Abound for Chupacabras," *The San Juan Star*, 3 Jan. 1996.

[2] Fernando Clemente, "De idioteces y supersticiones," *Claridad*, 24-30 May 1996, p. 13.

[3] John Marino, "The Chupacabras UFO/Moca Vampire/Garadiábolo Connection," *The San Juan Star Sunday Magazine*, 19 Nov. 1995, p. 3.

[4] Jorge J. Martín, "Orocovis!" *Evidencia OVNI*, No. 6, p. 2.

[5] Martín, "Orocovis!" p. 2.

[6] Bryan, C. D. B., *Close Encounters of the Fourth Kind: UFOs, Abductions, and the Conference at MIT* (New York: Knopf, 1994), pp. 304-305.

[7] Martín, "Orocovis!" p. 2.

[8] Jorge J. Martín, "Los Chupacabras: ¿Seres Extraterrestres o Manipulaciones Genéticas?" *Evidencia OVNI*, No. 8, p. 2.

[9] Martín, "Orocovis!" p. 2.

[10] Martín, "Los Chupacabras: ¿Seres Extraterrestres o Manipulaciones Genéticas?" p. 2.

[11] B. Ann Slate, "Gods from Inner Space," *SAGA UFO Report* 3, No. 1 (Apr. 1976), p. 37.

[12] Mark Chorvinsky, and Mark Opsasnick, "The Maryland Monster Cover-Up," *Fate*, Dec. 1990, pp. 65-67.

Chapter Thirteen

[1] Rollo Ahmed, *The Black Art* (New York: Paperback Library, 1968), n. pag.

[2] Ahmed, n. pag.

[3] John Mackin, *Strange Encounters* (New York: Ace Books, 1968), p. 35.

[4] Douglas Hill and Pat Williams, *The Supernatural* (New York: Signet, 1967), p. 182.

[5] Mike Marinacci, *Mysterious California* (Los Angeles: Panpipes Press, 1988), p. 53.

[6] J. J. Benitez, *La Quinta Columna* (Barcelona: Planeta, 1991), p. 282.

[7] Jorge J. Martín, "Yeti en Villalba?" *Enigma!* 1, No. 2, p. 3.

Chapter Fourteen

[1] Jacques Vallee, *Dimensions* (New York: Ballantine Books, 1988), n. pag.

[2] Coral E. Lorenzen, *Flying Saucers: The Startling Evidence of the Invasion from Outer Space* (New York: Signet, 1966), n. pag.

[3] Kevin Randle, "The UFO Kidnapping That Challenged Science," *Saga UFO Report*, 2, No. 3 (Summer 1975), p. 14.

[4] Daniel Rebisso-Giese, *Vampiros Na Amazonia* (Belem-Pará, 1991), n. pag.

[5] Ralph and Judy Blum, *Beyond Earth: Man's Contact with UFOs* (New York: Bantam Books, 1975), p. 143.

[6] Salvador Freixedo, *Defendámonos de los Dioses* (Madrid: Quintá, 1985), pp. 105-107.

[7] Wendelle Stevens, "Case of the Twin Flying Saucers," *Saga UFO Report*, 2, No. 3 (Summer 1975), p. 14.

[8] Salvador Freixedo, *La Granja Humana* (Mexico: Editorial Posada,

1989), p. 123.

[9] Antonio Las Heras, *OVNIs—Los Extraterrestres entre Nosotros* (Buenos Aires: Edad, 1992), p. 41.

[10] Salvador Freixedo, *Visionaries, Mystics and Contactees* (Lilburn, Georgia: Illuminet Press, 1992), n. pag.

[11] Correspondence with Dr. Rafael A. Lara Palmeros, 14 Nov. 1992.

[12] Luis Andrés Jaspersen, *El Lado Oscuro de los OVNI* (Mexico: Editorial Universo, 1982), p. 35.

[13] Jaspersen, p. 39.

[14] Leonard Stringfield *Status Report VII—UFO Crash/Retrievals: Search for Proof in a Hall of Mirrors* (Cincinnati, Ohio: the author, 1994), n. pag.

[15] Rafael A. Lara Palmeros, "The UFO Phenomenon in Mexico: The 1991 UFO Wave in Hidalgo," *Samizdat*, Summer 1995, pp. 5-6.

[16] Antonio Las Heras, *OVNIs—Los Extraterrestres entre Nosotros* (Buenos Aires: Edad, 1992), pp. 32-33.

[17] Las Heras, *OVNIs*, p. 37.

[18] Antonio Las Heras, *Respuestas al Triángulo de las Bermudas* (Buenos Aires: Edad, 1992), pp. 153-156.

[19] Correspondence with Dr. Ricardo C. Calderón.

[20] Salvador Freixedo, *Defendámonos de los Dioses* (Madrid: Quintá, 1985), p. 154.

[21] *Samizdat*, Year One (1993), p. 9.

[22] Las Heras, *OVNIs*, p. 26.

[23] Las Heras, *OVNIs*, p. 136.

[24] Las Heras, *OVNIs*, pp. 69-79.

[25] Freixedo, *La Granja Humana*, p. 103.

[26] Freixedo, *La Granja Humana*, pp. 104-105.

[27] Sebastián Robiou, *Manifiesto OVNI* (San Juan: Punto y Coma, 1979), n. pag.

[28] Robiou, pp. 172-218.

[29] Leonte Objio, "Llegaron los Vampiros!" *Contactos Extraterrestres*, 1978.

[30] Freixedo, *La Granja Humana*, p. 64.

[31] Freixedo, *La Granja Humana*, p. 65.

[32] Freixedo, *La Granja Humana*, p. 70.
[33] Juan José Benítez, *OVNIs—SOS a la Humanidad* (Barcelona: Plaza y Janés, 1989), p. 114.
[34] Benítez, pp. 129-133.
[35] Benítez, p. 37.
[36] Benítez, p. 95.
[37] Correspondence with Dr. Rafael A. Lara.
[38] Francisco D'Amico, *La Ciencia y el Fenómeno OVNI* (Mexico: Editorial Orion, 1979), p. 124.
[39] D'Amico, p. 127-28.

Chapter Fifteen

[1] Willie Durand Urbina, *Brightlights*, 1, No.1 (Jan. 1996), p. 18.
[2] Durand Urbina, p. 19.
[3] "¿Existen los Extraterrestres?" *El Show de Cristina,* WAPA, San Juan, Puerto Rico, 12 Nov. 1991.
[4] "¿Existen los Extraterrestres?"
[5] Correspondence with Dr. Rafael A. Lara.
[6] Correspondence with Richard Heiden.
[7] Manuel Carballal, *Secuestrados por los OVNIs* (Madrid: Espacio y Tiempo, 1992), p. 57.
[8] Carballal, p. 86.
[10] "¿Existen los Extraterrestres?"
[10] Carballal, p. 90.

Chapter Sixteen

[1] Correspondence with Dr.Oscar R. Padilla.
[2] Jean Alencar, "Casuistica ufologica revela hiperatividade alienigena no Brasil," *Revista UFO,* April 1994, p. 9.
[3] Salvador Freixedo, *Extraterrestres y Creencias Religiosas* (Mexico: Editorial Orion, 1973), n. pag.
[4] J. Blaschke, R. Brancas, and J. Martínez, *Los Dioses de Tassili: Astro-*

nautas en la Edad de Piedra (Barcelona: Martínez Roca, 1978).

[5] Aimé Michel, *The Truth About Flying Saucers* (New York: Pyramid Books, 1956), pp. 104-110.

[6] Juan G. Atienza, *En Busca de la Historia Perdida* (Madrid: Martinez Roca, 1982), p. 37.

[7] Antonio Ribera, *¿De Veras, Los OVNIs Nos Vigilan?* (Mexico: Posada, 1974), p. 29.

Works Cited

Books

Ahmed, Rollo. *The Black Art.* New York: Paperback Library, 1968.

Atienza, Juan G. *En Busca de la Historia Perdida.* Madrid: Martinez Roca, 1982.

Benitez, Juan José. *La Quinta Columna.* Barcelona: Planeta, 1991.

_____. *OVNIs—SOS a la Humanidad.* Barcelona: Plaza y Janés, 1989.

Blaschke, J., R. Brancas, and J. Martínez. *Los Dioses de Tassili: Astronautas en la Edad de Piedra.* Barcelona: Martínez Roca, 1978.

Blum, Ralph, and Judy Blum. *Beyond Earth: Man's Contact with UFOs.* New York: Bantam Books, 1975.

Bryan, C. D. B. *Close Encounters of the Fourth Kind: UFOs, Abductions, and the Conference at MIT.* New York: Knopf, 1994.

Carballal, Manuel. *Secuestrados por los OVNIs.* Madrid: Espacio y Tiempo, 1992.

Clark, Jerome, and Loren Coleman. *Creatures of the Goblin World.* Highland Park: Clark Publishing, 1978.

Corrales, Scott. *The Chupacabras Diaries: An Unofficial Chronicle of Puerto Rico's Paranormal Predator.* Bradford, Pennsylnania: Samizdat Press, 1996.

_____, ed. *Samizdat, Year One.* Bradford, Pennsylnania: Samizdat Press, 1993.

Davenport, Marc. *Visitors From Time: The Secret of the UFOs,* 2nd ed. Murfreesboro, Tennessee: Greenleaf Publications, 1994.

Francisco D'Amico. *La Ciencia y el Fenómeno OVNI.* Mexico: Editorial Orion, 1979.

Freixedo, Salvador. *La Granja Humana.* Mexico: Editorial Posada, 1989.

_____. *Defendámonos de los Dioses.* Madrid: Quinta, 1985.

_____. *Visionaries, Mystics and Contactees.* Lilburn, Georgia: Illuminet Press, 1992.

_____. *Extraterrestres y Creencias Religiosas.* Mexico: Editorial Orion, 1973.

Haley, Leah A. *Lost Was the Key.* Murfreesboro, Tennessee: Greenleaf Publications, 1993.

Hill, Douglas, and Pat Williams. *The Supernatural.* New York: Signet, 1967.

Jaspersen, Luis Andrés. *El Lado Oscuro de los OVNI.* Mexico: Editorial Universo, 1982.

Keel, John A. *The Mothman Prophecies.* New York: Signet, 1975.

Las Heras, Antonio. *OVNIs—Los Extraterrestres entre Nosotros.* Buenos Aires: Edad, 1992.

_____. *Respuestas al Triángulo de las Bermudas.* Buenos Aires: Edad, 1992.

Lorenzen, Coral E. *Flying Saucers: The Startling Evidence of the Invasion from Outer Space.* New York: Signet, 1966.

Mackin, John. *Strange Encounters.* New York: Ace Books, 1968.

Marinacci, Mike. *Mysterious California.* Los Angeles: Panpipes Press, 1988.

Michel, Aimé. *The Truth About Flying Saucers.* New York: Pyramid Books, 1956.

Rebisso-Giese, Daniel. *Vampiros Na Amazonia.* Belem-Pará, 1991.

Ribera, Antonio. *¿De Veras, Los OVNIs Nos Vigilan?* Mexico: Posada, 1974.

Robiou, Sebastián. *Manifiesto OVNI.* San Juan: Punto y Coma, 1979.

Stringfield, Leonard. *Status Report VII—UFO Crash/Retrievals: Search for Proof in a Hall of Mirrors.* Cincinnati, Ohio: the author, 1994.

Vallee, Jacques. *Dimensions.* New York: Ballantine Books, 1988.

Wilkins, Harold T. *Strange Creatures from Time and Space.* New York: Citadel Press, 1959.

Articles

"Stories Abound for Chupacabras." *The San Juan Star*, 3 Jan. 1996.

Alencar, Jean. "Casuistica ufologica revela hiperatividade alienigena no Brasil." *Revista UFO,* Apr. 1994, p. 9.

Associated Press. "Analizarán víctimas del Chupacabras." *El Vocero*, 15 Jan. 1996, p. 4.

_____. "Chupacabras incursiona en el Sur; mata 16 patos." *El Vocero*, 4 May 1996, p. 4.

_____. "Chupacabras limpia pico 20 gallinas." *El Vocero*, 10 May 1996, p. 10.

Anonymous. "Ovnis—Tema Para Una Conferencia." *El Vocero*, 2 Jun. 1995, n. pag.

Beardsley, Clarence. "Asocia OVNI con Chupacabras." *El Vocero*, 14 Nov. 1995, p. 4.

_____. "Chupacabras inspira a jóven estudiante teatro." *El Vocero*, 27 Nov. 1995, p. 31.

_____. "Pocos misterios han fomentado tanto interes como esta terrible criatura." *El Vocero*, 8 Feb. 1996.

Betancourt, Obed. "Chupacabras acosa a dos sujetos." *El Vocero*, 6 Nov. 1995, p. 12.

Candelas, Laura. "Nada inexplicable muerte de animales." *El Vocero*, 17 Jan. 1996, p. 12.

Cano, Arturo. "En el climax de un mito." *El Norte*, 11 May 1996, p. 23.

Chía, Juan. "Los seres humanos, nuevas víctimas." *Año Cero*, No. 6 (1996), p. 56.

Chorvinsky Mark. "Our Strange World." *Fate*, Oct. 1992, p. 32.

Chorvinsky, Mark, and Mark Opsasnick. "The Maryland Monster Cover-Up." *Fate*, Dec. 1990, pp. 65-67.

Clemente, Fernando. "De idioteces y supersticiones." *Claridad*, 24-30 May 1996, p. 13.

Crónica Policiaca, No. 4 (7 May 1996), p. 19.

Del Amo-Freixedo, M. "Un monstruo causa terror en Puerto Rico." *Enigmas*, No. 7 (1996), p. 46.

Durand Urbina, Willie. *Brightlights*, 1, No.1 (Jan. 1996), pp. 18, 19, 22.

Figueroa, Manuel. "¿Seres extraterrestres o engendros genéticos?" *Año Cero*, No. 6 (1996), pp. 52, 54.

Lara Palmeros, Rafael A. "The UFO Phenomenon in Mexico: The 1991 UFO Wave in Hidalgo." *Samizdat*, Summer 1995, pp. 5-6.

_____. Unpublished article for *Terra Incognita*, Mexico, 1995.

Mangual, Tomás de Jesús. "Chupacabras ataca manada Rincón." *El Vocero*, 27 Nov. 1995, p. 7.

_____. "Chupacabras deja marcadas huellas." *El Vocero*, 28 Nov. 1995, p. 8.

Marino, John. "The Chupacabras UFO/Moca Vampire/Garadiábolo Connection." *The San Juan Star Sunday Magazine*, 19 Nov. 1995, p. 3.

Martín, Jorge J. "Cadaver Extraterrestre Hallado en Salinas." *Evidencia OVNI*, No. 3, p. 4.

_____. "El fenómeno Chupacabras está ligado a estrellamientos de OVNIs en Roswell, Nuevo México, EE.UU." *Evidencia OVNI*, No. 10, p. 18.

_____. *Enigma!*, No. 23, p. 31.

_____. "Es todo un experimento de agencias de inteligencia de los EE.UU.?"

_____. "Los Chupacabras: ¿Seres Extraterrestres o Manipulaciones Genéticas?" *Evidencia OVNI*, No. 8, p. 2.

_____. "Orocovis!" *Evidencia OVNI*, No. 6, pp. 2, 17, 44.

_____. "¿Que son las extrañas criaturas vistas en Orocovis?" *Evidencia OVNi*, No. 6, p. 16.

_____. "Tambien Animales Imposibles ¿Que Ocurre en Puerto Rico?" *Evidencia OVNI*, No. 6, pp. 32-33.

_____. "Yeti en Villalba?" *Enigma!* 1, No. 2, p. 3.

Maymí, Javier. "Ama casa se topa con Chupacabras." *El Vocero*, 1 Jul. 1996, p. 4.

_____. "Chupacabras cambia dieta a patos." *El Vocero*, 19 Jun. 1996, p. 4.

Objio, Leonte. "Llegaron los Vampiros!" *Contactos Extraterrestres*, 1978.

Padilla, Oscar Rafael. "La huella radiactiva." *Año Cero*, No. 6 (1996), p. 59.

Perkins, David. "Heart of Weirdness." *Spirit—The Magazine of the Rocky Mountain Southwest*. Fall/Winter 1994-95, p. 24.

Ramírez, Julio Víctor. "Alcalde declina opinar sobre avistamientos OVNI." *El Vocero*, 8 Feb. 1996, p. 20.

_____. "Avistan OVNI sobre área montañosa de Patillas." *El Vocero*, 19 May 1995, n. pag.

_____. "Buscan insolito pajaro." *El Vocero*, 12 Mar. 1989, n.p.

_____. "Chupacabras asusta gallos pelea." *El Vocero*, 16 Nov. 1995, p. 11.

_____. "Chupacabras ataca gallos y perros." *El Vocero*, 19 Mar. 1996, p. 4.

_____. "Chupacabras de ronda por Maravillas." *El Vocero*, 12 Mar. 1996, p. 4.

_____. "Conejos y perro en dieta Chupacabras." *El Vocero*, 25 Jan. 1996, p. 79.

_____. "Encuentro cercano con Chupacabras." *El Vocero*, 11 Nov. 1995, p. 39.

_____. "Enorme OVNI ilumina montañas." *El Vocero*, 28 Sep. 1996, p. 8.

_____. "Reaparece Chupacabras en Isabela." *El Vocero*, 23 Oct. 1996, n. pag.

_____. "Reaparecen extraños seres y Chupacabras." *El Vocero*, 2 Oct. 1996, p. 8.

Randle, Kevin. "The UFO Kidnapping That Challenged Science." *Saga UFO Report*, 2, No. 3 (Summer 1975), p. 14.

Rivera Puig, Miguel. "4 patos víctimas del Chupacabras." *El Vocero*, 18 Jan. 1996, p. 28.

_____. "6 ovejas víctimas Chupacabras." *El Vocero*, 8 Dec. 1995, p. 11.

_____. "Chupacabras ataca a un mecánico." *El Vocero*, 23 Dec. 1995, p. 3.

_____. "Chupacabras mata patos Coronel." *El Vocero*, 12 Jan. 1996, p. 6.

_____. "Clama por captura Chupacabras." *El Vocero*, 11 Jan. 1996, p. 6.

_____. "Extraña criatura ataca ganado." *El Vocero*, 12 Dec. 1995, p. 6.

Rivera Renta, José. "Chupacabras se desquita con 4 gatos y 5 perros." *El Vocero*, n.d., n. pag.

Rodríguez, Marco. "Aumenta por Chupacabras vigilancia en Chapultepec." *Excelsior*, 11 May 1996, n. pag.

Rodríguez, Rubén Darío. "20 periquitos víctimas Chupacabras." *El Vocero*, 2 Nov. 1995, p. 4.

_____. "Avistan Chupacabras patio hogar ancianos." *El Vocero*, 9 Nov. 1995, p. 8.

_____. "Chupacabras activo en dos pueblos." *El Vocero*, 5 Jan. 1996.

_____. "Chupacabras ataca animales en Naguabo." *El Vocero*, 14 Dec. 1995, p. 4.

_____. "Chupacabras deja fuerte olor azufre." *El Vocero*, 3 Apr. 1996, p. 5.

_____. "Chupacabras desangra 9 ovejas y gansos." *El Vocero*, 1 Nov. 1995, p. 4.

_____. "Chupacabras mata mascota niña." *El Vocero*, 26 Jan. 1996, p. 5.

_____. "Chupacabras mete brazo en casa." *El Vocero*, 15 Nov 1995, p. 4.

_____. "Chupacabras se apunta 10 gallinas." *El Vocero*, 13 Apr. 1996, p. 4.

_____. "Chupacabras se oculta en cavernas." *El Vocero*, 10 Nov. 1995, p. 6.

_____. "Chupacabras vuelve a sus andadas." *El Vocero*, 8 Mar. 1996, p. 14.

_____. "Chupacabras vuelve dieta conejos." *El Vocero*, 1 Dec. 1995, p. 8.

_____. "Clarividente describe y dice cómo capturar al Chupacabras." *El Vocero*, 25 Nov. 1995, p. 4.

_____. "Clarividente dice es especie de vampiro asentado en El Yunque." *El Vocero*, 6 Dec. 1995, p. 8.

_____. "Examina DRN víctimas Chupacabras." *El Vocero*, 22 Nov. 1995, p. 6.

_____. "Eximen de culpa al Chupacabras." *El Vocero*, 8 Dec. 1995, p. 18.

_____. "Extraña nave en área Chupacabras." *El Vocero*, 8 Nov. 1995, p. 4.

_____. "Montan vigilancia para ver Chupacabras." *El Vocero*, 13 Dec. 1995, p. 6.

_____. "Piden Contralora pesquisa la cacería." *El Vocero*, 2 Nov. 1995, p. 4.

_____. "Quieren rebautizar al Chupacabras." *El Vocero*, 19 Dec. 1995, p. 5.

_____. "Reaparece Chupacabras en San Lorenzo." *El Vocero*, 7 Sep. 1996, p. 5.

_____. "Reaparece el Chupacabras." *El Vocero*, 29 Apr. 1996, p. 4.

_____. "Reaparece la bestia en otro "junker." *El Vocero*, 7 Nov. 1995, p. 5.

_____. "Un perrito, 30 gallinas se suman a víctimas raro ser." *El Vocero*, 23 Nov, 1995, p. 4.

_____. "Ve posible Chupacabras sea un ser extraterrestre." *El Vocero*, 27 Dec. 1995, p. 12.

_____. "Vinculan a brujería matanza novillos." *El Vocero*, 24 Nov. 1995, p. 2.

Slate, B. Ann. "Gods from Inner Space." *SAGA UFO Report*, 3, No. 1 (Apr. 1976), p. 37.

Steinberg, Jim. "Mendota Rooster's Demise Stirs Talk of Chupacabras." *Fresno Bee*, 18 May 1996, n. pag.

Stevens, Wendelle. "Case of the Twin Flying Saucers." *Saga UFO Report*, 2, No. 3 (Summer 1975), p. 14.

Suárez, Rafael. "Añaden pavo a lista muertes misteriosas." *El Vocero*, 3 Feb. 1996, n. pag.

_____. "Sigue pesquisa víctima Chupacabras." *El Vocero*, 26 Jun. 1996, p. 16.

Other sources

"¿Existen los Extraterrestres?" *El Show de Cristina.* WAPA, San Juan, Puerto Rico. 12 Nov. 1991.

"Interview With Daniel Perez." *OVNIs Confidencial.* WUNO-AM, San Juan, Puerto Rico. 6 Oct. 1995.

Conference hosted by Stan Gordon, Greensburg, Pennsylvania, Aug. 1994.

Correspondence with Bruno Cardeñosa.

Correspondence with Dr.Oscar R. Padilla.

Correspondence with Dr. Rafael A. Lara Palmeros.

Correspondence with Dr. Ricardo C. Calderón.

Correspondence with Richard Heiden.

Gordon, Stan. "UFOs in Relation To Creature Sightings in Pennsylvania." MUFON UFO Symposium, 1974.

Martín, Jorge J. Telephone conversation. Nov. 1995

OVNIs Confidencial. WUMO-AM, San Juan, Puerto Rico, 21 Dec. 1995, 10:30-11:30 PM.

Senderos. WUNO-AM, San Juan, Puerto Rico, 2 Jun. 1995.

Index

Index

Index

Index

Index

Index

Index

Index

Index

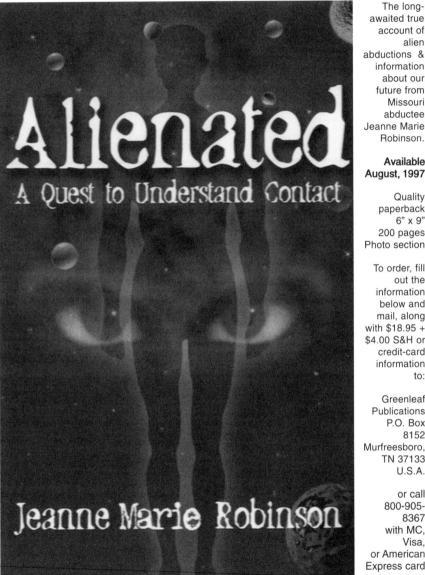

VISITORS FROM TIME

New Revised Edition from Greenleaf Publications!

The Secret of the UFOs
Marc Davenport

VISITORS FROM TIME
The Secret of the UFOs

Marc Davenport

Here is the most thoroughly documented book available in the UFO subject concerning the connection between UFOs and time travel! A must for every serious and not so serious scholar of ufology!

The Book Shopper®
A Division of Greenleaf Publications

So busy that you cherish every second of leisure time?
Want someone else to take care of unpleasant tasks for you?
Loathe traffic, crowds, and waiting in line?
Lack transportation?
Stumped every time you must buy a gift for someone?

Never fear! The Book Shopper® *is here!*

We established our company with your needs in mind. You can now buy books by simply dialing our toll-free number. We'll ship right to your home or work place! *We'll even gift wrap or ship to a third party at no extra charge if you like!*

📖 Novels 📖 Cookbooks 📖 Romances 📖 Westerns

📖 Children's books 📖 Sports Books 📖 Any kind of book!*

1-800-905-8367

(615-896-1549 outside the U.S.)

*applies only to books currently in print and carried by major U.S. distributors. It does not include out-of-print titles.